G000038153

In Nomine Patris

In the Name of the Father

In the Name of the Father

Homilies for Sundays and Feast Days in the
Extraordinary Form Calendar

Edited by
Julien Chilcott-Monk

CANTERBURY
PRESS
Norwich

© The Contributors 2010

First published in 2010 by the Canterbury Press Norwich
Editorial office
13–17 Long Lane,
London, EC1A 9PN, UK

Canterbury Press is an imprint of Hymns Ancient and Modern Ltd
(a registered charity)
13A Hellesdon Park Road,
Norwich, NR6 5DR

www.scm-canterburypress.co.uk

All rights reserved. No part of this publication may be reproduced,
stored in a retrieval system, or transmitted,
in any form or by any means, electronic, mechanical,
photocopying or otherwise, without the prior permission of
the publisher, Canterbury Press.

The Contributors have asserted their right under the Copyright,
Designs and Patents Act, 1988,
to be identified as the Contributors of this Work

British Library Cataloguing in Publication data

A catalogue record for this book is available
from the British Library

978 1 84825 027 7

Typeset by Regent Typesetting, London
Printed and bound in Great Britain by
CPI Antony Rowe, Chippenham SN14 6LH

to
Fr Dominic Jacob
of the
Congregation of the Oratory,
whose idea I have been privileged to edit

Contents

Foreword

by the Archbishop of Westminster

For all disciples of the Lord, the words of the Scriptures are the starting point for so much of meditation and reflection. When we take these words and let them echo within our hearts, we are nurtured in our quest for God and in our task of opening ourselves to allow the Word to find a home in us.

For many people their most constant hearing of the words of Scripture takes place in the context of the Church's liturgy. In the celebration of Sundays and Feast Days, the Church presents to us a selection of texts that highlight certain central truths of the faith, and open up pathways of meditation and devotion.

I am grateful to all who have contributed to this book, which contains meditations on the liturgical selection of scriptural texts for important Feasts and Sundays throughout the year. In offering these thoughtful sermons, the contributors help us all to enter more deeply not only into the words and events of Our Lord's life, but also into the saving mystery which they open up for us. I am sure that many priests will find the sermons in this book a great help. And the book will be welcomed by all who wish to meditate privately on these texts, not least in preparation for the celebration of Mass on these Sundays and Feast Days.

While the book is structured around the Calendar of the Extraordinary Form of the Mass, it is also applicable, of course, to the celebration of these same Feasts in the Ordinary Calendar and where the texts accord with the Proper of the Day in the Ordinary Form of the Mass. I welcome this book as a contribution to the important task of understanding the fundamental unity of the one Roman Rite of the Mass, even when expressed in two Forms. It is the mystery of faith that holds us in the firm unity of the Church, and this publication can help to emphasize that fundamental unity which is one of God's greatest gifts to us.

May the Lord bless all who use this book and, under the inspiration of the Holy Spirit, may these words lead us more deeply into the mystery of our salvation.

+ Vincent Nichols
St Martin de Porres 2010

Preface

by Monsignor Conlon

The claim is sometimes made that good preaching is the particular gift of those who would be considered – in the strictly denominational sense – as evangelicals. Measured perhaps by the standards of the presumption that many people are frequently touched by an emphasis upon the extravagant gestures; engagement of the emotions; and the urgent appeals to sentiment rather than to reason, some of the practitioners of these beguiling arts may well carry off the prize for persuasion. Preaching, however, is as much a matter of agency as of artistry. As in the rest of the liturgy, the preacher is an instrument whose human gifts have been voluntarily placed at the disposal of Christ's Church, of which he is the servant not the proprietor. Effective preaching needs to engage in a manner that provokes a spirit of docility and humility in the one preaching and of a desire to be receptive and reactive on the part of the listeners. Both should appreciate the sanctity and otherness of the One who is the ultimate source of the subject, and acknowledge that although the words and gestures are being conveyed by a human and fallible agent, those expressions are the only elements of the sermon that owe their origin to him. The substance of this material should stem from God's own revelation of truth, from the lived experience and liturgical expression of the Church through all the centuries of her existence.

There is a story told of a famous preacher of the twentieth century who though invited to participate in a church ceremony was told that his oratory was not required on that occasion. This information was conveyed to him by the priest in a note which read, 'I will preach myself.' The famous preacher returned it with the words, 'Better to preach Christ Jesus.' It may be apocryphal, but it is also cautionary. The temptation to be over-personal and autobiographical when preaching is all too prevalent at a time when reality shows and probing interviews are fashionable and frequent. It is a temptation to be avoided. To some extent, the Ordinary Form of the Mass, when celebrated forward facing, can place an unfortunate emphasis on personal presentation. This, in turn, can lead to a type of preaching which relies heavily on style rather than content, though obviously not in every case. The urge to achieve engagement and empathy with the congregation can easily extend to an exercise in egotism, which lacks objectivity. At the lowest level, the emphasis becomes one of entertainment without embracing the challenge of exhortation to obedience, sacrifice and self-control. Some forms of preaching thought to be pastorally effective remain only on the level of the ethical and humanitarian and ignore the doctrinal and catechetical. The moment of attention to the clerical obligation to edify and educate the assembled flock can also provide an excuse or opportunity to project acerbity and animosity towards particular groups or individuals in place of exhortations to the pursuit of virtue and encouragement to rely more readily upon the grace of God. It is all too easy for any preacher to fall into one or other of such categories, as between the stools of sentimentality on the one hand and severity on the other.

Preaching is an awesome responsibility as well as an urgent obligation that should never be taken lightly, or exercised casually. To maintain the best standards, we rely on sources outside ourselves to derive ideas and material. This book of short exhortations has been written – with one exception – by a variety of priests from the perspective and experience of their own pastoral appointments. The subject in every case is the Proper of a particular Sunday or Feast in the Church's liturgical year. It is primarily, though not exclusively of course, as the Archbishop points out in his Foreword, for use with the Missal of the Gregorian Mass – *Mass in the Extraordinary Form* – as issued in its amended form by Blessed Pope John XXIII in 1962, and now again sanctioned for universal use in the document *Romanum Pontificum* by the Holy Father Pope Benedict XVI in 2007. The blessing bestowed upon the Church by that permission to offer the ancient Mass more frequently and freely is celebrated in these newly composed sermons for the benefit of all who cherish and seek to extend knowledge of it. Because the rite itself is one that rightly relegates the priest to a presence that is utterly dependent upon rubrics that are historically reverent, it stimulates a preaching style that seeks to reflect the classical tradition and content of that exercise in charitable communication between a pastor and his flock. Everyone who uses this manual brings independently his own particular gifts and mode of expression and may adapt any phrase or sentence in it to his own vocabulary according to his needs and his custom. The texts may be preached verbatim or serve as spiritual reading sources from which ideas or themes may be drawn. All who are priests in the great tradition of the Church recognize and wish only to fulfil the duty to inform, inspire and educate the people to whom they are sent. May these examples of simple sermons, based on the faith of the Church reflected in her liturgy and tradition, be of some use to all who discover them.

Antony F. M. Conlon
Our Lady of Sorrows 2009

Introduction

Many of the Feast Days that can be celebrated on a Sunday are included in this book together with the Sundays of the Seasons. However, the First and Second Sundays after Pentecost are not included, as Trinity Sunday occurs on the First Sunday and the Feast of Corpus Christi is now commonly celebrated on the Second Sunday. The Sunday after the Ascension is not included, as Ascension Day is commonly celebrated on that Sunday. If these omissions are regarded as deficiencies in the book, they may be remedied in a future supplement along with the feasts of the Patrons of the United Kingdom and some of the other saints not included. Omitted also are sermons for the Good Friday Liturgy of the Lord's Passion and the Easter Vigil, whose ceremonies speak more eloquently than the finest preacher. The additional material included for each day is intended to serve those using the book for meditation and contemplation. This material comprises prompts and nudges, nothing more.

The writers are listed with the briefest of biographies, together with a note of their contributions. Inevitably, the styles vary as does the length of the sermons. I was anxious in my dual role of editor and compiler merely to attempt some general consistency. I am most grateful to the contributors for their goodwill and hard work. Most were engaged upon other writing projects when I pestered them unmercifully.

I do not wish to repeat what has been written in the Foreword and in the Preface. The Archbishop and Fr Conlon have made it clear that the sermons may be used with the Ordinary Form of the Mass and this is certainly so; but the idea behind the book was first to assist the priest who was becoming acquainted or reacquainted with the Mass in the Extraordinary Form, and for those priests whose first language was not English, who were beginning to celebrate in the Extraordinary Form.

For the sake of consistency I have employed the Douay-Rheims translation of the Holy Bible throughout, except where stated otherwise. The translations by J. M. Neale and others, of the office hymns, are to be found in *The Hymner,* published in 1905 by the Plainsong and Medieval Music Society, and in the *English Hymnal,* published in 1906 by Oxford University Press. The verses by Blessed John Henry Newman are to be found in his *Verses on Various Occasions,* published by Burns Oates & Co. in 1868. The Sarum sequences are to be found in *The Sarum Missal in English,* published by The De La More Press in 1911.

Royalties from the sale of this book will benefit the Reaffirmation and Renewal Campaign of the Oxford Oratory, 25 Woodstock Road, Oxford OX2 6HA.

Julien Chilcott-Monk
St Thomas Becket 2009

About the Contributors

FR JEROME BERTRAM, Cong. Orat., was born in Sussex in a Holy Year; served Mass before the 'Cultural Revolution'; lived through all the liturgical changes and observed their effect on the faith and the practice of the laity. Fr Jerome is a member of the Oxford Oratory, a Fellow of the Society of Antiquaries, and a prolific author.

- ✠ The Vigil of the Nativity
- ✠ The Holy Name
- ✠ The Epiphany
- ✠ The Third Sunday after the Epiphany
- ✠ Quinquagesima
- ✠ Easter Morning
- ✠ The Third Sunday after Easter
- ✠ The Eleventh Sunday after Pentecost
- ✠ The Nineteenth Sunday after Pentecost
- ✠ The Nativity of St John the Baptist

JULIEN CHILCOTT-MONK is an author, composer and choral director, who was born in Somerset and lives in Hampshire.

- ✠ The Third Mass of the Nativity
- ✠ Sexagesima
- ✠ Corpus Christi
- ✠ The Purification of the Blessed Virgin Mary
- ✠ St Peter and St Paul
- ✠ St Michael the Archangel

✠ The Kingship of Our Lord Jesus Christ
✠ Remembrance Sunday

FR ANTONY CONLON studied for the Priesthood at the English College, Valladolid, Spain (1972–77) and The Pontifical Gregorian University in Rome (1985–88); ordained to the Priesthood in Westminster Cathedral by Cardinal Basil Hume OSB in 1979. He served as assistant priest at Marylebone, Camden Town and as Rector of Bunhill Row (1991–2001); and has been chaplain to the Oratory School at Woodcote since 2001. He was Chaplain of Magistral Grace in the Sovereign Military and Hospitaller Order of Malta in 1980; Conventual Chaplain *ad honorem* 1994; Chaplain to the restored Grand Priory of England (SMOM) since 1994; and Ecclesiastical Knight of the Constantinian Order of St George. Fr Conlon has completed a research study of Queen Mary Tudor's Catholic Counter-Reform.

✠ The First Mass of the Nativity
✠ The Circumcision of Our Lord
✠ Septuagesima
✠ The Fourth Sunday after Easter
✠ The Ninth Sunday after Pentecost
✠ The Seventeenth Sunday after Pentecost
✠ The Feast of the Most Precious Blood
✠ The Immaculate Conception

FR RICHARD DUFFIELD, Cong. Orat., the provost of the Birmingham Oratory, was for nine years Parish Priest of the Oxford Oratory. Born in York, he was educated at Ampleforth and read English at St Anne's College, Oxford. He completed his studies for the Priesthood at the Angelicum in Rome and Blackfriars in Oxford.

✠ The Second Mass of the Nativity
✠ Sunday within the Octave of the Nativity
✠ The Feast of the Holy Family

- ✠ The Fourth Sunday after the Epiphany
- ✠ Trinity Sunday
- ✠ The Eighteenth Sunday after Pentecost
- ✠ The Transfiguration of Our Lord

FR SEÁN FINNEGAN is Parish Priest of the parish of Our Lady, Queen of Peace, Adur Valley, in the Diocese of Arundel and Brighton, and also teaches Church History at St John's Seminary, Wonersh. He has served in several locations within and out of the Diocese.

- ✠ The Seventh Sunday after Pentecost
- ✠ The Eighth Sunday after Pentecost
- ✠ The Tenth Sunday after Pentecost
- ✠ The Twenty-fourth Sunday after Pentecost

FR STEWART FOSTER was ordained as a Servite Friar in 1992, having studied for the Priesthood at Heythrop College, University of London, and Blackfriars, Oxford. He was incardinated into the Diocese of Brentwood in 1998. He is Diocesan Archivist, editor of *Catholic Archives*, a Fellow of the Royal Historical Society and holds a Doctorate in Educational History from the University of Hull. Fr Foster is the Bishop of Brentwood's Co-ordinator for the Extraordinary Form of the Mass.

- ✠ The First Sunday of Advent
- ✠ The Sixth Sunday after Epiphany
- ✠ The Feast of Pentecost
- ✠ The Twenty-second Sunday after Pentecost
- ✠ Common of the Dedication of a Church

FR KEVIN W. A. HALE was born and raised in East London. After completing his theological studies at Allen Hall Seminary, he was ordained priest for the Diocese of Brentwood in the Parish of Our Lady of Lourdes, Wanstead, in 1984. He served as Assistant Priest in Ilford, Rayleigh and Colchester. From

1994 to 2003 he was Parish Priest of St Edward's Romford, and is currently Parish Priest of Our Lady of Lourdes, Leigh-on-Sea.

✠ The Second Sunday of Advent
✠ The First Sunday after Easter
✠ The Sixth Sunday after Pentecost
✠ The Fourteenth Sunday after Pentecost

FR DOMINIC JACOB, Cong. Orat., was born in London and graduated from St David's University College, Lampeter, in 1982, in which year he entered the Congregation of the Oratory of St Philip Neri, Birmingham. After studies at St Mary's College, Oscott, he was ordained priest in 1989. Fr Dominic was among the group of Fathers sent to help establish the Oratory in Oxford in 1990, where he is currently Vice-Provost. He is Chaplain to St Philip's School, London.

✠ The Third Sunday after Pentecost
✠ The Fourth Sunday after Pentecost
✠ The Assumption of the Blessed Virgin Mary
✠ The Feast of All Saints

FR NICHOLAS SCHOFIELD read history at Exeter College, Oxford, and trained for the Priesthood at the Venerable English College in Rome. He is Parish Priest of Uxbridge, and Archivist of the Archdiocese of Westminster. He is co-author of *The English Cardinals* (2007) and *The English Vicars Apostolic* (2009).

✠ The Twenty-first Sunday after Pentecost
✠ The Exaltation of the Holy Cross

FR DANIEL SEWARD, Cong. Orat., is a priest of the Oxford Oratory. He was born in Ndola, Zambia, and studied at Trinity College, Oxford, Blackfriars, Oxford, and at the Angelicum in Rome. He was ordained in 2001. He has worked as a school chaplain, and is now Parish Priest of the Oxford Oratory.

- ✠ Ash Wednesday
- ✠ The First Sunday in Lent
- ✠ The Second Sunday in Lent
- ✠ The Third Sunday in Lent
- ✠ The Fourth Sunday in Lent
- ✠ Passion Sunday
- ✠ Palm Sunday
- ✠ The Mass of the Lord's Supper

FR MATTHEW TALARICO is a Canon of the Shrine and Institute of Christ the King, Chicago.

- ✠ The Fifteenth Sunday after Pentecost
- ✠ The Sixteenth Sunday after Pentecost
- ✠ The Twenty-third Sunday after Pentecost

FR ANTON WEBB, Cong. Orat., is Assistant Parish Priest of the Oxford Oratory and Catholic Chaplain to the Campsfield House Immigration Removal Centre. He read theology and religious studies at Jesus College, Cambridge, before moving to Oxford.

- ✠ The Third Sunday of Advent
- ✠ The Second Sunday after Epiphany
- ✠ The Fifth Sunday after Epiphany
- ✠ The Fifth Sunday after Easter
- ✠ The Twelfth Sunday after Pentecost
- ✠ The Twentieth Sunday after Pentecost

FR RICHARD WHINDER read history at King's College, London, and studied for the Priesthood at the Venerable English College in Rome. He was ordained in 2001 as a priest of the Archdiocese of Southwark. He has worked in parishes in Canterbury and Norbury, and is currently Assistant Priest in New Malden, Surrey.

- ✠ The Fourth Sunday of Advent
- ✠ The Second Sunday after Easter

Dominica Prima Adventus
The First Sunday of Advent

*'Maranatha!'** ['Come, Lord Jesus!']

Proper of the Day: Introit: *Psalm 24:1, 3, 4*
                                  Epistle: *Romans 13:11–14*
                                  Gradual: *Psalm 24:3, 4*
                                  Alleluia: *Psalm 84:8*
                                  Gospel: *Luke 21:25–33*
                                  Offertory: *Psalm 24:1–3*
                                  Communion: *Psalm 84:13*

✠

'Verba autem mea non transibunt.'†

The Gospel appointed for today's Mass is one of foreboding: Our Lord enumerates the momentous signs that will announce the end of the world. That Advent is ushered in with such a warning leads the Church to her only possible response: *'Maranatha!'* ['Come, Lord Jesus!']. The signs of the end of time also indicate that mankind's liberation is near at hand, for these happenings are portents of the coming Kingdom of God. Advent is, therefore, above all a season of expectation and hope: the Church awaits the coming of the Kingdom, just as she prepares for the birth of the Saviour.

Yet Advent is equally a time for intercession and for beseeching God's good mercy that his promise will be fulfilled in and through ourselves, unworthy of him as we are. *'Ad te levavi animam meum: Deus meus, in te confido, non erubescam.'* ['To thee have I lifted up my soul: in thee, O my God, I put my trust,

---

* 1 Corinthians 16:22.

† Luke 21:33: 'My words shall not pass away.'

let me not be ashamed.'] With these words from the Introit the whole Advent cycle begins on a note of confidence and hope – not *self*-confidence, which is the message of the world, but trust in God's merciful love. Indeed, throughout the Old Testament, through the Patriarchs and Prophets, to the very time of Our Lord himself, by way of the preaching of St John the Baptist, such confidence and hope has been voiced by those who know that only, and precisely, is *God* our Saviour.

The salvation promised us is recapitulated in the Epistle of the Mass, as St Paul bids us to rise from sleep and to cast off the works of darkness.* In the Gospel, despite the dramatic warnings issued by Jesus, there is also the promise of the fulfilment of the work of redemption. Advent, as the proximate preparation for Christmas, seeks to prepare the soul not only for the Feast of the Nativity itself, but for the appropriation of the very redemption for which the Incarnation is purposed. Just as in Lent and Holy Week, it is important for us to remember that the Crucified Lord is the Child of Bethlehem, so now in Advent the Church recalls that the One long expected is he who will suffer and die for our sake.

Advent, therefore, although not a penitential season in quite the same sense as Lent, brings with it a certain starkness and clarity of purpose. Indeed, it is hardly possible to pray *Adveniat* [Come], unless there is envisaged a true and effective preparation, in soul, mind and body, for the arrival of the Saviour. The violet vestments, the omission of the Gloria at Mass, the muting of the organ – each of these is a sign of expectation, of awaiting someone who will transform the whole of creation, making all things new.

Today's Gospel closes with Our Lord promising that his words will endure for ever. For that reason Advent should motivate us to reconsider our lives, to seek pardon for our sins, and to prepare for the Feast of Christmas not in the way that the world bids us, with its message of rampant, yet empty, materi-

---

* Romans 13:11, 12.

alism, but with a joyful expectation of the twofold Coming of Christ in time and at the close of the age.

For further reflection:

> *Thou for ever our salvation,*
> *Thou the life of all creation,*
> *Thou the hope of restoration,*
> *Thou the never-failing light.*

(from the Sarum sequence)

'In thee, O my God, I put my trust, let me not be ashamed.' Even better, perhaps, 'Let me never blush with shame – help me never to have cause to blush with shame.'

Stir up thy power, we beseech thee, O Lord, and come.

(from the Collect of the Day)

Dominica Secunda Adventus
The Second Sunday of Advent

'People of Sion, behold the Lord shall come to save the nations.'*

Proper of the Day:	Introit: Isaiah 30:30; Psalm 79:2
	Epistle: Romans 15:4–13
	Gradual: Psalm 49:2, 3, 5
	Alleluia: Psalm 121:1
	Gospel: Matthew 11:2–10
	Offertory: Psalm 84:7, 8
	Communion: Baruch 5:5; 4:36

---

* Isaiah 30:30.

'Sed quid existis videre? Hominem mollibus vestitum?'*

Modes of dress tell much about a person, or so it is thought. It was Shakespeare who wrote: *'For the apparel oft proclaims the man.'†* But it is certainly not the case with some of the saints. For instance, St John the Baptist appeared as someone with a complete disregard for convention in his appearance; he did not appear to give any consideration to what people thought of him, and he might have been the sort of person who would cause embarrassment. Sometimes John the Baptist even seems to be portrayed as something of a madman ranting and railing against the sins of the times. But the Gospel portrait of John is not that of a man out of his mind; like he for whom he was a herald, John was the sign of contradiction.

Our world needs signs of contradiction still. We do not need to be sociologists to observe that society has been beguiled with material things, and how when the things of this world fail us, we turn to different forms of escapism to anaesthetize the pain. The Prophets of the Old Testament warned of the evils facing the people then; those warnings translate today into our respect for the dignity of every person, and the cherishing of the gift of life God has freely given us. The dramatic conflict between cultures of death and life, those who have and those who have not, is something that deeply concerns all people who believe in the Truth. The rising tide of the breakdown in relationships, the decline of marriage and family life – together with the decline in the practice of religion – all tell us that something is not right in the Western world.

Something of the reason for this is, we can be certain, the fear we all have of explaining and speaking the Truth, whatever the cost. To be a public Catholic today means to be a sign of contradiction to our generation and society. To be a

---

* Matthew 11:8: 'But what went you out to see? A man clothed in soft garments?'
† Hamlet I.iii.

Catholic today means to be counter-cultural, since it means to live and communicate the Truth: the Truth for which John the Baptist and the Apostles after him gave their blood. The cost of following Christ in any era is the same – at least it should be. It is a cost that asks for nothing less than everything. It may be that as we are not threatened with dungeon, fire and sword, we shall never bother to test what we do believe and whether we can answer the demands of that belief. The sobering thought is . . . maybe not.

What will increase the Kingdom of God on earth is our steadfastness. Blessed Mother Teresa of Calcutta often used to say to her sisters: *'God does not want our success, only our faithfulness.'* Fidelity is required of us on every level of our lives; and God only asks that we keep trying. It is not easy for a priest to measure success, though he can readily identify failure. Doctors, lawyers and teachers, on the other hand, may be able to measure the results of their profession but it can never be so for the priest. And John the Baptist seemed to fail. When your head ends up on a dish it is a fair conclusion. But he had not been ignored; the world had changed because of him, and the world was prepared, because of him, to receive the Redeemer.

John the Baptist would not have been a universally popular preacher, as the only way to be popular with everyone is never to challenge, to be bland, to say nothing. The Catholic Church can never be accused of blandness. We are not called to give blandness to the world, but to give salt and light, to give meaning to the existence of our fellow men and women; we are called to make our presence felt. So whether it is wearing a crucifix to work, or placing it upon the walls of our homes, wearing a miraculous medal, or a Roman collar, or ringing our bells before Mass, all of this makes us visible and audible, and the Church learned a long time ago that it pays to advertise.

Around this time of Advent, there occurs the great festival of the Immaculate Conception of Our Blessed Lady; this means that she was conceived without original sin, perfect from the moment of her existence in the womb of St Anne. This was so that she could be the God-bearer. It is a day each year when we consecrate our parishes, our homes and families to her Immaculate Heart. It was at Lourdes that Our Lady spoke those words to St Bernadette, which the Church had long believed: 'I am the Immaculate Conception.' In this time of Advent, she will direct us to focus on what is most important, on what is vital – Jesus, our Lord and Redeemer.

For further reflection:

> *Lo! To grant a pardon free,*
> *Comes a willing Lamb from Heaven;*
> *Sad and tearful, hasten we,*
> *One and all, to be forgiven.*
> > *(from En clara vox redarguit – tr. JHN)*

What will increase the Kingdom of God on earth, is our steadfastness.

Stir up our hearts, O Lord, to prepare the ways of thine only-begotten Son.
> *(from the Collect of the Day)*

Dominica Tertia Adventus
The Third Sunday of Advent
(Gaudete Sunday)

*'Behold, our God will come, and will save us.'**

Proper of the Day: Introit: Philippians 4:4–6; Psalm 84:2
Epistle: Philippians 4:4–7
Gradual: Psalm 79:2, 3
Alleluia: Psalm 79:2
Gospel: John 1:19–28
Offertory: Psalm 84:2, 3
Communion: Isaiah 35:4

✠

'Ipse est, qui post me venturus est.'†

Today, St Paul, in both the Introit and the Epistle, exhorts Christians to let their modesty be known to all men. This seems something of a contradiction because modesty is having a humble opinion of one's abilities and accomplishments, not wishing to noise them abroad. However, true modesty is to be found precisely in obeying St Paul's injunction by expending our energy in giving glory to God rather than to ourselves. We *must* be seen inasmuch as Christ shines through us. The more we become like Christ, the more we manifest him to the world. In his self-effacement, St John the Baptist gives heroic witness to the self-emptying of Christ himself, *'who'*, as St Paul tells us, *'being in the form of God ... humbled himself, becoming obedient unto death, even to the death of the cross'.‡* We need only to turn to the way in which John, in today's Gospel, answers the questions of the priests and Levites sent to him from Jerusalem.

---

* Isaiah 35:4.
† John 1:27a: 'The same is he that shall come after me.'
‡ Philippians 2:6, 8.

'*Who art thou?*' '*I am not the Christ.*' Notice that St John the Baptist is not asked, '*Art thou the Christ?*', but, '*Who art thou?*' Yet he is quick to say, '*I am not the Christ.*' True humility is interested in truth and is quick to defend and proclaim it. He knew well of their suspicion that he might be the Messiah, so he wished to strike at the heart of their suspicion. '*I am not the Christ.*' They must look to another: John is not the Christ.

'*Art thou Elias?*' '*I am not.*' In response to the first question, John could proclaim the simple truth that he is not the Christ, but the answer to the second question is more complex. This is that Our Blessed Lord himself says elsewhere, '*If you will receive it, he [John] is Elias that is to come.*'* The Baptist replied that he is not Elias to clear up any misunderstanding; he is not *literally* Elias. (Elias was to come to herald the Lord's coming in power and glory. This we know as our Lord's *Second* Coming.) John the Baptist was to herald the Lord's First Coming in the flesh. In this way he is certainly *like* Elias for he heralds the Messiah. That is why the Angel tells Zachary, John's father, that John '*shall go before [the Lord] in the spirit and power of Elias*'.† When Our Lord says that the Baptist *is* Elias, he is speaking figuratively.

But there is another reason why the Baptist was keen not to be taken for Elias. Elias was to be privileged to herald the Second Coming of the Messiah on account of Elias's own greatness.‡ In denying that he was Elias, John wished to free himself from the danger of his works magnifying himself, rather than God. John was a great man in the eyes of some of his contemporaries purely by his being the son of a priest. The Angel had told his father that John '*shall be great before the Lord*'.§ In his modesty, John saw that whatever task we are called to do for the Lord, however exalted, it is a duty for which we should not expect praise, even if carried out well. In this, he gave witness to what Our Lord would later teach in his public ministry:

* Matthew 11:14.
† Luke 1:17.
‡ Ecclesiastes 48:1, 3, 4, 11, 15.
§ Luke 1:15.

*'when you have done all these things that are commanded you, say: "We are unprofitable servants; we have done that which we ought to do."'**

'Art thou the Prophet?' 'No.' Some Jews believed that another prophet – probably Moses – would come with Elias. The Baptist denies any connection with being *the* Prophet. What amazing depths of humility, when Christ himself says of John: *'he is more than a prophet'.*† John the Baptist *is* a prophet but his response to the Jews was not intended as an untruth. He wished to show that it is from Christ and his Holy Spirit that we exercise the divine gifts and all goodness. Jesus, in his humanity, is the Prophet of prophets.‡ The Baptist teaches us that we should praise God who is the origin and source of all good, rather than to praise those who exercise the gifts. In his desire to show that all he said and did was of Christ and for Christ, John considered himself to be even less than a man. He saw himself as a mere voice. This voice existed for the sole purpose of heralding Christ's coming and preparing the people to meet him. In this, John teaches us that true humility makes us desirous to see God praised and magnified in all the actions and activities of our lives. We are entirely God's creatures.

True modesty and true humility boast of nothing except God and his gracious gifts. We should observe that modesty and humility have nothing to do with self-loathing. Although we should lament our many sins and do penance, we should also recognize that we are creatures of Almighty God, and find our peace and consolation in the fact that he loves us and wants us in his Kingdom. The Baptist may sometimes come to us as a harsh and exacting figure, yet even he can find time to rejoice and be glad, since all true joy is found in Christ. John delights that the Saviour has come, and likens himself to a friend waiting for the bridegroom to come. *'The friend of the bridegroom who standeth and heareth him, rejoiceth with joy because of*

---

* Luke 17:10.
† Matthew 11:9.
‡ Luke 7:16.

{ 9 }

the bridegroom's voice. This my joy therefore is fulfilled.'* And
that is just as well, especially on this Gaudete Sunday.

For further reflection:

Thou who dost each earthly throne
Rule by thy right hand alone,
Raise up thy power and shine,
Show thy flock the face divine.
Saving gifts on him bestow
Whom the prophets did foreshow.
From the palace of the sky,
Jesu, to our land draw nigh.

(from the Sarum Sequence)

Let us rejoice!

By the grace of thy Visitation, enlighten the darkness of our
minds.

(from the Collect of the Day)

Dominica Quarta Adventus
The Fourth Sunday of Advent

'The heavens show forth the glory of God and the firmament
declareth the work of his hands.'†

Proper of the Day: Introit: Isaiah 45:8; Psalm 18:2
                             Epistle: 1 Corinthians 4:1–5
                             Gradual: Psalm 144:18, 21
                             Alleluia: cf Hebrews 10:37
                             Gospel: Luke 3:1–6
                             Offertory: Luke 1:28, 42
                             Communion: Isaiah 7:14

---

* John 3:29.
† Introit of the Day and Advent Prose.

'Parate viam Domini: rectas facite semitas ejus.'*

A dvent is an *uncomfortable* season, which is, perhaps, why so many of our contemporaries choose to ignore it and jump immediately to the pleasures of Christmas. Yet, as fallen human beings, we need occasionally to allow ourselves to be made uncomfortable, to be challenged by the Word (the Logos) of God and the call to sanctity. Advent provides us with just such an opportunity.

In the Divine Office at this season, the lessons are taken chiefly from the Prophet Isaiah from whose book comes today's Introit: *'Rorate caeli . . .'* ['Drop down ye heavens . . .']. Isaiah's insistence on a salvation we cannot provide for ourselves becomes the hallmark of this season; we wait, arms outstretched, for the Lord. Yet the Lord's answer, when it comes, is also in the form of a challenge. The Gospel of the First Sunday of Advent is that rather terrifying prophecy concerning the end of the world: *'There shall be signs in the sun, and in the moon, and in the stars; and upon the earth distress of nations . . .'†* Over the weeks that follow, the Gospels each Sunday are dominated by the figure of John the Baptist, the last prophet of the Old Testament and the first martyr of the New, a man whose life and mission are supremely well adapted to overthrow our worldly-minded complacency. The Second Sunday of Advent finds him in prison, sending his disciples to confirm whether Our Lord was indeed the long-awaited Messiah. On the Third Sunday, we heard his giving testimony to our Saviour and to his own relationship to him: *'The same is he whose shoes I am not worthy to unloose.'‡* Finally, today, we see the dramatic opening to his ministry – his sudden springing forth from his hiding place in the wilderness, proclaiming repentance and the hope of forgiveness.

---

* Luke 3:4 'Prepare ye the way of the Lord, make straight his paths.'
† Luke 21:25.
‡ John 1:27.

Why, we might wonder, do the Advent Gospels present John's prophetic activity in this peculiar order? First, we see him in prison, then freely preaching, and now we witness the beginning of his ministry. It is, surely, back to front. Yet it is not the only aspect of the Advent liturgy which runs contrary to our normal thinking. After all, the season begins with a prophecy of the Second Coming* and ends on Christmas night, with the birth of Christ in his First Coming. Again, it is counter-intuitive. But it is, perhaps, deliberately so. Advent, once again, is intended in some way to be *uncomfortable*, to challenge our normal ways of thinking. Above all, it should tear us away from our preoccupation with this passing world and concentrate our minds on that which is truly important – the world which is still to come.

The Gospel we have just heard reminds us, of course, that the Incarnation was an event which happened very much in the world. It was an historical event. St Luke lists for us the temporal authorities who governed when the Baptist began his prophetic ministry as well as the religious authorities of the Old Covenant. Cardinal Baronius, in the sixteenth century, father of Church history and disciple of St Philip Neri, went still further in writing the Christmas Proclamation of the Roman Martyrology, which is used in the Office of Prime (and often sung before Midnight Mass). In this reading, Baronius does his best to pinpoint exactly the moment of our Lord's appearing in the world of classical antiquity: '. . . *in the one hundred and ninety-forth Olympiad; in the year seven hundred and fifty-two from the founding of the city of Rome . . .*'†, and so on.

Yet, while these readings remind us, quite rightly, of the historical nature of the Incarnation, they remind us also of the transitory nature of worldly greatness. For where is now the Roman Empire? Where is the Principality of Galilee? Who would even have heard of Philip or Lysanias if they had not been of the family of the unfortunate Herod the Great? All

---

* Luke 21:25–33.

† From the entry for 25th December in the Roman Martyrology.

these kings and kingdoms have passed away but the Kingdom of God endures.

We are all born into this world, and must live out our faith in this world, yet we must never allow ourselves to become too comfortable here. Advent reminds us of this, and so too does John the Baptist. He, who prepared the way of the Lord, died for that same Lord in a prison cell. Not for nothing is the deacon's singing of the Saviour's Nativity from the Proclamation of Baronius reminiscent of the singing of the Passion. The path from Bethlehem leads to Calvary, and we as Christians are called to carry our cross. And yet we do so in hope, knowing that the things of this world are of little value, compared with the promise of heaven, which lies ahead. Does not the Gospel today end with the promise: '*And all flesh shall see the salvation of God*'?

For further reflection:

'*O Emmanuel, our King and Lawgiver, the desire of the nations and the Saviour thereof, come to save us, O Lord our God.*'*
(*The Great 'O' antiphon for 23rd December*)

Advent is the call to sanctity, for spiritual refreshment before we celebrate the Nativity of our Saviour.

---

* Isaiah 7:14; 33:22.

In Vigilia Nativitatis Domini
The Vigil of the Nativity

'Lift up your gates ... and the King of glory shall come in.'*

Proper of the Day: *Introit: Exodus 16:6, 7; Psalm 23:1*
                              Epistle: Romans 1:1–6
                              Gradual: Exodus 16:6, 7; Psalm 79:2, 3
                              Alleluia: from an unknown Gallican source
                              Gospel: Matthew 1:18–21
                              Offertory: Psalm 23:7
                              Communion: Isaiah 40:5

✠

'Noli timere accipere Mariam.'†

Just as the yearnings of all creation were fulfilled in Mary, so the expectations of Israel were to be fulfilled in Joseph. Joseph it was who completed the prophecies that the Son would be born from the line of David. His obedience, his free consent was needed before what was *'promised before by the prophets'*‡ could come to pass. For it was Joseph who, in fear and humility, first shrank from the responsibility that was his; it was the Angel who gave him the courage to accept his vocation.

This Gospel is one that has been subject to very different interpretations. There have been those like St Augustine who thought that Joseph mistrusted Our Lady and wished to repudiate her, to send her away and renounce all responsibility for her, leaving her to bear her child in solitude and disgrace. That is hardly the action of a *'just man'*, nor would it in any way have protected her from shame. Yet for long that was the common interpretation, and the explanation, perhaps, of why there was no devotion to St Joseph until the late Middle Ages. Even now

---

* Psalm 23:7.

† Matthew 1:20: 'Fear not to take unto thee Mary.'

‡ Romans 1:2.

most translations of the Scriptures choose words that support this interpretation, speaking of *'putting her to shame'*, or even *'divorcing her informally'*. It is difficult, on St Augustine's reading, to feel any admiration for Joseph.

But if we look at writers earlier, and later, than Augustine, we find a very different view. It was the third-century commentator Origen who wrote: *'He wished to send her away because he recognized that a great mystery had been fulfilled in her, which he deemed himself unworthy to approach.'** St Bernard, in one of his lovely sermons on the Virgin Mother, takes up the theme and tells us: *'He wished to put away his spouse for the same reason on account of which Peter begged of the Lord to leave him, exclaiming "Depart from me, O Lord, for I am a sinful man" and on account of which the Centurion prayed that he would not enter his house, saying "Lord, I am not worthy that thou shouldst enter under my roof". Thus Joseph also, considering himself unworthy and a sinner, said to himself that it was not fitting for a man like him to live any longer in such intimate relations with one so great and exalted, whose sublime dignity inspired him with awe.'†*

Now we can believe that Joseph is a saint! His feelings towards Our Lady were not of anger and disgust, but feelings of wonder, awe, humility and fear. That is why the Angel says to him: *'Fear not.'* He knows, he believes that she is with child *'of the Holy Ghost'*, but he is afraid, knowing himself to be unworthy to receive her under his roof. He is unwilling, also, for her to become a celebrity, or to be held up as an example, anxious to shield her from public admiration. For that reason he plans to send her away privately to some secret location, to conceal her, to protect her. Vain hope! She is destined to become the greatest celebrity the world has ever known, to be admired and imitated more than any other child of Eve.

Nor can St Joseph escape the great vocation destined for him: *'Thou,'* says the Angel, *'thou shalt call his name Jesus.'* It is his

---

* Catena Aurea.

† Second Sermon on the Virgin Mother, tr. by a priest of Mt Melleray.

responsibility to give the child a name, the *'name which is above all names . . . in heaven, on earth and under the earth'.** When Joseph stands by at the child's circumcision and proclaims the name, Jesus, he is, in the eyes of the Jewish Law, proclaiming his own responsibility for the child, and giving him the whole of his inheritance. It is in that moment, the giving of the name, that Joseph makes Jesus the Son of David.

Grace is God's free gift to us, his first call towards us, but we must respond to that grace if it is to bear fruit. The eternal Son of God could not become the Son of Man until Our Lady said, *'Let it be done to me according to thy word!'* He could not become the Son of David had Joseph not obeyed the call of the Angel and publicly acknowledged the child as his own. By Our Lord Jesus Christ, as St Paul says in today's Epistle, *'We have received grace and apostleship for obedience to the faith.'*† Our part is to obey the faith which is given us by God; without our co-operation, grace cannot force us.

St Joseph, therefore, shows us that we need not be afraid, even though we know well how unworthy we are to receive the Son of Mary under our roof. We need not shrink back, fearing to enter God's Church. If we have once dared to enter, we need not fear to approach the life-giving sacraments he offers us. They are for us precisely because we are not worthy; the call of faith, to which we must respond, is the call to allow Christ into our lives, to let the King enter in triumph.‡ Of we obey that summons, if we accept the free gift of grace which God offers us, with faith and love, then in us the prophecy will be fulfilled that *'all flesh shall see the salvation of our God'.*§

How can we think ourselves unworthy, despite all our weakness and our sins, for *'the earth is the Lord's . . . and all they that dwell therein'.*¶ He knows well enough how feeble we are, how frail our nature, for he made us. He understands us

---

* Philippians 2:9–11.
† Romans 1:6.
‡ Offertory of the Day.
§ Communion of the Day.
¶ Introit of the Day.

far better than we can understand ourselves. That is why he comes to rescue us from our sins and weakness, to blot out our wickedness, our stupidity and our pride. In obedience to his call, we can welcome him with joy, gladly receive him into our hearts, take him to ourselves, and so draw the breath of new life. Tomorrow we celebrate his coming to our world long ago in Bethlehem, but today and every day we rejoice that he comes to us, the King of Glory, the Child in the manger, the familiar guest in our hearts.

For *further reflection:*

Come, thou Redeemer of the earth,
And manifest thy virgin-birth:
Let every age adoring fall;
Such birth befits the God of all.

(from Veni Redemptor gentium – tr. JMN)

In obedience to his call, we can welcome him with joy, gladly receive him into our hearts, take him to ourselves.

Grant, Almighty God, that we may joyfully receive the eternal gifts of thy Son.

(from the Secret)

In Nativitate Domini – ad Primum Missam
The Nativity of Our Lord – at the First Mass

'Thou art my Son, this day have I begotten thee.' *

Proper of the Day: Introit: Psalm 2:7, 1
                      Epistle: Titus 2:11–15
                      Gradual: Psalm 109:3, 1
                      Alleluia: Psalm 2:7
                      Gospel: Luke 2:1–14
                      Offertory: Psalm 95:11, 13
                      Communion: Psalm 109:3

☩

'et reclinavit eum in praesepio'†

The contrast between the awesome authority of an imperial edict involving vast territories and many peoples, and the arrival in Bethlehem of a simple Jewish couple expecting a child, seems at first extraordinary. Yet St Luke tells us that is why they were there when Mary's child was born. It was no accident but a part of divine revelation that it happened in that place and at that time. The city of David had long ago been prophesied as the birthplace of the Saviour. The time also was of God's own choosing. Just as he used a decision of the Roman Emperor to order it so that Mary and Joseph should be in Bethlehem when the birth was due, so the other social and political circumstances of the time were directly selected as part of his design.

The peoples of the Mediterranean world into which Our Lord was born had never before been so closely linked by language, law and culture. At the same time, the Jewish religion was to be found linking communities throughout the Roman Empire. In his infinite wisdom, God used the unifying aspects

---

* Introit of the Day.

† Luke 2:7: 'and laid him in a manger'.

{ 18 }

of this society into which to launch his great plan of redemption and rescue for mankind. Though imperfect as are all human societies, yet it was to provide fertile ground for the gospel seed when it came to be planted. Sin and evil also reigned and the majority of people were steeped in idolatry and superstition. But it was precisely these and other such evils that the Son of Man came to deal with face to face, as it were. Where darkness and despair abounded there would be light and hope. In a cave that sheltered animals, the Divine Infant let forth his first cry. His first human utterance was a sound that pierced the night and signified the end of Satan's tyranny over mankind. No wonder it was answered by the Angels with a chorus of heavenly rejoicing heard by simple shepherds. That same voice would one day announce the coming of the Kingdom, and later speak the words that shall be spoken again this night at Mass, to make him once again really and truly present as he was to the shepherds who came to adore him.

As we kneel to acknowledge this great mystery, we recall his infinite love manifested in the great humility that he showed by becoming as we are, though without any trace of sin. The Christ-Mass that we celebrate takes us back to the manger in Bethlehem and also to the foot of the cross at Calvary. In both places we meet Our Lady through whom it all became possible. If we let her, she will teach us and lead us to know and love him better. We need not envy those who, we are told, were among the few to visit and acknowledge Our Lord in the manger. Beautiful as those moments must have been for them, they are mirrored in the gracious opportunities which are available also to us. Let us but consider carefully how he is never far from where we may find him; sometimes but a short distance from our homes or places of work or leisure.

The manger and the cross unite in the Tabernacles in every Catholic Church throughout the world. Christ present under the appearance of bread remains waiting for those with loving hearts to seek him. The Angels glorify him in the Most Holy Sacrament as they did while he lay asleep in the manger or in Mary's arms. Every worthy Communion and every loving visit to a church relives that precious gift and rejoices his and Mary's heart. St Paul tells us in the Epistle of this Mass, *'We should live soberly and justly and godly in this world . . .'* This implies daily asking for God's grace to aid us. Then we can come with faith and love into his presence and rejoice that, like the shepherds at Bethlehem, we too have been led by faith to know and see what many have missed or simply failed, through ignorance, to seek.

For further reflection:

> *Who was before all time*
> *Is born of purest Maid;*
> *Glory to God in heights sublime,*
> *Peace comes the world to aid.*
>
> > *(from the Sarum Sequence)*

The Christ-Mass that we celebrate takes us back to the manger in Bethlehem, and it also takes us to the foot of the cross at Calvary.

Grant that by thine infinite grace we may be found like unto him in whom our nature is united to thee.

> *(from the Collect of the Day)*

In Nativitate Domini – ad Secundam Missam

The Nativity of Our Lord – at the Second Mass

*'He shall be called Wonderful, God, the Prince of Peace, the Father of the world to come.'**

Proper of the Day: Introit: Isaiah 9:2, 6; Psalm 92:1
                       Epistle: Titus 3:4, 7
                       Gradual: Psalm 117:26, 27, 23
                       Alleluia: Psalm 92:1
                       Gospel: Luke 2:15–20
                       Offertory: Psalm 92:1, 2
                       Communion: Zechariah 9:9

✠

'sed secundum suam misericordiam salvos nos fecit per lavacrum regenerationis et renovationis Spiritus Sancti'†

You will remember from *Brideshead Revisited*, how amazed Charles Ryder is the first time he discusses the Catholic faith with Sebastian. *'You can't seriously believe it all . . . about Christmas, and the star and the three kings and the ox and the ass. You can't believe things because they are a lovely idea.'* In the end, of course, this is exactly how Charles himself comes to believe. He is an artist who sees the beauty of the Catholic faith even as it is expressed by some very flawed characters indeed. That fact alone makes the novel one of hope for flawed Catholics everywhere.

This morning's Epistle tells us that God saved us *'not by the works of justice which we have done, but according to his*

---

* Isaiah 9:6b.

† Titus 3:4: 'but according to his mercy, he saved us, by the laver of regeneration and renovation of the Holy Spirit'.

mercy he saved us by the laver of regeneration and renovation of the Holy Spirit'. Perhaps that is rendered more succinctly in *'not thanks to anything we had done for our own justification but in accordance with his own merciful design'*. St Paul here is giving us a key to understand our experience of the beauty of our faith. God made us in his image and likeness and able to recognize him in the design, in the beauty of his creation and, still more, in the wonder of the Incarnation of his Son. When we come to a well-made crib, we are moved with a childlike wonder at the beauty of the Incarnation, the Word made flesh. We are able to capture, briefly, the experience of the shepherds. On seeing him, they discovered the truth of what had been told them about this child.

St Paul puts things in a very theological way, giving us reason for the hope we have, expressing it in a way that we can communicate easily with others. Ever since, theologians have reasoned in a similar way showing how goodness, beauty and truth as we find them in the world around us make visible to us invisible attributes of God. We call them *transcendentals* because they reveal God to us. St Gregory the Great encapsulates this theology in the Preface he wrote for the Christmas Mass: *'In him we see our God made visible and so are caught up in love of the God we cannot see.'*

When the shepherds came to the stable at Bethlehem and discovered the truth of what they had been told, they did not immediately formulate a doctrine of the Incarnation or frame an argument for God's own merciful design. But they did see at once that what they saw with their eyes in the stable was in full accord with the message they had heard from the Angels. How do we respond to the beauty of our faith, to the childlike wonder that we experience each year when we come to the crib or attend a Christmas Mass? The modern man, the young Charles Ryder, wants to dismiss it, to relegate it to the world of make-believe, suitable for children but not for the modern man. But this was not the response of the shepherds who went out and told their story to the amazement of all who heard it. Still less was it the response of Our Blessed Lady, who treasured up all these sayings *'and pondered them in her heart'*.* Perhaps we should trust our feelings too when we come to the crib and find that in our encounter with Mary and Joseph, and the child lying in the manger, all that we have been told is true after all.

✠

For further reflection:

> *And while the Angels in the sky*
> *Sang praise above the silent field,*
> *To shepherds poor the Lord most high,*
> *The one great Shepherd was revealed.*

(from A solis ortis cardine – tr. JE)

When the shepherds came to the stable at Bethlehem they saw at once that all was in accord with the message they had heard from the Angels.

O wonderful, mysterious generation! O most astonishing Nativity! O glorious child! O Deity incarnate!

(from the Sarum Missal)

In Nativitate Domini – ad Tertiam Missam
The Nativity of Our Lord – at the Third Mass

'Sing ye to the Lord a new canticle: because he hath done wonderful things.'

Proper of the Day:　　Introit: Isaiah 9:6; Psalm 97:1
　　　　　　　　　　　Epistle: Hebrews 1:1–12
　　　　　　　　　　　Gradual: Psalm 97:3, 4, 2
　　　　　　　　　　　Alleluia: Psalm 97:2
　　　　　　　　　　　Gospel: John 1:1–14
　　　　　　　　　　　Offertory: Psalm 88:12–15
　　　　　　　　　　　Communion: Psalm 97:3

✠

'In principio erat Verbum . . .'†

The Word was before all things – before our solar system, before the wider universe and the knowable and unknowable space between, beyond and within. In the vastness of it all we can easily be confused by this small word. Does it simply mean *Scripture*, for instance? After all, as it was revealed to John to pass on to us, we ought to be able to understand something of its meaning and the truth of it – at least to some small degree.

For all the immensity of God, we can, nevertheless, grasp something of the idea of the eternal Trinity bound together in a love so intense we cannot fathom. The *Word*, the *Logos*, in the meaning of the glorious acclamation at the beginning of St John's Gospel, is nothing less than the *Wisdom* of God we hear often spoken of in the Old Testament. Yet, it is much more than that – and we struggle to define the indefinable – it is a *promise*, and *command* of Divine Authority; it is an *idea*; it is the Divine

---

* Introit of the Day.

† John 1:1: 'In the beginning was the Word . . .'

Intention; and it is that *Intention* living with God the Father from the very beginning, wrapped up in the love of God the Father and the Holy Spirit, who is gradually revealed through the prophets to a people chosen to be the first recipients of God's outpouring revelation. That *Intention*, that *Idea*, that Son of God the Father, is the Word here spoken of in St John's Gospel. Of course, it was not until the Word was expressed in the very flesh of mankind that we could begin to understand a little of the glory of the eternal Trinity. This Divine Intention was expressed in flesh from the moment of conception within God's chosen vessel, Our Blessed Lady, and was subsequently brought forth and laid in a manger to be sniffed and snorted at by the lower orders of his own creation. And so, a human baby brings God to earth. The Divine Intention was ever the Incarnation, to be made flesh and dwell among us.

At Christmas, we kneel alongside those simple, but privileged rustics; later, we kneel with those honourable and honoured wise men; later still, beside Mary and John at the foot of the cross, and we worship the Son who is the Word. These events in Christ's life on earth took place in time, in our time, though not in our span. We pray to the child Jesus as we pray to Christ crucified, to Christ as he says 'Mary' in the garden. All episodes in the life of Jesus reveal the Saviour to us and we rightly keep these pictures in our mind. Here, after all, is the life of God on earth, experiencing the human condition, to be rejected, to offer himself to the Father as a ransom and in exchange for the sin of mankind. All this was bound up in the child as he lay in the manger, as it was bound up within the Heavenly Father as the Word, before all things were made. Christ, now joined in one with his Bride, the Church, remains with us in that body and, particularly, in the Most Holy Sacrament of the Altar, a gift of utmost generosity.

✠

For further reflection:

> Affections must be weaned away from sin
> So shall we gain that peace within
> Reserved for those the pure in heart;
> Lo! earth is joined with things divine,
> In this respect all lays combine,
> In which we take a part.
> O man, rejoice, and ponder this accord;
> O flesh, rejoice, associate with the Word.
>
> (from the Sarum Sequence)

The Word is the Son of God expressed in the flesh of man.

Grant, Almighty God, that this celebration of the birth of thine only-begotten Son in the flesh may set us free from waywardness.

(Cf the Collect of the Day)

Dominica infra Octavam Nativitatis
Sunday within the Octave of the Nativity

'God sent his Son, made of a woman, made under the law, that he might redeem them who were under the law . . .'*

Proper of the Day: Introit: Wisdom 18:14, 15; Psalm 92:1
Epistle: Galatians 4:1–7
Gradual: Psalm 44:3, 2
Alleluia: Psalm 92:1
Gospel: Luke 2:33–40
Offertory: Psalm 92:12
Communion: Matthew 2:20

---

* Galatians 4:4, 5.

'Ecce positus est hic in ruinam, et in resurrectionem multorum in Israel; et in signum cui contradicetur.' [*]

How quickly in the Christmas season we are reminded of the cost of our redemption: *'Behold, this child is set for the fall, and for the rise of many in Israel; and for a sign which shall be contradicted.'* The Gospel carries us forward to Our Lord's Presentation in the Temple, the feast which ends the Christmas season, and anticipates Lent. It is a feast that, like today's readings, brings with it a penitential aspect: *'Like funeral lights for Christmas gone, old Simeon's tapers shine.'* Christmas has not gone by any means, but the feasts of St Stephen and St Thomas of Canterbury that we have just celebrated remind us that discipleship does not come without a cost.

We should not be surprised. Before the coming of Our Lord, we find in Ecclesiasticus: *'Son, when thou comest to the service of God . . . prepare thy soul for temptation. Humble thy heart and endure . . . For gold and silver are tried in the fire, but acceptable men in the furnace of humiliation.'* [†] The Christmas season includes examples of courageous martyrs, who shed their blood for Our Lord, sometimes after lives of great suffering. Two of the supporting characters in today's Gospel are Simeon and Anna, who show us a rather different kind of trial – that of patient waiting and endurance. Either or both these kinds of suffering may be our lot in life, but some suffering there must be if we are truly to be called Our Lord's disciples. *'If any man will come after me, let him deny himself, and take up his cross, and follow me.'* [‡]

So, if we are to be sons, we must accept the inheritance that follows. St Paul tells us that the man or woman who comes into property while still a child has no more liberty than one of the servants. Every man and woman has inherited property

---

[*] Luke 2:34: 'Behold, this child is set for the fall, and for the rise of many in Israel; and for a sign which shall be contradicted.'

[†] Ecclesiasticus 2:1, 2, 5.

[‡] Matthew 16:24.

{ 27 }

from God. We are born in his image and likeness, and into a world he has created for our use. In Baptism, God gives us the gift of faith; we are born again in new life as his sons. Yet, how many of us continue to live as if this had never happened, living infantile lives, toiling away at the childish ways of the classroom and nursery. We accept the good things God gives us as our right but seldom move beyond our love of creation to the full and proper love of the creator. Our faith fails to grow through the failure to exercise it.

Truly accepting the inheritance that comes from God, the one that will last beyond the end of creation, means first of all embracing the life of Our Lord in our own lives, being prepared to be *'a sign which shall be contradicted'*.* It can mean bearing witness to Christ and his Resurrection, as St Stephen, or shunning compromise and putting the demands of the Church and of our faith even above our friends, as St Thomas of Canterbury. It can mean long lives of patient waiting and suffering, sometimes in the face of the derision of the world, as it did with Simeon and Anna. It is certain that in this world, where our faith is largely ignored when it is not being openly attacked, there will be plenty of opportunity to exercise this second aspect of our inheritance, in order to fulfil the duties that come – as duties always will – with the rights of inheritance.

If all this seems like darkness and gloom, then, in a sense, it is because it is precisely where God is to be found, where Simeon and Anna found him, where the saints and martyrs of the Church found him. Christmas, the coming of the Lord in flesh, occurs at the darkest time of the year.

However, the Introit gives us both the theme of this Mass and a glimpse of what lies ahead: *'While all things were in quiet silence and the night was in the midst of her course, thine Almighty Word, O Lord, leaped down from heaven from thy royal throne.'†* Then the psalm speaks of what lies beyond the inheritance of suffering: *'The Lord hath reigned, he is clothed*

---

* Luke 2:34.

† Wisdom 18:14, 15.

with beauty: the Lord is clothed with strength . . .' This is the lot of those who accept the inheritance God gives to them in Christ, with its duties as well as its rights. *'Therefore I endure all things for the sake of the elect, that they also may obtain the salvation, which is Christ with heavenly glory. A faithful saying: for if we be dead with him, we shall live also with him.'**

✠

For further reflection:

> *Sleep, Holy Babe. Ah, take thy brief repose.*
> *Too quickly will thy slumbers break*
> *And thou to lengthened pains awake*
> *That death alone shall close.*
> (Revd Edward Caswell, Cong. Orat.)

Our faith fails to grow through the failure to exercise it.

May our vices be removed and our just desires fulfilled.
(from the Post Communion Collect)

---

* 2 Timothy 2:10, 11.

In Circumcisione Domini et Octava Nativitatis

The Circumcision of Our Lord and the Octave of Christmas

'All the ends of the earth have seen the salvation of our God.'*

Proper of the Day: Introit: Isaiah 9:6; Psalm 97:1
Epistle: Titus 2:11–15
Gradual: Psalm 97:3, 4, 2
Alleluia: Hebrews 1:1, 2
Gospel: Luke 2:21
Offertory: Psalm 88:12, 15
Communion: Psalm 97:3

✠

'Vocatum est nomen ejus Jesus.'†

The well-known Christmas song 'The Twelve Days of Christmas' reminds us that in the past the festivities were spread over a longer period than is customary today. The truth is that few people now could sustain it for so long. There may be various reasons for this. The cost of keeping the party going would be more than most of us could bear. It is also true that the impact of feast days on all our lives has been blunted by the fact that we have so many other celebrations and *non*-celebrations of all kinds throughout the year. Even, dare one say it, the many Christmas parties and dinners that are hosted throughout the season of Advent. By the time we arrive at the actual feast day, many people enjoy the break from work and simply wish to get over the festivities quickly. This is a sad reflection on current attitudes to feasting and to religious festivals. Christmas and

---

* Psalm 97:3.

† Luke 2:21: 'His name was called Jesus.'

{ 30 }

the days following it are festivals of faith as much as of food. Observing them in the right spirit does not necessarily mean sitting down to another Christmas dinner every day. It means giving time away from normal routine of work to enjoy the goodness of God and having greater opportunity to render him thanks appropriately.

Today, we celebrate the Feast of the Circumcision of Our Lord, the Naming of Jesus, the Octave Day of Christmas. What is an octave? It is one of the most ancient customs which we trace far back to the Old Testament itself, to the primitive times of Jewish worship and law. The great feasts of the Bible were prolonged for eight days to emphasize their importance and solemnity. Scholars tell us that there was also another reason. The scattered community of the Jews at various times in their history meant that sometimes the actual date of a festival was uncertain, give or take a few days. Having eight days in which to keep it could guarantee that it would be kept on the actual day during that week. In biblical times these things were not insignificant. The various festivals marked not only the intervention of God in the history of the people but also marked their identity as chosen and different from all other races.

In contrast to the exclusive faith of the Jewish nation, we are conscious of the universality of our faith and of the Church that proclaims it. The message of Christmas is not for the few but for the many. That is our identity. Our cultural roots and social and political systems are the result of centuries of Christianity. Today for many will be just New Year's Day – a public holiday like any other. For us, it is much more. It marks the beginning of another twelve months in *Anno Domini*. It is from the birth of Christ that we date all our years. Our sometimes godless society needs reminding of these things from time to time. We as individuals and as a community of souls redeemed by our Saviour can take the opportunity of this feast of the Naming of Jesus to re-dedicate ourselves to him for this coming year, and make appropriate resolutions to do better during it. May the grace of God, effective in this Holy Mass, be with us throughout this coming year and lead us effectively to a deepening of our faith and our greater love for God and our neighbour.

For further reflection:

> *O blessed day, when first was poured*
> *The blood of our redeeming Lord!*
> *O blessed day, when first began*
> *His sufferings for fallen man.*
>
> (from Felix Dies quem proprio)

It is from the birth of Christ we date our years.

O God, who givest leave to celebrate this octave of our Saviour's birth, grant that as we may ever be renewed by the communion of his body and blood, so we may be defended by his Divinity.

(from the Sarum Missal)

In Festo Sanctissimi Nominis Jesu
The Holy Name of Jesus

'Amen, amen I say to you, if you ask anything of the Father, he will give it you in my name.'

Proper of the Day:	Introit: Philippians 2:10, 11
	Epistle: Acts 4:8–12
	Gradual: Psalm 105:47; Isaiah 63:16
	Alleluia: Psalm 144:21
	Gospel: Luke 2:21
	Offertory: Psalm 85:12, 5
	Communion: Psalm 85:9, 10

This feast of the Holy Name of Jesus is of comparatively recent origin, and has in its short life wandered about the Calendar rather like the journey from Nazareth to Bethlehem and from Bethlehem to Egypt. Only in 1721 was it inserted into the Calendar of the Universal Church, replacing the Second Sunday after Epiphany, and it was Pope Pius X who moved it to the Sunday within the Octave of the Circumcision, to fill the curious gap left in the 1570 Missal which made no provision for that Sunday at all. Since then it has suffered a period of occlusion, before reappearing on 3rd January. Yet devotion to the Holy Name is most associated with that extraordinary revival of lay Catholic piety preached by saints such as St Bernardino of Siena† and St John of Capistrano‡ in the fifteenth century. In England the feast was well established, and appears in the Sarum Missal on 7th August, although with a rather different Proper, including the sequence – *Dulcis Jesu Nazaremus.*

The great preachers emphasized that the name represents the person, and that when we do honour to the name of Jesus we acclaim him as truly the Saviour. For that is what the name Jesus means. It incorporates the letters of the sacred name of the Lord revealed to Moses, with the addition of two letters to make it possible to pronounce. It is no different from the name we write as Joshua, for both are attempts at putting the same Hebrew characters into our alphabet. The name Joshua was given by Moses to his servant when he was sent along as the thirteenth man in the expedition to spy out the land of Canaan.§ The name Joshua, or Jesus, means 'the Lord saves'. We, therefore, are not saved by our own sword or by our armies, but by God himself, who scatters our enemies and brings us into the Promised Land. That is why it is one Joshua who leads

---

* Philippians 2:10a: 'That in the name of Jesus every knee should bow . . .'
† 20th May.
‡ 23rd October, formerly 18th March.
§ Numbers 13:16.

{ 33 }

the Children of Israel across the Jordan into Palestine;* it is another, together with the priests, who leads the returning exiles home after the Babylon-ish Captivity.†

It is in the *name* of Jesus that we call upon the Father with utter confidence, for he himself has promised: '*Amen, amen I say to you, if you ask anything of the Father, he will give it you in my name. Hitherto you have asked nothing in my name; ask, and you will receive, that your joy may be full.*'‡ The apostles were not slow to invoke that name: '*In the name of Jesus Christ of Nazareth, walk!*'§ And when the priests asked them: '*By what power or by what name did you do this?*' they answered boldly: '*Be it known to you all, and to all the people of Israel, that by the name of Jesus Christ, whom you crucified, whom God raised from the dead, by him this man is standing before you well.*'¶

St Peter is bolder yet. Not only is he glad to be able to invoke the name of Jesus, and see sickness dispersed, demons banished, the dead raised to life – he continues to proclaim: '*there is no other name under heaven given among men by which we must be saved*'.** Jesus Christ of Nazareth, and he alone, is the salvation of the Lord. He is not a Saviour only for the Galileans, or only for the Jews, but he comes to save all men of every tribe and race and people and language. No one is excluded from his saving work, for he is the new Adam, come to right the wrongs unleashed in the world by our common ancestor. Salvation through him is offered '*to the Jew first, and also to the Greek*',†† and everyone of any nationality '*who calls upon the name of the Lord will be saved*'.‡‡

---

* Joshua 3.
† 1 Esdras 3:2 (Ezra).
‡ John 16:23–24.
§ Acts 3:6.
¶ Acts 4:7, 10.
** Acts 4:12.
†† Romans 1:16.
‡‡ Romans 10:13.

The reason for this is that Jesus is the Word incarnate. Just as Israel affirmed of old, *'The Lord our God is one Lord'*,* so the Word is *'the only-begotten Son of the Father'*.† There is only one God; God is incarnate only once; only once and for all does Christ offer the supreme sacrifice on our behalf. His covenant is an eternal covenant, and of his reign there shall be no end. To look for any other name is to look for an Anti-Christ – and there have been false Christs in plenty. To say that his salvation is only for a few, only for one group or other, is to deny our common descent, and our common brotherhood in Christ. For that reason the Gradual chant calls on the Lord to save us *'and gather us from among the nations'*‡ [*'congrega nos de nationibus'*]. Again, the Communion chant declares: *'All the nations thou hast made shall come and bow before thee, O Lord.'*§ Just as there is only one Creator God, and we are all his children, so there is only one Saviour, and we are all his brethren. His Father is offered to us as *our* Father; his Mother as the Mother of all the faithful.

And for this reason we honour the name of Jesus. *'That in the name of Jesus, every knee should bow'*¶ [*'In nomine Jesu omne genu flectatur'*], writes St Paul to the Philippians. Our physical gestures of respect when we pronounce or hear that name are only an outward sign of inner respect, the deep love we feel for him. The sacred texts of the Old Testament speak again and again of the reverence due to the *name* of God, that unutterable name which tells us of who he is and of how he is the one who is to come. *'Let all flesh bless his holy name'*,** *'and I will glorify thy name for ever'*.†† The name of God is full of awe, and none shall dare to utter it in vain.‡‡ Yet it is a name of

---

* Deuteronomy 6:4.
† John 1:14.
‡ Psalm 105:47.
§ Psalm 85:9, 10.
¶ Philippians 2:10a.
** Psalm 145:21.
†† Psalm 85:12.
‡‡ Exodus 20:7.

delight – *'thy name is as oil poured out'*,* *'for thou, O Lord, art sweet and mild: and plenteous in mercy to all that call upon thee'.*† Now that the name of Jesus has been given to us, God is no longer far away, no longer separated from us by the impassable gulf between Creator and creation, for the Word has been made flesh, and has dwelt among us.‡ As a small child he is given to us, as Son of Man he is born for us, and *'his name was called Jesus, which was called by the angel, before he was conceived in the womb'.*§ O come, let us adore him!

✠

For further reflection:

> *Sweet is the name, sweet the surname,*
> *No one such title can proclaim,*
> *Surpassing all beside.*
> *It sinners soothes, and gives them cure,*
> *Comforts the just, and makes them sure,*
> *Whatever may betide.*
> *Unto this name be honour paid,*
> *Which evil spirits, sore afraid,*
> *Dread, and before it quail:*
> *This is the name which brings salvation,*
> *The only certain consolation*
> *To aid when sad hearts fail.*
>
> (from Dulcis Jesu Nazaremus)

Now that the name of Jesus has been given to us, God is no longer far away.

O God ... mercifully grant that we who venerate his holy name on earth may fully behold him in heaven.

(from the Collect of the Day)

---

* Canticle of Canticles 1:2.
† Psalm 85:5.
‡ John 1:14a.
§ Luke 2:21b.

In Epiphania Domini
The Epiphany of Our Lord

*'All they from Saba shall come, bringing gold and frankincense and showing forth praise to the Lord.'**

Proper of the Day: *Introit: Malachi 3:1; Psalm 71:2*
                            Epistle: Isaiah 60:1–6
                            Gradual: Isaiah 60:6, 1
                            Alleluia: Matthew 2:2
                            Gospel: Matthew 2:1–12
                            Offertory: Psalm 71:10, 11
                            Communion: Matthew 2:2

✠

'Inundatio camelorum operiet te . . .'†

The Magi are pagans, Gentiles, outsiders and foreigners, men from the East, worshippers of fire, dreamers after stars. Yet they come to worship the Lord in a humble house at Bethlehem, where his own people knew him not.‡ St Matthew, himself a tax-collector and acquainted with pagans, tells us this story as a message of hope for all those who had considered themselves excluded from hope, of faith for those who did not share the faith of God's people.

It was in the days of King Herod – himself an outsider and more than half a pagan – that the Wise Men came to find the Christ. They were led by a star, in their foolishness, following a point of light in the night sky, but in their wisdom they came upon the Sun of Righteousness, rising into the dawn of a new day. So it is that God can lead outsiders to the home of truth, pagans to true religion, star-gazers to the real light. False reasoning can often lead to a true conclusion. In God's providence those who follow false religions and false sciences can eventually

---

* Isaiah 6:1.
† Isaiah 60:6: 'The multitude of camels shall cover thee . . .'
‡ Cf John 1:1–14.

{ 37 }

find the truth, but once that truth is found, how could they return to the shadows and faint images they had left behind? That is why the Magi returned *'by a different way'* – no longer astrologers and pagans; they had found the true Way.

Our Lord told the crowds: *'Many shall come from the East and the West, and shall sit down with Abraham, and Isaac and Jacob in the Kingdom of Heaven but the children of the Kingdom shall be cast out into the exterior darkness.'** So often Our Lord has to remind them of this until at last it is too late – his parable of the vineyard ends with the stark warning: *'The Kingdom of God shall be taken from you, and shall be given to a nation yielding the fruits thereof.'*†

Now the priests and Pharisees recognize that he is speaking of them, but they still will not recognize who he is. *'He came unto his own, and his own received him not.'*‡ But the Magi, who had never belonged to God's people, came from far in the East to receive him and welcome him.

The Pharisees conspired against him because he spoke of heaven opening to the Gentiles, and of all nations hearing the call of God. Yet this was nothing new, nothing contradictory to the traditions of Israel, if only the scribes and Pharisees had bothered to read their own Scriptures. Abraham was called by God with a promise: *'In thy seed shall all the nations of the earth be blessed.'*§ And his seed was to be as many as the stars of heaven: *'Look up to heaven and number the stars if thou canst.'*¶

The Star itself was, perhaps, foretold by the pagan prophet Balaam, who looked far into the future for the coming of the Christ: *'I shall see him, but not now: I shall behold him, but not near. A star shall rise out of Jacob and a sceptre shall spring up from Israel.'*** In today's lesson, Isaiah sings of the light from

---

* Matthew 8:11, 12.
† Matthew 21:43.
‡ John 1:11.
§ Genesis 22:18.
¶ Genesis 15:5.
** Numbers 24:17.

Jerusalem which will illuminate all those nations that had formerly been in darkness. Salvation comes to the pagans from the Jews,* and that is precisely the meaning of God's choice of that people. Israel was chosen, not to keep God's grace to himself, but in order that through Israel all nations might be saved. As Isaiah says: *'And the Gentiles shall walk in thy light, and kings in the brightness of thy rising.'†* In many places Isaiah and the other prophets speak of the pagan nations being drawn to the God of Israel, but somehow, by the time of Our Lord, the scribes had forgotten that and had come to believe that God loved Israel to the exclusion of others.

It is often pointed out that St Matthew does not mention kings, nor camels, in his account of the coming of the Magi. It is Isaiah who supplies those details: kings coming from afar, and a positive inundation of camels, not to mention *'dromedaries of Madian and Epha'.‡* The coming of the Magi is a fulfilment of those prophecies, although, like the coming of Our Lord himself, not in a form that the scribes can recognize. A group of oriental sages (possibly even without camels) coming unannounced to Jerusalem, does not look quite like the splendid picture drawn by Isaiah of a triumphant royal progress, just as a swaddled babe in a manger was not easily recognized as the Christ. The wisdom of the Magi is shown in the fact that when they found him, they knelt without question, and adored him; not in the royal palace at Jerusalem, but in Bethlehem they found him. *'Behold, the Lord, the Ruler is come . . . Give to the King thy judgement, O God.'§* But it is a helpless baby King, a Ruler bound in swaddling clothes.

The scribes in Jerusalem knew that it was in Bethlehem that the Christ was to be born, but they were unconcerned, and would not stir an afternoon's walk to see him, when the Magi, the pagans, had travelled so far, risked so much, opened their hearts to the light of the Truth, given up earthly treasures in

---

* Cf John 4:22.

† Isaiah 60:3.

‡ Isaiah 60:6.

§ Introit of the Day.

{ 39 }

exchange for him *'who by these same gifts was signified, is sacrificed and received'.** What a contrast there is between God's own people – indifferent, suspicious, even hostile – and the generous journey of those who had been considered aliens and strangers. St Matthew returns to this theme many times in the Gospel, from that initial list of ancestors where he draws attention to the foreign women, Rahab, Ruth and the wife of the Hittite, from whom Our Lord, by Joseph's adoption, claims descent; and ending with the great command to go out: *'Teach ye all nations.'*†

The Truth is the same for all nations – no matter where people come from, the message is for them. There is only one Way to salvation, through the Incarnation of the Word of God. Those who do not yet fully know that Word may still be saved by following the Truth as far as they *do* know him, but once they have found that Truth they may not go back to their shadows and images, for it is in the Child of Bethlehem that all peoples find eternal life.

✠

For further reflection:

> *Lo, sages from the East are gone*
> *To where the star hath newly shone:*
> *Led on by light to Light they press,*
> *And by their gifts their God confess.*
> *(from Hostis Herodes impie – tr. PD)*

The Magi returned by a different way, no longer astrologers; they had found the true Way.

Grant, O God, we may be led by the star to contemplate the beauty of thy majesty.
(from the Collect of the Day)

---

* Secret of the Day.
† Matthew 28:19.

Sanctae Famillae Jesu, Mariae, Joseph
The Holy Family Jesus, Mary, Joseph

'The father of the just rejoiceth greatly, let thy father and thy mother be joyful, and let her rejoice that bore thee.'*

Proper of the Day: Introit: *Proverbs 23:24, 25; Psalm 83:2, 3*
                              Epistle: *Colossians 3:12–17*
                              Gradual: *Psalm 26:4; 86:5*
                              Alleluia: *Isaiah 45:15*
                              Gospel: *Luke 2:42–52*
                              Offertory: *Luke 2:22*
                              Communion: *Luke 2:51*

✠

'Super omnia autem haec, caritatem habete, quod est vinculum perfectionis.'†

Pope Paul Sixth's address, which forms the second reading for the Feast of the Holy Family, in the Novus Ordo Divine Office, must have been inspired by the Mass for the feast as the Holy Father knew it in those days. It is a beautiful meditation on the life in the home at Nazareth. Pope Paul wrote: *'The home of Nazareth is the school where we begin to understand the life of Jesus – the school of the Gospel.'*

It is true, perhaps, that some of the newer feasts of the liturgy may tend to be rather didactic, morally edifying, rather than mystical. But in the case of the Mass of the Holy Family, it can be most helpful. Although this kind of inspiration may be quite new to the *liturgy*, it does have a rather older pedigree in meditative prayer, especially in the tradition begun by St Ignatius of Loyola. This practice of imagining oneself to be in, say, a Gospel scene – in the Bethlehem stable or the Bethlehem house, at Nazareth in the workshop, in Jerusalem with the teachers in

---

* Proverbs 23:24, 25.

† Colossians 3:14: 'But above all these things have charity, which is the bond of perfection.'

the Temple – gauging one's reactions and then drawing a lesson from it is not always an easy exercise. But at this time of the year, with the crib still in church to help us, most can find themselves transported to contemplate the Holy Family there in Bethlehem and, later, in Nazareth. We can draw from the exercise spiritual sustenance for our lives. Pope Paul drew three lessons from the imaginative reconstruction of the life of the Holy Family: a lesson of silence, of family life, and of work.

A beautiful crib will always help us learn a lesson of silence and contemplation – the sight of Our Blessed Lady and St Joseph fondly regarding their child in the crib, gazing in amazement like any parent, but gazing also in the knowledge that this child is the Son of God. It is a lesson – perhaps above all to parents – to see in the unique life of their offspring, another independent and irreplaceable image of God himself. That intense awe that parents feel at the sight of the new life they have, by the privilege of sharing in God's creative power, brought into the world, is just a pale reflection of the awe we shall all feel when one day, God willing, we see God himself, face to face. We should try to make time in our lives for silence to make space to contemplate God's glory and his gifts to us.

Pope Paul speaks of the lesson of family life, of its sacredness and inviolability, of its importance in the social order. St Paul's words to the Colossians in today's Epistle give the best guidance. Compassion, kindness, humility, gentleness and patience, a generosity modelled on the generosity God has shown us; forbearance, charity and gratitude. These are the examples that the members of a Christian family should give to each other, and to the world. The Gospel encourages children in respect for the authority of their parents after Our Lord's own example. None of this is to set an unrealistic standard or to expect perfection. There will be daily failures and we should not be discouraged. God does not expect perfection but perseverance. Those who persevere in these virtues to the end, beginning with them anew every day, are the ones who will be saved.

Finally, the Holy Father Pope Paul draws a lesson from the value of work. God became man in a family who worked for its living in Nazareth – a home had to be kept, mouths had to be fed, and charity had to be given. By doing this, Our Lord, in some sense, undid the curse that had attached to work since the Fall, and dignified it and associated it with a share in the creative activity of God. Work is noble, not as an end in itself, nor as a result of its economic worth, but rather because it derives its value from the value of those for whose sake it is undertaken.

Contemplating the scene in the crib and listening to the lesson of this Mass, may we see in our families and in our world, the opportunities God gives us to create as he creates, to be generous as he is generous.

For further contemplation:

In stature grows the heavenly child,
With death before his eyes;
A Lamb unblemished, meek and mild
Prepared for sacrifice.

The Son of God his glory hides
With parents kind and fond;
And he who made the heaven abides
In dwelling-place beyond.

(from Divine, crescebas Puer – tr. JC)

There will be daily failures and we should not be discouraged. God does not expect perfection but perseverance.

May we be taught by the example of thy Holy Family.

(from the Collect of the Day)

Dominica II Post Epiphaniam
The Second Sunday after Epiphany

*'Let love be without dissimulation.'**

Proper of the Day: Introit: Psalm 65:4, 1, 2
                            Epistle: Romans 12:6–16
                            Gradual: Psalm 106:20, 21
                            Alleluia: Psalm 148:2
                            Gospel: John 2:1–11
                            Communion: John 2:7–11

✠

'Omnis terra adoret te Deus.'†

At the Epiphany, Christ was made manifest to the whole world, represented by the Magi from the East. Today's Mass celebrates the manifestation of his divine sovereignty over all creation by recounting the *'beginning of miracles'‡* at the Wedding Feast of Cana. Christ shows that he is the very God who governs *'all things both in heaven and on earth'§* by dispensing with the ordinary laws of nature in changing the water into wine.

Our Lord never manifests his power and strength without at the same time showing his gentleness and humility. Although the Eternal Son took flesh of the Virgin Mary and became man solely through the omnipotence of God, he came to teach us that the way to the Father is not through power and command but through the virtues of humility and obedience. Seeing his mother's solicitude over the bride and groom, undoubtedly wishing them to be spared the embarrassment of a seemingly inhospitable wedding feast, he approved her concern. His *'hour*

---

   * Romans 12:9.
   † Psalm 65:4: 'Let all the earth adore thee, O God.'
   ‡ John 2:11.
   § Collect of the Day.

is not yet come',* but he chooses to work his first miracle in obedience to his mother's wishes. By this he demonstrates that only through the agency of human meekness will the power and the glory of God shine through.

The miracle of Cana completes the three miracles that the Church from ancient times has seen in the Epiphany as manifesting Christ's power and divinity to the world – the other two comprise the day the star led the Wise Men to Christ and the day Our Lord chose to be baptized by John in the Jordan.

There is yet another manifestation at Cana during this wedding feast. It is not divine, yet serves the divine purpose in perfect co-operation with it. In itself it is nothing, but in union with Our Lord it is everything, and indeed takes its source and vigour from him. This is, of course, the Blessed Virgin's unique role in the plan of the redemption of man from sin. Already at the Annunciation, Mary declares herself to be *'the handmaid of the Lord'*.† She dedicates her whole being to God in her assent: *'Let it be done to me according to thy word.'*‡ But lest we should think that this special role of assistance would finish with the Incarnation, the Miracle at Cana shows the role of being God's handmaid to be permanent.

'The mother of Jesus was there. And Jesus also was invited.'§ The Lord of all things visible and invisible is invited to a banquet, yet his invitation is secondary to Mary's own. She provides the context for Our Lord's first miracle. Indeed, she brings the problem of the failed wine to his attention. And because she is the more prominent guest, his apparent secondary place facilitates his message that only through the agency of human meekness will the power and the glory of God shine through.

Though Mary is very much Jesus' mother, even here her solicitude for the married couple and their guests points towards the time when she will be Mother of the Church, of all those

* John 2:4.
† Luke 1:38.
‡ Luke 1:38.
§ John 2:1b, 2a.

redeemed in Christ. The concern in Mary's heart for the happiness of the young couple resonates with the deeper desire in Our Lord's heart for the salvation of all mankind. *'Whatsoever he say to you, do ye.'**

'Woman, what is that to me and to thee? My hour is not yet come.'† The *hour* to which Jesus refers is the hour of his Passion. Cana is a foreshadowing of that hour and of Mary's role in it. Now she intercedes with Jesus that he will save the hosts' embarrassment by changing water into wine; then, as she witnesses the blood and water flowing from his side, she will pray that men and women will be saved from their sins inasmuch as they accept the fruits of redemption produced in abundance from the Cross. Mary's role at Cana and Calvary is unique, yet it is the duty of each and every one of us as we hear Holy Mass, to pray for the conversion of sinners and for the forgiveness of sins.

✠

For further reflection:

The Lamb of God is manifest
Again in Jordan's water blest,
And he who sin had never known
By washing hath our sins undone.

Yet he that ruleth everything
Can change the nature of a spring,
And gives at Cana this for sign –
The water reddens into wine.

(from Hostis Herodes impie – tr. PD)

Today we celebrate the manifestation of Jesus' divine sovereignty over all creation and the foreshadowing of his Passion.

---

* John 2:5.
† John 2:4.

'I will tell you what great things the Lord hath done for my soul.'

(from the Offertory of the Day)

Dominica III Post Epiphaniam
The Third Sunday after Epiphany

'Be not overcome with evil, but overcome evil with good.'

Proper of the Day: Introit: Psalm 96:7, 8, 1
Epistle: Romans 12:16–21
Gradual: Psalm 101:16, 17
Alleluia: Psalm 96:1
Gospel: Matthew 8:1–13
Offertory: Psalm 117:16, 17
Communion: Luke 5:22

'Cum descendisset Jesus de monte . . .'†

O ur Lord came down from the mountain where he had been instructing his disciples, and is confronted with the practical calls of charity, the efficacious love of neighbour which alone can demonstrate that we truly love God. *'He that loveth not his brother whom he seeth, how can he love God whom he seeth not?'‡* asks St John. We must spend time sitting at the feet of Our Lord listening to him – a time of study and meditation, of contemplation and adoration – but after that we must come down from the mountain and apply ourselves to the needs of our brethren. At the end of Mass we are sent out onto the mission, *ite missa est.*

---

* Romans 12:21.

† Matthew 8:1: 'When Jesus was come down from the mountain . . .'

‡ 1 John 4:20.

Not our brethren alone, but our enemies, not our friends and neighbours alone, but those we despise, or who despise us – these must be the objects of our charity. *'If thy enemy be hungry, give him to eat,'* says St Paul, adding rather mischievously, *'for doing this, thou shalt heap coals of fire upon his head.'* The reference is, of course, to the book of Proverbs,* but it must refer also to the cleansing coal of fire in Isaiah, the purification by fire, which renders us worthy to see God. Even if the enemy is really a sinner, truly malicious and at enmity with God, our acts of kindness may give him the possibility of purification, may bring him back to God who alone can repay us for our deeds. But if he will not listen, and will not recognize the love of God, then his condemnation is on his own head.

In the Gospel, Our Lord is confronted with two requests for healing, one from the leper, representative of sin, the other from the centurion, symbol of infidelity. The leper is an outcast from society, despised by the self-righteous because the mere fact that he has this disease shows that he is, doubtless, a sinner. Any contact with him would bring defilement – but the Lord heals him with a touch, that touch of God which reverses contagion and confers healing and forgiveness. The centurion is the enemy, the oppressor, and he is also a pagan, the one who does not believe in the faith of Israel. Contact with him too would be defiling, and he knows full well that a devout Jew should not enter under his roof, but the Lord offers at once to come to that house. He speaks to the centurion face to face. In the presence of the living God, no defilement can exist; his presence alone is enough to dispel contagion and to make the unclean clean.

The leper recognizes Our Lord immediately for who he is: *'Domine'* he calls him, knowing instinctively, through the voice of conscience within him, that this is the Lord God of Israel, the God of Abraham, Isaac and Jacob. The centurion also recognizes his authority, he too calls him *'Lord'*, and perceives that this is one who is 'under authority', for Jesus is ever obedient to

---

* Proverbs 25:22.

the Father, but has 'soldiers under' him, for he commands the winds and the sea and they obey him. The pagan discerns this through conscience; he may not have been instructed in the true faith, but knows the Truth when he sees it. Blessed John Henry Newman tells us that every man has by nature a conscience, and St Paul teaches that the pagans can know God *'because the knowledge of God is clear to their minds; God himself has made it clear to them; from the foundations of the world men have caught sight of his invisible nature, his eternal power and his divineness, as they are known through his creatures'.**

The leper submits to the will of God. *'If it be thy will'*, he prays. He does not try to impose his will on God, he prays like Our Lady, *'be it done unto me according to thy will'*, and like Our Lord himself in the Garden of Gethsemane. His request is conditional on the will of God, as all our requests must be. Here is his humility, and the humility of the centurion is shown in his unwillingness to trouble Our Lord, *'say but a word'*, *'I am not worthy'*. He does not directly ask for a cure, he simply tells Our Lord that the servant is ill, and waits until Our Lord offers to come and cure the boy himself before suggesting even so much as a word. God's will is proclaimed by Our Lord: *'It is my will, be thou made clean'*, and *'I will come and heal him'*.

The leper has total confidence in the power of Christ: *'Thou hast power to make me clean.'* He does not expect Our Lord to turn to any other power, he is not asking him to pray for him, for he knows that this son of man has his own authority, the Son of God is able to do all things. The centurion too has utter confidence in the power of Our Lord to do anything, to command sickness and health as he commands Angels. Neither shows the slightest hesitation, both affirm that Our Lord can do what they ask.

Our Lord asks the leper to say nothing, but to show himself to the priests in testimony. The time is not yet ripe for his true nature to be publicly proclaimed before the people: *'go and show thyself to the priest'*, observe the rituals prescribed in the

---

* Romans 1:20, 21 (R. Knox version).

Old Law, for the New Covenant has not yet been proclaimed. Let the priest alone hear the story, and maybe he will listen and believe; if he does not, his condemnation is on his own head. The leper is an Israelite, more devout, more faithful than the majority of the priests and the scribes. His healing is evidence that God's power is active in Galilee, if only they will believe.

The centurion, the unbeliever, has more faith than the most faithful of Israel. Before even hearing Our Lord preach, before witnessing any sign, he has believed. *'I have not found so great faith in Israel'*, Our Lord says. Thus the prophecies are fulfilled. *'The Gentiles shall fear thy name, O Lord.'** *'The right hand of the Lord hath exalted me.'*† In the trust of the leper we see how *'Sion heard, and was glad'*, and in the faith of the centurion: *'let the earth rejoice'*.‡ The message is first offered to the Jews, and on their behalf the leper accepts it. After them the gospel is extended to all nations, and for them the centurion speaks. Yet, as so often in St Matthew's Gospel, there is a warning that many of God's own chosen people will refuse to believe, and their places will be taken: *'Many [who] shall come from the East and the West, and shall sit down with Abraham and Isaac and Jacob.'*§

✠

For further reflection:

Firmly I believe and truly
God is Three, and God is One;
And I next acknowledge duly
Manhood taken by the Son.

Simply to his grace and wholly
Light and life and strength belong,

---

* Psalm 101:16.
† Psalm 117:16.
‡ Psalm 96:7, 8, 1.
§ Matthew 8:11.

And I love supremely, solely,
Him the Holy, him the Strong.

(JHN)

The centurion, the unbeliever, has more faith than the most faithful of Israel.

I shall not die, but live, and shall declare the works of the Lord.

(from the Offertory of the Day)

Dominica IV Post Epiphaniam
The Fourth Sunday after Epiphany

'What manner of man is this, that the winds and the sea obey him?'*

Proper of the Day: As for Dominica III Post Epiphaniam except:
                                   Epistle: Romans 13:8–10
                                   Gospel: Matthew 8:23–27

✠

'Plenitudo ergo legis est dilectio.'†

St Augustine says, *'Love [God] and then do what you will.'‡* At first glance we might think that that means we can do whatever we like so long as one element in our lives is loving God – going to Mass, maybe, or being faithful in our prayers. But of course loving God can never be just one element in our lives. Love of God pervades the whole of our lives – or it should. When we love God we want what he wants. Our wills

---

* Matthew 8:27.

† Romans 13:10: 'Love therefore is the fulfilling of the law.'

‡ In Epist. Joann. Tractatus vii:8.

are conformed to his. So, loving God means doing his will in everything we think or do or say. So, 'Love [God] and then do what you will' in reality is a demand to give ourselves wholly to him. Real love tolerates no half measures. Its nature is to give completely. A lover wants to give himself or herself wholly to the beloved.

Today's Epistle looks rather like St Augustine's dictum. Three times St Paul seems to be setting rather limited, even realistic goals: 'Owe no man any thing . . . He that loveth his neighbour, hath fulfilled the law . . . The love of our neighbour worketh no evil.' Pay your debts, do a few good deeds, do not hurt anyone. That is the Christian faith. Nothing more? Just as St Augustine's phrase, when we think that we have found a relatively easy ride, there is that word 'love' to break open the limitations of the law and of our expectations and open up a whole new perspective on the world.

No sooner has St Paul said, 'Owe no man any thing', than he says, 'but to love one another'. This is a debt we never stop owing. It is an unlimited and endless duty which is fulfilled (but never ended) by loving God and our neighbour with our whole heart and our whole strength for ever. We always owe love and we never pay off the debt, but unlike ordinary debts, it comes as a joy to realize this. Where should we be if no more love were expected of us, if we had done everything and paid off the debt? We should be dead – and not in heaven.

As St Paul says famously in the first Epistle to the Corinthians: 'Charity never faileth', or 'love never ends'. How can it? God is giving it to us always so that we can pass it on in our turn. In the very demand to love, God promises to give love to us. And his word is more reliable than our miserly hearts that look so readily to find a way of doing just what we want to do or of setting ever narrower limits to our duties and responsibilities.

At the end of today's Epistle, St Paul tells us: 'Love therefore is the fulfilling of the law.' This is because love is the very mystery of God himself who is love itself. It is always something more than the rational order of the universe, the rules for keeping human society running smoothly, more than the sum of the duties we owe our neighbour. If this seems rather repetitive to us, recall what the tradition tells us about St John who, at the end of his life, repeated over and over again to his disciples: '*Little children, love one another.*' When his disciples asked him why he always preached the same thing, he replied that it was the commandment of the Lord, and that was enough.

Love is a debt that will never be paid because God is love and is infinite and eternal. He is the love that, in the words of Dante, *'moves the sun and the other stars'*,* the love that, in our own more prosaic way, *'makes the world go round'*.

For further reflection:

> The Faith that first must be possess'd,
> Root deep within our inmost breast:
> And joyous Hope in second place,
> Then Charity, thy greatest grace.

(Aeterna caeli Gloria)

Where should we be if no more love were expected of us?

Grant us health of mind and body, that what we suffer for our sins, we may overcome by thy help.

(from the Collect of the Day)

---

* Paradiso xxxiii:145.

Dominica V Post Epiphaniam
The Fifth Sunday after Epiphany

*'Let the word of Christ dwell in you abundantly, in all wisdom: teaching and admonishing one another in psalms, hymns, and spiritual canticles.'**

Proper of the Day: As for Dominica III Post Epiphaniam except:
                              Epistle: Colossians 3:12–17
                              Gospel: Matthew 13:24–30

✠

'Sinite utraque crescere usque ad messam.'†

U nusually, Our Lord continues, after today's portion of the Gospel, to interpret for his disciples the parable of the good and bad sower: *'He that soweth the good seed is the Son of man. And the field is the world. And the good seed are the children of the kingdom. And the cockle are the children of the wicked one. And the enemy that sowed them is the devil. But the harvest is the end of the world. And the reapers are the Angels. Even as the cockle therefore is gathered up and burnt with fire; so shall it be at the end of the world.'‡* There is a difficulty here. Consider the cockle – it is a weed. It signifies *'the children of the wicked one'*. Now, cockle begins and ends as cockle; it cannot change into wheat. So Our Lord would seem to be teaching that bad people are born that way, and that there is no possibility of repentance for them. In other words, some people are predestined to Hell.

This cannot really be the message of the parable, since the possibility of predestination to Hell is odious to the whole purpose of Christ's earthly life and mission. He came to preach repentance for the forgiveness of sins, and conversion of the

---

  * Colossians 3:16.
  † Matthew 13:30: 'Suffer both to grow until the harvest.'
  ‡ Matthew 13:37–40.

heart to the God *'who will have all men to be saved and to come to the knowledge of the truth'.* * The heresy of the doctrine of predestination to evil was denounced in the sixth century at the Second Council of Orange, and also in the sixteenth century at the Council of Trent. A parable is a useful device by which Our Lord describes, in situations familiar to the minds of his audiences, what the Kingdom of Heaven is like. It is not a question of what the Kingdom of Heaven *is* but what the Kingdom of Heaven is *like*. A parable is not intended to fit what it is describing in every detail. Our Lord preaches many parables concerning the Kingdom; only by putting them all together may we begin to catch a glimpse of the whole picture rather than one small detail within the painting.

The indisputable fact is that there is nothing in God's creation that was created evil. At the end of God's act of creation, Holy Scripture is clear: *'God saw all the things that he had made, and they were very good.'*† Since God is the sole creator, nothing exists that has not been made by God. So, all creation is good from the beginning. God's act of creating did not, of course, cease with the book of Genesis: every new life comes from God, is created by God. And at the conception of every new human life in its mother's womb, God breathes into that life the gift of a soul. It is true that human life born from the womb is infected with the guilt of original sin, but the image of God in the soul has only been distorted by original sin, rather than obliterated. It follows that no human being is intrinsically evil. All are called to life.

Our Lord comes to sow the seed of his *Word* – that is, not only what he *says*, but what he is – into the hearts of man. In the vocabulary of today's Gospel parable, it is our receptivity – our desire or lack of it – for Christ's Word, which contributes to whether or not one matures as wheat or cockle. No one begins as cockle but may well become so later.

* 1 Timothy 2:4.
† Genesis 1:31.

Except for the grace of God, and our openness to its operation in our lives, we should all end up as the cockle, giving way *'to the wicked one'*. Before our baptism, we *'were by nature children of wrath'*.* However, relying *'wholly on the hope of God's heavenly grace'*,† the sanctifying grace we first receive in baptism, allows us to become *'the children of the kingdom'*.‡

Our Lord tells the parable of the cockle precisely because he wishes to draw our attention to the abundance of his divine mercy. He wishes to *'suffer'* the cockle *'to grow'* with the wheat *'until the harvest'*; and he delays any weeding out of evil men in case they might repent and turn back to him. *'The Lord delayeth not his promise, as some imagine, but dealeth patiently for your sake, not willing that any should perish.'*§

✠

For further reflection:

Jesu, the hope of souls forlorn.
How good to them for sin that mourn;
To them that seek thee, O how kind,
But what art thou to them that find?

No tongue of mortal can express,
No letters write its blessedness;
He only who hath proved it knows
What bliss from love of Jesus flows.

(from Jesu, dulcis memoria)

There is nothing in God's creation that was created evil.

May thou mercifully absolve us from our sins, and thyself direct our inconstant hearts.

(from the Secret of the Day)

---

* Ephesians 2:3.
† Collect of the Day.
‡ Matthew 13:38.
§ 2 Peter 3:9.

Dominica VI Post Epiphaniam
The Sixth Sunday after Epiphany

May we be fed with heavenly delights.*

Proper of the Day: As for *Dominica III Post Epiphaniam* except:
Epistle: *1 Thessalonians 1:2–10*
Gospel: *Matthew 13:31–35*

✠

'donec fermentatum est totum'†

In the Epistle appointed for today's Mass, St Paul teaches the new Christians of Thessalonika that it is fitting to rejoice in the truth that they have been called and chosen by God. He also makes it clear that an essential ingredient of their newly given faith is the gift of being able to recognize that God works in *his* way and not according to man's expectations. The Thessalonians had proved particularly receptive to the gospel, and the Apostle reminds them of the power of the Trinitarian God working in and through them such that, difficulties not-withstanding, substantial numbers had been brought to faith in Christ.

Today's Gospel reinforces this very point as we listen to Our Lord teaching the crowds by means of parables, wherein he likens the Kingdom of Heaven to a grain of mustard seed and also to leaven hidden in a measure of meal. Jesus Christ is the Incarnate Word of God and it is he who brings that Word to man. The task of the Apostles, both in biblical times and throughout the ages in and through the Church, is to continue Christ's mission of preaching the Gospel. The Word of God, like the seed and the leaven but only more so, bears the power to infuse all around it and to bring to fulfilment and comple-tion. Like the earth in the case of the mustard seed, or the

---

* Cf Postcommunion.
† Matthew 13:33: 'until the whole was leavened'.

dough of the leaven, the environment for the Word of God is precisely the receptivity of the human soul, which is converted to Christ by the power of that same Word.

The Epistle and Gospel should thus encourage each one of us, according to his or her own vocation, to continue the preaching of the Word of God and likewise to recognize its power in our own lives. Indeed, the history of the Church, both collectively and in terms of its individual members, bears ample testimony – especially in the lives of the saints – to the transforming power of the Word, not least in times and places where, humanly speaking, there seemed little likelihood of success. We have only to think of those many situations where, confronted by an unbelieving or irreligious audience, the preaching of the gospel of Christ and the reception of the Sacraments, has won God for whole nations. But that is the point: it is *God's* power and *his* grace which matter. The proper response given to man is to co-operate with the divine initiative and to remove every hindrance to the working of the Holy Spirit.

Indeed, the Collect of the Mass beseeches of God the same: *'ut semper rationabilia meditantes'*, that is, that we may always think what is right and reasonable, and thereby please him in what we say and do. For it is only by active co-operation with grace and by the conscious submission of ourselves to that same grace, especially the Sacrament of Confession, that we stand any chance of becoming that which he has called us to be: *'followers of the Lord . . . a pattern to all that believe'* serving *'the living and true God'*.*

✠

For further reflection:

> *Pour on us of the Grace*
> *The everlasting spring;*
> *Lest our frail steps renew the trace*
> *Of the ancient wandering.*

---

* 1 Thessalonians 1:6, 7, 9.

May faith in lustre grow,
And rear her star in heaven,
Paling all sparks of earth below,
Unquench'd by damps of even.

(from Immense caeli conditor – tr. JHN)

The Word bears the power to infuse all around it and bring to fulfilment and completion.

Grant that we may accomplish, both in words and works, that which is pleasing in thy sight.

(from the Collect of the Day)

Dominica in Septuagesima
Septuagesima Sunday

'In my affliction I called upon the Lord and he heard my voice from his holy temple . . .'*

Proper of the Day: Introit: Psalm 17:5–7, 2, 3
                     Epistle: 1 Corinthians 9:24–27; 10:1–5
                     Gradual: Psalm 9:10, 11, 19, 20
                     Tract: Psalm 129:1–4
                     Gospel: Matthew 20:1–16
                     Offertory: Psalm 91:2
                     Communion: Psalm 30:17, 18

✠

'Sed castigo corpus meum . . .'†

Those who are observant or know about these things will quickly notice that the colour of the vestments is no longer green but violet. You will also notice that the Alleluia and its verse have been replaced by a Tract. The Alleluia will not be heard again until the Easter Vigil. We are entering into a

---

* Introit of the Day.

† 1 Corinthians 9:27: 'But I chastise my body . . .'

solemn season of preparation and penance. If you know your catechism well, or if you are still at school and are being taught to know about your faith properly, you will know that we are all flawed in a particular way. We tend to want to do things that are not good, and to go against God's plan for us and the world in which we live. This problem goes back to Adam and Eve. The Holy Bible tells us that the first man and woman were created free and with easy access to God, whom they served simply by being as they were. But they wanted more and so they rebelled. They sought to reap greater rewards for their existence than God had already given, even to the extent of wanting equality with him in knowledge and power. The Devil led them on. They did not know that by refusing to obey God they would reduce themselves in status and disable their ability to use properly the freedom God gave them. This original sin of theirs is at the heart of what is wrong with us. That defect could only be remedied by one who was free from it and also strong enough to overcome all its evil effects.

The story of how and why he did this and our continuing need to remember it and to make it known to others is what this season sets out to relate. Just as the Chosen People of old yearly celebrated their festivals of salvation and rescue by God, so we do likewise, following millennial liturgical and spiritual traditions. The festivals of ancient times celebrated symbolic events that marked the various stages of salvation history. With the coming of Christ, the meaning of those events became clearer and ancient prophecies fulfilled. This Septuagesima Sunday begins the cycle of remembrance and recall which will take us back to the beginnings of man's fall and its consequences, and forward to the foundation of the Church. Through the same rituals, which originated with Christ and his Apostles, we relive the saving words and actions by which we were redeemed and the Church herself came into being in the first Christian century.

St Paul, in today's Epistle, says, *'But I chastise my body . . .'* This chastising of the body means training ourselves to be less greedy and less demanding. The Gospel parable tells us about the owner of a vineyard who condemned the greed and envy of those who resented what others received. The generosity of the giver in hiring them was overlooked. God is the real owner in this story and the vineyard is the world in which he has placed us. We have no right to demand anything from him more than he generously allows. Such envy and greed brought down our first parents. This day marks the beginning of our annual cycle of coming to terms with the reality of our own share in the sin of the world for which Our Lord suffered and died. If we do as we are meant to in these weeks, we shall not only receive grace and healing from God, but also be better disposed to take part in the Paschal celebration at the end of it. Through the Church, our Saviour invites us to accompany him in prayer and self-denial on a journey that took him from the serenity of a carpenter-shop at Nazareth to public acclaim and then utter abandonment on a cross outside Jerusalem. Through it he achieved victory over death and sin, and by it he offers no less to you and to me.

For further reflection:

> *Be none submerged in sin's distress,*
> *None lifted up in boastfulness;*
> *That contrite hearts be not dismayed,*
> *Nor haughty souls in ruin laid.*
> > *(from Magnae Deus potentiae – tr. JMN)*

If we are envious and greedy we place ourselves before God as surely as did Adam and Eve.

Cleanse us and graciously hear us.
> *(from the Secret of the Day)*

Dominica in Sexagesima
Sexagesima Sunday

*'We have heard, O God, with our ears: our fathers have declared to us.'**

Proper of the Day: Introit: Psalm 43:23–26, 2
                      Epistle: 2 Corinthians 11:19–33; 12:1–9
                      Gradual: Psalm 82:19, 14
                      Tract: Psalm 59:4, 6
                      Gospel: Luke 8:4–15
                      Offertory: Psalm 16:5, 6, 7
                      Communion: Psalm 42:4

✠

'Vobis datum est nosse mysterium regni Dei.'†

W as there some exasperation in Our Lord's voice, perhaps, when he answered his disciples? He was training them for what was to come; he was making them understand slowly and surely. They would be fully enlightened only after his death and Glorious Resurrection. He had taught his close disciples and his other followers in parables – a common enough convention at the time. *'Master, what did this parable mean?'* Had they suspected there was a deeper meaning? After all, on the face of it, it is one of those parables whose point is most easily identified. Is the answer Jesus gives simply humorous or is he in earnest? *'You are to know the secrets of the Kingdom; others, well I teach them only in parables so that the true meaning is hidden from them.'* The purpose of a parable is to convey to the audience a particular point. Is our Lord *really* saying: *'Why do you think that I preach in parables – simply so that I am not understood? Wake up!'* Without further ado, he proceeds to explain what each component of the story might mean. The

---

* Psalm 43:2.

† Luke 8:10: 'To you it is given to know the mystery of the Kingdom of God.'

explanation does not alter the point of the parable of course; it merely gives an idea or two as to the likely causes of failure of the seed. That we all need to prepare an uncluttered home for God's word is clear. We need to be receptive. That we need to cultivate the soil, kill the weeds and water well is obvious. Even the slowest wit would have grasped all that, surely. Did the disciples look at each other dimly, suddenly smile as the light dawned, nod and say: 'O yes, *now you put it like that, we see*'? Probably not.

Is there a deeper meaning? Is there something here that would only strike the disciples after the Resurrection? Is the parable *really* only about the word of God as contained in the Scriptures, and about bothering to spend time in careful contemplation? Maybe it is, but the true answer to the question probably lies in Jesus' first words after the disciples have made the request for further and better particulars. '*To you it is given to know the mystery of the Kingdom of God.*' Jesus is now talking about hearts rather than minds, for it is in the heart that territory for the Kingdom is won. The disciples have now moved on to higher things, the next stage in their development. And who enters the heart to claim it for the Kingdom? Why, Christ himself, the true Word of God, the Word who came down from Heaven and brought God to man. Here was that Word discoursing with these simple Galileans. The *Word* of God now bears the meaning revealed a little later to John and contained in the prologue of his Gospel, and heard at the end of every Mass in this Form. The full thrust of it all probably initially passed the disciples by, but it remained latent within.

So now the parable can be understood in a rather different light. The difficulties faced by the seed are now the trials and tribulations of Jesus' own ministry, which highlight the difficulties to be faced in the future by the Apostles – the shallow ground, those amused by spectacular tricks, and the enemies of Christ who would seek out the Apostles and take their lives. The parable now makes clear that in the near future the Word, the Christ, would be choked by the forces of evil; he would be silenced by the unholy alliance of High Priest and Roman Governor with the help of the fickle crowds manipulated by the authorities. But Christ himself would, by then, have been firmly planted in some of the hearts, and territory for the Kingdom of God won. The Apostles would have their corner stone in place as the life-blood from Christ's body on the cross spilled out and nourished Holy Church. They would now *know* the mystery of the Kingdom. *Knowledge* of the Kingdom is more than cognizance; it is oneness with the Kingdom, not a mere acquaintance with the idea of it. *Knowledge* of the Word is, therefore, an intimate relationship with the Word, an intimacy that allows Christ to gain territory for the Kingdom of God within our very selves.

We are on the threshold of the season of Lent. It is time to consider how best to prepare our minds for the teaching of Holy Church, and our hearts to be a place where Christ can find a permanent home. *'To you is given to know the mystery of the Kingdom of God.'*

✠

For further reflection:

> *Illuminate our hearts within,*
> *And cleanse our minds from stain of sin;*
> *Unburdened of our guilty load*
> *May we unfettered serve our Lord.*

Knowledge of the Word is an intimate relationship with the Word.

'Perfect thou my goings in thy paths that my footsteps be not moved: incline thine ear and hear my words.'*

---

* Psalm 16:5.

Dominica in Quinquagesima
Quinquagesima Sunday

*'In thee, O Lord, have I hoped, let me never be confounded.'**

Proper of the Day: Introit: Psalm 30:3, 4, 2
                            Epistle: *1 Corinthians 13:1–13*
                            Gradual: *Psalm 76:15, 16*
                            Tract: *Psalm 99:1, 2*
                            Offertory: *Psalm 118:12, 13*
                            Communion: *Psalm 77:29, 30*

✠

'Videmus nunc per speculum in aenigmate.'†

Those who think they can see are often blind; those who know they cannot see may have greater clarity to perceive. Those who pride themselves in their wisdom are often those who know nothing, for only those who know themselves to be fools for Christ's sake are truly wise.

The blind man in today's Gospel is more perceptive than all the people of Jericho. They see only Jesus of Nazareth, but he knows this is the Son of David. They see only a wandering prophet, but he acknowledges him as Lord. They might expect to hear from him some instructive words, or perhaps accept alms from the Apostles' common purse, but he is utterly confident in calling upon him *'that I may see'*.

The Apostles themselves see only *'through a glass in a dark manner'*. For the third time, Our Lord has told them plainly that he is going up to Jerusalem, to be betrayed, to suffer, to die, to rise again, but they understand nothing; they imagine this is just another of his mysterious sayings, which he will eventually explain to them. What he tells them literally, they think is a parable. He performs miracles before their eyes, but

---

* Psalm 30:2.
† 1 Corinthians 13:12: 'We see through a glass in a dark manner.'

they are unable to see that this is something that only God can do: it is the common people, the *plebs,* who magnify Our Lord as God, and give praise to him.

The blind man of Jericho is a model of Christian prayer, a prayer made in love. For love *'beareth all things'* – the blind man accepts his poverty and does not ask for money or material goods. Love *'believeth all things'* – the blind man acclaims Our Lord as *'Son of David'* and *'Lord'*. Love *'hopeth all things',* just as the blind man hopes *'that I may see'*. He continues to pray despite the throng, the crowd of followers and spectators, those in front who bid him be silent, those behind who press on him and trample over him. Through it all, he continues his litany: *'Jesus, Son of David, have mercy on me!'*

Our prayer must be infused with charity like this. As we pray, we too must endure all things, accepting the will of God, praying always, *'Thy will be done.'* We too must believe all things, acknowledging our Saviour as truly Lord and God, accepting his word, whether welcome or unwelcome; his Truth, however obscure or difficult to understand. We too must hope all things, praying with perfect confidence for the gift of eternal light, praying in the faith that makes us whole.

And we continue to pray despite the crowds who tell us to be silent. When we pray, we are surrounded and oppressed and trampled by distractions and teeming imaginations, crowds of thoughts that seem to stifle our pleas, and leave us discouraged, tempted to abandon our prayer, and to be silent. But through it all we must keep praying, calling out over and over: *'Jesus, Son of David, have mercy on me!'*

Perseverance is the secret in prayer – perseverance, informed by hope, hope instructed by faith. We call out, *'Be thou unto me a God, a protector . . .',** for we believe that our Saviour is the Son of God, and: *'Thou art the God who alone dost wonders . . .',†* *'know ye that the Lord is God . . .'‡* Faith believes

---

* Introit of the Day.

† Gradual of the Day.

‡ Tract of the Day.

all things: we can be confident in the teaching Our Lord has given us in his Church, while at the same time admitting that we see only in part, we understand only in part. If we begin to imagine that we really understand, that we already have all wisdom, then we simply deceive ourselves. Part of our faith must be the realization that we still have so much more to learn. The Pharisees and the learned men in the Gospels are called blind because they imagine that they can see so clearly; they are shown to be ignorant because they pretend to themselves that they know.

Prayer hopes all things: we come before God with the assurance that what he wants for us is the best that could possibly come upon us. We do not set our hopes on things of this world, on money or power or influence, we set our hopes on what we know for certain God wills for us. *'In thee, O Lord, have I hoped, let me never be confounded . . .'** *'Teach me thy justifications.'†* *'The Lord gave them their desire: they were not defrauded of that which they craved.'‡* We pray with total confidence for the light that has come into the world.

Love endures all things. Even though we have to follow Our Lord to Jerusalem, to be handed over to the Gentiles, to be mocked and scourged and spat upon, we follow him still, glorifying God. Even if we have to give away all we have, to surrender our bodies to be burnt, we love him still. The things of this world, our possessions, our health, our life itself, are all expendable: what we can never lose is our love, our hope, our faith.

Love is not an abstraction, a concept, an idea: Love is a Person, the Person of the Son of God made flesh for us. When we pray, we open our hearts to the love of God, so that he can fill us to overflowing, so that his love can spread through us to all we meet. We invoke the true Light that enlightens all men, and that Light shines in us and through us, so that all men can

---

* Introit of the Day.
† Offertory of the Day.
‡ Communion of the Day.

see our good works and glorify our Father in heaven. Prayer is putting ourselves at God's disposal, for his own kind purposes, until the first great commandment, the love of God, drives us inevitably to fulfil the second, the love of neighbour.

In three days we begin Lent. We shall reflect on our need for God's love, for the healing of our blindness, the enlightenment of our darkness, the instruction of our ignorance. And we reflect on his Passion, his journey to Calvary, his offering of himself for our benefit. It is with joy that we reflect on this: *'Sing joyfully to God, all the earth: serve ye the Lord with gladness. Come into his presence with exceeding great joy.'** Already in anticipation we can celebrate the fruit of that bitter Passion, his rising to the new life that we are called to share, his liberation from death, which is the pledge of our own Resurrection, his gift of grace that fills us already in this life as we follow through our Lent of earthly existence towards the Easter that is to come.

✠

For further reflection:

> *Let every soul thy law obey,*
> *And keep from every evil way;*
> *Rejoice each promised good to win,*
> *And flee from every mortal sin.*
> *(from Telluris ingens Conditor – tr. Anon)*

Those who know themselves fools for Christ's sake are truly wise.

We beseech thee, O Lord, graciously hear our prayers and . . . guard us from all adversity.
> *(from the Collect of the Day)*

---

* Tract of the Day.

Feria IV Cinerum
Ash Wednesday

'For the good which I will, I do not; but the evil which I will not, that I do.'*

Proper of the Day: Introit: Wisdom: 11:24, 25, 27; Psalm 56:2
                      Epistle: Joel 2:12–19
                      Gradual: Psalm 56:2, 4
                      Tract: Psalms 102:10; 78:8, 9
                      Gospel: Matthew 6:16–21
                      Offertory: Psalm 29:2, 3
                      Communion: Psalm 1:2, 3

✠

'Cum jejunatis, nolite fieri sicut hypocritae, tristes.'†

We ought to be able to look forward each year to this season of Lent even though our three exercises of prayer, fasting and almsgiving are associated in the minds of the world with abject misery. However, this is not the note that is struck on this day of penance. We do penance not to become sad like the hypocrites and the pagans, but so as to attain joy. Our Lord tells us not to have a sad countenance, and the Preface for Lent tells beautifully of the benefits that will come to us from the observance of this time: *'who by this bodily fast dost curb our vices, lift our minds, bestow strength and rewards through Jesus Christ our Lord'.* What are these rewards that we hope to receive? Simply, the treasure of which today's Gospel speaks – that which rust and moth shall never consume.

The season of Lent reminds us that we are like athletes who must train and deny themselves now in the hope of future victory. St Paul uses this image several times: *'I have fought a good fight, I have finished my course, I have kept the faith.'‡*

---

* Romans 7:19.
† Matthew 6:16a: 'And when you fast, be not as the hypocrites, sad.'
‡ 2 Timothy 4:7.

And he reminds the Philippians that they must keep up that fight, *'forgetting the things that are behind, and stretching myself to those that are before, I press towards the mark, to the prize . . .'** The collect after the imposition of ashes speaks of the *'Christian's war of defence with holy fasts'* and *'the battle with the spirits of evil'*. Lent is a re-engagement of that warfare against sin and temptation and our own vices. At the same time, this battle does not only bring us joy in the future, but it also sets us free now.

Consider those who do not pray, who do not deny themselves, who do not give to others. It is surely the vast portion of humanity who put their trust in treasures of this world rather than those of heaven. Do they bring happiness? It cannot be said that happiness is a notable feature of our society, because it seeks fulfilment only in what is transitory, in things that can never ultimately be grasped. The pleasures of the flesh are brief and illusory when they are separated from the love of God, which gives them meaning. Sexual lust is an ache that can never be satisfied because it has no goal. It trivializes the human person so that he loses his own dignity and degrades the objects of that lust. There are many other aspects of selfish worldliness we could consider, but none is so typical of the emptiness of our age than the celebration of lust which is all around us. In the media, in contemporary culture and even in schools and families, the gratification of lust is presented as good and even as a human right.

What are the consequences? – divorce, abortion, prostitution, sexual abuse and violence. Do these things bring happiness? The question is absurd. In the following of Christ, however, we find a remedy, for he seeks to liberate us from the selfishness that brings such misery. He gives us a new perspective: *'For where thy treasure is, there is thy heart also.'†* When our sole aim is to accumulate wealth, to dominate others, or to enjoy vain pleasure, those good things God has created for our

---

* Philippians 3:13, 14.
† Matthew 6:21.

use become our slave-drivers. He who is addicted to drink, or drugs, or gambling, does not have a choice whether or not to follow his compulsion. He relinquished that freedom long ago in the successive wrong choices that led to his addiction. The problem all of us have is that we are addicted to sin. We call this concupiscence, and it is a consequence of original sin. With the Apostle, we can all say: *'but the evil that I will not, that I do'.** Whenever people hear this quotation for the first time, they say that it is as if Paul were speaking from their own heart. The more that we sin, the more enslaved we become and the less free we are to change.

This is the purpose of our Lenten warfare: that we should be set free from all the demons that enslave us. Just as the Olympic marathon runner trains first by running small distances, so our Lenten exercises are meant to train us and strengthen us for the real fight against our vices. Moreover, the more that we are set free from our domination by the things of this world, the more that we shall be able to enjoy them as God intended. Our Lord was condemned as a wine-bibber and a glutton,† but in fact he was able to choose freely when to make use of his creation and so truly see its goodness. This reward we too can receive if we keep this season faithfully.

The Gospel tells us to hide our fasting and good works not only to save us from pride and ostentation, but also so that we can confound those who would portray our religion as gloomy. And we know that the opposite is true. It is only those who can forsake the world who place a true value upon it, and only those who have mastered themselves who are truly free. This Lent we have an obligation to be joyful because we have found a treasure which is everlasting. Therefore, today's reminder that we are dust and shall return to dust is not an invitation to despair, but to hope. By placing the frailty of our existence before us, the Church shows that there is something more than

---

* Romans 7:10b.
† Luke 7:34.

our sins and failings – there is mercy and forgiveness. And so *'be not as the hypocrites, sad'.**

For further reflection:

> *O thou Chief Cornerstone; Right Hand of the Father:*
> *Way of Salvation; Gate of life Celestial.*
> *Cleanse thou our sinful souls from all defilement.*
> *Sins oft committed now we lay before thee;*
> *With true contrition now no more we hide them;*
> *O Redeemer, grant us absolution.*
> *Hear us, O Lord, have mercy on us,*
> *For we have sinned against thee.*
>
> (from Attende Domine)

This is the purpose of our Lenten warfare: that we should be set free from all the demons that enslave us.

May we undertake with due piety this period of fasting.
(from the Collect of the Day)

✠

---

* Matthew 6:16a.

Dominica I in Quadragesima
The First Sunday in Lent

*'He that dwelleth in the aid of the Most High, shall abide under the protection of the God of Heaven.'**

Proper of the Day: Introit: Psalm 90:15, 16, 1
                               Epistle: 2 Corinthians 6:1–10
                               Gradual: Psalm 90:11, 12
                               Tract: Psalm 90:1–7, 11–16
                               Gospel: Matthew 4:1–11
                               Offertory: Psalm 90:4, 5
                               Communion: Psalm 90:4, 5

✠

'Si Filius Dei es, mitte te deorsum.'†

So, St Matthew tells us, the Devil tempts Our Lord in the wilderness. In five weeks' time, we shall hear from the same Gospel a very similar taunt: *'And they that passed by, blasphemed him, wagging their heads, and saying: "Vah! Thou that destroyest the temple in three days, dost rebuild it: save thy own self: if thou be the Son of God, come down from the cross."'‡*

Both in the desert and on the Cross, the powerful in this world mock the most powerless human being and are delighted to find that the all-powerful God has made himself weak. The Devil is undoubtedly very powerful on earth: it is he who has persuaded humanity to worship the emptiness of money, to squander the image of God in human life by war, violence and murder of the unborn, and to live in a non-stop frenzy of noise and frivolity that drowns out the quiet voices of truth, goodness and beauty. The Devil's most powerful trick is to convince us that he does not exist – an amazing feat given what we see daily in our own lives.

---

* Psalm 90:1.

† Matthew 4:6: 'If thou be the Son of God, cast thyself down.'

‡ Matthew 27:39, 40.

On Ash Wednesday we heard about our 'Christian warfare' against evil. This warfare is the task we have to undertake during Lent. We do not need the weapons of strength, but those of weakness – the same used by Our Lord in the wilderness and on the Cross. He could have blasted Satan straight back to Hell. He could have summoned far more than legions of Angels; but instead, he was weak. When he stood before Pilate, he was silent. When they hammered nails through his hands and feet, he prayed: *'Father, forgive them for they know not what they do.'* The weapons of weakness we are given to fight against evil are those we took up on Wednesday: prayer, fasting and almsgiving. All three of them might appear to diminish us, but they are the only means by which we shall overcome sin.

In his thirty-three years on earth, Our Lord made himself weak and vulnerable. He became hideous and disfigured and so utterly human. We can easily forget Our Lord's real humanity. The account of his forty days in the desert takes only a part of a page in the Gospel, and so we might think of his saying no to temptation as easy. This is not what the Scriptures say. Our Lord was tempted. Just like us, he was attracted by sin, but he did not. The fact that Our Lord was tempted to turn the stones into bread means that he wanted to do it. Of course he did, after forty days without food, but he knew that this was not his Father's will and that the first stage in this great battle was to demonstrate that there is more than bread alone. The world both worships and despises the human body and is convinced that there is no higher good than sensual pleasure. We know, however, that our bodies are temples of the Holy Spirit. This is why fasting is the first of the three weapons in our Lenten warfare. By doing without something – even something small – we are attesting to the reality of a spiritual world which is greater and more real than the flesh. Of course, it is our motive that is important here. If you arrive at Easter Sunday as a size zero supermodel, then you may have already had your reward. We do not fast to lose weight – that may be an added bonus – but to strengthen our souls for the fight. If we can say no to something that is good – chocolate or alcohol or television – then we shall also find it easier to resist temptations to sin.

The temptations to misuse power are the most difficult that the Devil proposes to Christ: *'All these will I give thee, if falling down thou wilt adore me.'* Even Satan can tell the truth, and here he does, for all the glory of the kingdoms of the world does belong to him. Who can doubt his power when we see the vast unhappiness caused by those who do not love God and neighbour? How tempting it must have been for Our Lord to accept this easy way out and to relieve the suffering of his people by showing his glory now. Instead, he chooses the way of weakness; he chooses to suffer and die. These temptations of Christ at this recorded moment must be only a glimpse of those he faces throughout thirty-three years. If temptations beset the Son of God, then we too must expect them. It matters whether or not we give in to temptation because good and evil are realities: we have to take sides in the fight.

After fasting, the next weapon is almsgiving: giving of ourselves to others to show that we are not the centre of the universe. The people of Israel were told to bring the first-fruits of their produce to the Lord; not what was left over, or what they could spare, but the best.

The greatest of the three weapons and the purpose for which Our Lord went into the desert, is prayer. If we try to do good and avoid evil on our own, we will fail. Each morning, St Philip Neri used to say: *'Lord, do not put any confidence in me, for I am sure to fail if thou dost not help me.'* Another of St Philip's sayings was: *'There is nothing the Devil fears so much, or so much tries to hinder, as prayer.'* So we must make the battle of prayer one in which we do not relent. The best possible Lenten practice would be to come to daily Mass or to pray daily before the Blessed Sacrament. We will always lose the struggle if we fight on our own, but by the weakness and humility of Christ, we have a certain victory. In this life the battle never ends but we have a leader who has shown us the key to success: *'The Lord thy God shalt thou adore, and him only shalt thou serve.'*

For further reflection:

> *Remember thou, though frail we be,*
> *That yet thine handiwork are we;*
> *Nor let the honour of thy name*
> *Be by another put to shame.*
>
> *(from Ex more docti mystico – tr. JMN)*

The greatest of our three weapons is prayer.

Grant that what we strive to obtain from thee by abstinence, we may achieve by good works.

(from the Collect of the Day)

Dominica II in Quadragesima
The Second Sunday in Lent

'In thee, O my God, I put my trust: let me not be ashamed.'*

Proper of the Day:	Introit: Psalm 24:6, 3, 22, 1, 2
	Epistle: 1 Thessalonians 4:1–7
	Gradual: Psalm 24:17, 18
	Tract: Psalm 105:1–4
	Gospel: Matthew 17:1–9
	Offertory: Psalm 118:47, 48
	Communion: Psalm 5:2–4

✠

'Levantes autem oculos suos, neminem viderunt, nisi solum Jesum.'†

The Transfiguration is one of the Mysteries of Light because it enlightens us as to who Our Lord is. The disciples have

---

* Psalm 24:2.
† Matthew 17:8: 'And they lifting up their eyes saw no one, but only Jesus.'

come to faith that he is the Christ, the Son of the Living God, and now they hear confirmation of this fact in the voice of the Father from Heaven: *'This is my beloved Son, in whom I am well pleased.'* St Matthew shows us that this luminous event came when Our Lord was travelling towards Jerusalem, towards his Passion and death. That is why the Church presents the Transfiguration to us at this stage of Lent: like Peter, James and John, we need to be reminded of who the Lord really is, and to be prepared for the Cross. Christ revealed himself upon Mount Tabor so as to strengthen the disciples' faith when they saw him disfigured, bloody, wounded and derided on Calvary. Of course, for Peter and James this did not work: they still ran off, terrified and dismayed; but for John at least, this glimpse of divine glory upon the mountain sustained him through the agony of the Crucifixion.

We too need to remember the glory so as to pass through the pains and trials of this life. The young St Bernadette of Lourdes was told by Our Lady: *'I do not promise you happiness in this life, but in the next.'* Our faith does not give us freedom from suffering and anguish now – rather the opposite – but the promise of future glory which we are given, is meant to strengthen us for the trials of life, as St Paul writes to Timothy: *'labour with the Gospel, according to the power of God'.**

Peter, who had not yet caught on to this truth, tried to detain Moses, Elijah and the Lord on the mountain by offering to set up three tents – but when the moment of glory had passed, they still had to go back to the plain. The brilliant light had gone, and when the disciples looked up *'they ... saw no one, but only Jesus'.* So for us, there may be moments of transfiguring light now, but it is in the gloom of the world that we actually have to live. Our task is to bring that light into the darkness. Blessed John Henry Newman wrote a well-known and beautiful prayer:

---

* 2 Timothy 1:8b.

Stay with me and then I shall begin
to shine as thou shinest;
so to shine as to be a light to others . . .
Make me preach thee without preaching –
by my example and by the catching force,
the sympathetic influence of what I do . . .

And the Blessed Mother Teresa of Calcutta used to say this prayer every day. In one of her letters she wrote:

Daily we pray: 'Let them look up and see only Jesus', but how often do we see only Jesus in us? Do we see him in using our eyes, mind, and heart, as his own? Are we so given to him that we find his eyes look through ours, his tongue speaking, his hands working, his feet walking, his heart loving? Do we really see only Jesus in us?

How do we do this? It is not in the extraordinary, mystical, luminous way of Mount Tabor, but rather in the ordinary, banal events of daily life. We do not need to do great things, but little things with great love. In Mother Teresa's own life, we can see two great virtues – difficult but simple – which we could each imitate and so become the Light of Christ to others. Those virtues are cheerfulness and kindness. For many years, Mother Teresa's inner life was one of great darkness. She felt abandoned and cut off from God, and yet all through this she radiated joy and cheerfulness. The smile hid her interior desolation and enlightened others. '*When I see someone sad,*' she would say, '*I always think, she is refusing something to Jesus.*' Smiling and being cheerful – these we must keep doing through the miseries of our lives. Again, Mother Teresa said:

Cheerfulness is often a cloak which hides a life of sacrifice, continual union with God, fervour and generosity. A person who has this gift of cheerfulness very often reaches a great height of perfection. For God loves a cheerful giver.

{ 78 }

Cheerfulness means looking out from ourselves and acting rather for the benefit of others. It leads on to kindness. It is so often so easy to be clever, but so much more important to be kind. Kindness is that 'catching force' of which Newman spoke. No kind action stops with itself; it always leads to another. When we act kindly we are showing Christ to the world. We can begin with our thoughts – by putting the best possible interpretation on the actions of others, for example – and this leads on to our words. It is always better to remain silent than to say something unkind. Father Faber once said:

> No one was ever converted by a sarcasm – crushed, perhaps, if the sarcasm was clever enough – but drawn nearer to God, never. Kindness has converted more sinners than zeal, or eloquence or learning, and these have never converted anyone unless they were kind also . . .

Cheerfulness and kindness would give value to all our other spiritual practices this Lent – and they are two virtues of which we are all capable. We must look beyond the difficulties of our lives to the glory of the life to come, and show the radiance of Our Lord's glory to the world. If we are gentle, if we are kind, if we smile, if we are cheerful, then we shall be able to shine as he shines, and others will look up and see 'only Jesus'.

✠

For further reflection:

> We see a dazzling sight
> That shall outlive all time,
> Older than depth or starry height,
> Limitless and Sublime.
>
> To Jesus, who displays
> To men his beaming face,

Be, *with the Father, endless praise,*
And with the Holy Ghost.

(from 'The Transfiguration' – JHN)

We do not need to do great things, but little things with great love.

O God, keep us within and without . . .

(from the Collect of the Day)

Dominica III in Quadragesima
The Third Sunday in Lent

'Mine eyes are ever towards the Lord: for he shall pluck my feet out of the snare.'*

Proper of the Day: Introit: Psalm 24:15, 16, 1, 2
Epistle: Ephesians 5:1–9
Gradual: Psalm 9:20, 4
Tract: Psalm 122:1–3
Gospel: Luke 11:14–28
Offertory: Psalm 18:9, 11, 12
Communion: Psalm 83:4, 5

✠

'Qui non est mecum, contra me est: et qui non
colligit mecum, dispergit.'†

Two weeks ago we saw Our Lord go into the wilderness and defeat Satan, who tempted him. Today we see that the great battle between good and evil goes on, and that each of us must enlist on one side or the other. St Ignatius of Loyola, in

---

* Psalm 24:15.

† Luke 11:23: 'He that is not with me is against me: and he that gathereth not with me scattereth.'

his Spiritual Exercises, instructed his readers to imagine them-selves in the presence of two great armies – one, the forces of Hell, assembled with their standards and banners, and the other, the soldiers of Jesus Christ. St Ignatius suggests that with this scene before our minds, we make a definitive choice to enlist with the armies of Heaven, to put on the armour of grace and to resolve to follow the commands of our divine Captain. In the sacrament of Confirmation we become soldiers of Christ. Perhaps we shy away from such militaristic language, but it is a certain truth that we are engaged in warfare against Satan and his legions of Hell. While we know what the ultimate out-come of this battle will be, there remains a doubt as to the side on which we shall find ourselves at the Last Trump. It is for this reason that we must make that decision to fight under the standard of Christ.

When we look at the history of any great war, there are usu-ally significant and decisive battles that determine the outcome of the conflict. These might compare with the major decisions and temptations that we face in our lives. Some of us may have had, or will have, the opportunity to answer God's call in a dramatic and decisive way – for example by joining the Catholic Church, by accepting a vocation to the priesthood or religious life, or by rejecting some grave temptation or state of sin that would result in spiritual ruin. Battles like these are not won unless the morale of the troops has been built up by training and by instilling loyalty and discipline. It is possible to lose a war by a gradual, almost imperceptible ebbing away of confidence, or by failing to reinforce weak areas. It is an axiom that a chain is only as strong as its weakest link or that we only have to find the chink in someone's armour to bring about his downfall. So it is with our struggles. There is a danger of think-ing that because we have made a major decision to serve God that we are safe and that no more needs to be done. We are all at risk of becoming lukewarm. We should remember the words addressed to the Church in Laodicea in the book of the Apocalypse: *'I know not your works, that thou art neither cold* nor hot. I would thou wert cold or hot. But because thou art lukewarm, and neither cold nor hot, I will begin to vomit thee out of my mouth.'*

Our Lord does not invite us to do so much for him and no more. He tells us: 'Be you therefore perfect as also your Heavenly Father is perfect.'† This is not to say, of course, that if we are not perfect then we should give up now. On the contrary, it is never by our own efforts that we are saved but by God's grace alone. St Philip Neri used to say that very often we are left with one fault – or more – precisely so that we do not become proud and self-reliant, but realize our total dependence upon grace. Perfection, however, is a goal at which we should aim and we should not be satisfied with anything less. It is not enough for us simply to steer clear of mass-murder, when Our Lord tells us: 'Whosoever is angry with his brother shall be in danger of the judgement.'‡ Our struggle must be ceaseless and uncompromising because, as St Peter reminds us: 'Your adversary the devil, as a roaring lion, goeth about seeking whom he may devour. Whom resist ye, strong in faith.'§

Again, St Philip said that on the days when we are to receive Holy Communion, we should expect more temptations than usual. St John Vianney knew that when he was disturbed and thrown about at night by the Devil, he should expect some particularly great sinner to come to confession the next day. Our perseverance in grace thus far is never any guarantee of the future, and indeed we should be most afraid when we have received more than ordinary grace. When Cardinal Baronius finished his tremendous historical work, The Annals of the Christian Church, and presented them to St Philip, the saint said not a word, but sent him off to serve fifteen Masses as a penance. Philip knew that the vainglory was the greatest danger to the soul.

* Apocalypse 3:15, 16.
† Matthew 5:48.
‡ Matthew 5:21.
§ 1 Peter 5:8.

'He that is not with me is against me.' At every moment of our lives we have a choice to make by our thoughts, our words and our actions, and these choices all have eternal consequences. Despite all this, we ought not to be afraid or downhearted, when we have a Captain in the fight from whom all strength may be drawn. St James gives the best advice when he says: *'Be subject therefore to God, but resist the devil, and he will fly from you. Cleanse your hands, ye sinners and purify your hearts ye double-minded. Be humbled in the sight of the Lord and he will exalt you.'**

For further reflection:

> *Give us the self-control that springs*
> *From discipline of outward things,*
> *That fasting inward secretly*
> *The soul may purely dwell with thee.*
> *(from Audi benigne Conditor – tr. TAL)*

We are all at risk of becoming lukewarm.

Stretch forth the right hand of Thy Majesty to be our defence.
(from the Collect of the Day)

---

* James 4:7, 8, 10.

Dominica IV in Quadragesima
The Fourth Sunday in Lent

*'I rejoiced at the things that were said to me: we shall go into the house of the Lord.'**

Proper of the Day: Introit: Isaiah 66:10, 11; Psalm 121:1
                            Epistle: Galatians 4:22–31
                            Gradual: Psalm 121:7
                            Tract: Psalm 124:1, 2
                            Gospel: John 6:1–15
                            Offertory: Psalm 134:3, 6
                            Communion: Psalm 121:3, 4

✠

'Colligite quae superaverunt fragmenta, ne pereant.'†

Today's Gospel tells us of the great miracle of the multiplication of the loaves and fish, at the feeding of the five thousand. Here we see a powerful prefiguring of the institution of the Holy Eucharist, in the action of blessing, breaking and distributing the bread and the fish; and in the careful collection of the fragments at the end of the meal. Our Lord shows us how the fragmentation of his body in fact brings about the unity of the Church.

At the end of this episode, Our Lord has to escape into the hills to prevent the crowd from making him king. Later on, the crowds will manage to catch up with him, and he is rather sceptical of their motives. *'I say to you, you seek me, not because you have seen miracles, but because you did eat of the loaves and were filled.'‡* Probably like us, the crowds had taken a short-sighted view, considering only their immediate needs, and not looking beyond what they could see before their eyes. It is true that in the first place Our Lord fed them in the wilder-

---

* Psalm 121:1.

† John 6:12b: 'Gather up the fragments that remain, lest they be lost.'

‡ John 6:26.

ness simply because they were hungry and he wished to provide for their physical needs. However, the feeding of the five thousand was also a sign of the Kingdom. The loaves and the fish point beyond themselves to the central purpose of Christ's life: that he might give us eternal life. In the same way, he invites us to look beyond the concerns and troubles of our everyday lives and to see that our supernatural life is the one which is truly important. The loaves and the fish brought nourishment to the bodies of the people, but they were also symbols of the Eucharist, which Our Lord would later institute at the Last Supper. In this meal, the Mass, we are all fed with one loaf, though we are many, and all who eat the Body of Christ are sustained and strengthened for their journey to the heavenly homeland, just as the people of Israel were fed with manna for their long passage to the Promised Land.

When we look at all the different ways in which God has revealed himself throughout human history, we can see that he always has to use his own creation in order to communicate with us. We are unable to understand or know God as he truly is in himself, and so he uses the works of nature to give a dim reflection of his glory: burning bushes, earthquakes, winds, fires and manna from heaven are all natural signs that raise our minds beyond ourselves to the majesty of God who made them. The problem with these signs is that we are usually so impressed by them that we fail to look beyond their own glory. The Israelites saw Mount Sinai smoking and shaking when Moses went to receive the Ten Commandments, but this did not stop them from having a golden calf made. So, in the New Testament, God gives us a sign that does more than point to a greater reality: he gives us himself in the forms of bread and wine, and these signs actually are the God who created the Universe. This is why Our Lord says: *'I am the bread of life. He that cometh to me shall not hunger.'** Unlike the manna in the desert, which fed the people only for a short time, in the

---

* John 6:35.

Blessed Sacrament we are given the same Lord upon whom we hope to gaze for all eternity. The only difference is that in heaven we shall see him as he truly is, whereas now he comes to us hidden under these sacramental forms. Here again, God uses the ordinary – the bread and wine – in order to raise us to the supernatural.

The purpose of the Mass, then, is that by coming to share in this Bread of Life, the whole of our lives ought to be transformed. Our Lord feeds us with himself so that we may live in a new way, so that the ordinary events and actions of our lives may be divinized, made holy, by his grace. St Paul urges the Ephesians not to go on living the aimless kind of life that the pagans live. When we stop to think of how most human beings live, perhaps ourselves included, we realize that their lives have no point to them. They are like those Israelites who disobeyed the instructions of Moses and went out to gather more manna than they needed for one day. All that happened was that the extra food bred worms, and became foul. So also, when we seek only after the things of this world, none of them can satisfy us. They only fester and disappoint. The only food that can truly bring happiness is the Bread of Life. What must happen when we try to live according to this new life, St Paul tells us, is that our minds have to be renewed by a spiritual conversion so that we can put on the new self that has been created in God's own way, in the goodness and holiness of the truth.

The strength to live in this way is given us by the Eucharist. If only we made full use of all the graces given to us in just one reception of Holy Communion, we would have enough to become saints. As it is, Our Lord constantly feeds us with himself so that we may share his life and become more like him. To allow this to happen, we need to have our eyes fixed on heavenly things. If we make our communion, and then forget about it for the rest of the week, then we have lost sight of what is really important. If we realize that just as bread and wine are transformed into something of infinitely more worth, so also our ordinary lives can be changed so that they reflect the very life of God himself, and then we shall know how to work for food that endures to eternal life.

Here, in the Mass, we come into the presence of the One who is more valuable than the whole of the world, and he gives himself to us as our food. Here is a marvel beyond anything else. If we wish to be saints, we could begin by trying to realize how great are the gifts that God has given us.

For further reflection:

> *Therefore we before him bending,*
> *This great Sacrament revere:*
> *Types and shadows have their ending*
> *For the newer Rite is here;*
> *Faith, our outward sense befriending,*
> *Makes the inward vision clear.*
>
> (from Tantum ergo – tr. JMN)

If only we made full use of all the graces given to us in just one reception of Holy Communion, we would have enough to become saints.

'May we always receive thy gifts, O merciful God, with a steady faith.

(Cf Postcommunion Collect of the Day)

Dominica de Passione
Passion Sunday

'Send forth thy light, and thy Truth: they have conducted me, and brought me unto thy holy hill and into thy Tabernacles.'*

Proper of the Day: Introit: Psalm 42:1, 2, 3
Epistle: Hebrews 9:11–15
Gradual: Psalm 142:9, 10; 17:48, 49
Tract: Psalm 128:1–4
Gospel: John 8:46–59
Offertory: Psalm 118:7, 107
Communion: 1 Corinthians 11:24, 25

✠

'Jesus autem abscondit se, et exivit de templo'†

Apparently these last words of today's Gospel are one reason why all the images are veiled in the church from now until the end of Holy Week. *'Jesus hid himself . . .'* The mysteries of the Lord's death and Resurrection are to be revealed to us by the liturgy once more, and so first the glories must be hidden. Christ's glory will be most fully seen when he hangs rejected and despised upon the Cross, because it is there that God's infinite love for humanity is most effectively demonstrated. The Son of God empties himself of everything out of love for us; he submits to the basest torture and he becomes the lowest and most degraded of all his creatures. This last fortnight of Lent – Passiontide – is characterized by a more intense concentration upon the sufferings of Our Lord and by an attempt to share with him in some small measure his Passion. The liturgy helps us to live through the events of our salvation as they unfold. In this, we imitate St Paul, who said that he lived out the sufferings of Christ in his own body; who wanted to share his

---

* Psalm: 42:3.
† John 8:59: 'but Jesus hid himself, and went out of the temple'.

sufferings by reproducing the pattern of his death. As we join our Saviour on his journey towards Calvary, we at least have the advantage over his first companions in that we know that Easter comes at the end of our pilgrimage. Nevertheless, it is still difficult for us to understand the intensity of those sufferings. We all instinctively recoil from violence and bloodshed, and yet these are the very images the Church gives us to contemplate during Passiontide.

Modern people tend to think that there is no worse fate than to suffer, whereas our forebears thought that they could form noble characters by taking cold baths. We are more likely to pamper our bodies, telling ourselves, *'I'm worth it!'* So the sight of a man who goes willingly and silently to his agonizing death is inexplicable and shocking. That this man is also the Son of God makes us ask terrible questions about the nature of God himself. That God should become a human being at all is surprising. That he should become a man of sorrows can only make us take notice.

How different is the Christ described in the Passion narratives from the God of majesty and power we might expect; but how right it is that he should confound our expectations. Isaiah says: *'Verily thou art a hidden God, the God of Israel, the saviour.'** Unlike the false gods of the cultures around Israel, who were portrayed with terrifying aspect but in fact had no substance at all, the God of Israel deliberately concealed himself. He was known only to one insignificant nation, to those who listened to the still, small voice; and when the High Priest entered the Holy of Holies once a year on the Day of Atonement, as described in today's Epistle, he found there only an empty whitewashed room. So too, when he came upon this earth, the Son of God did not glorify himself, but he showed clearly to those who were listening who he was: *'Before Abraham was, I am.'* These words rang in the ears of his hearers as a direct claim to be the same God who told Moses: *'I am'*: the only name by which he could be known. The Jews picked up stones at this

---

* Isaiah 45:15.

point because Our Lord had claimed divinity. He slipped away because his hour had not yet come, but the essential ground for his final conflict had been prepared.

This question – who is Jesus? – is the central question of our lives. It is right that we should confront it at the beginning of Passiontide. Very often, like the inhabitants of Judea two-thousand years ago, we want to have a God who manifests himself beyond doubt and who vanquishes our enemies. Instead, our God is One who lies hidden, who conceals himself in the littleness of bread and wine, and who forces us to make our way to him by faith. Yet, like those who stood in the Temple and heard him say, *'Before Abraham was, I am'*, we have quite enough to make our faith certain.

That certainty comes not only from the rational arguments in favour of our religion, but also from the certainty of knowing Christ through the sacraments of the Church. When the High Priest went into the sanctuary, he bore in a symbolic way the sins of all the people. The blood which was so essential to every Old Testament sacrifice was shed because blood was the life of the victim. Yet no number of the lives of sheep, oxen or heifers could ever be a worthy offering to the God who is beyond everything in this world. Only Christ, the true and eternal High Priest, shedding his blood and pouring out his life once and for all upon the Cross, can reconcile God and man. For Christ to die once was enough; but he gives us access to this offering by renewing it daily in the Mass, and continuing to offer his death until the end of time.

It is this that makes the Crucifixion more than an historical event: we are not less privileged than the centurion who saw the blood and water flowing from his side and knew that this was indeed the Son of God. Here, in the Mass, the veil of the sanctuary is torn in two, and our High Priest, who hid and went out of the man-made Temple, leads us into a greater and more perfect tabernacle, not made with human hands.

✠

For further reflection:

> *O Tree of beauty, Tree of Light!*
> *O Tree with royal purple dight!*
> *Elect on whose triumphal breast*
> *Those holy limbs should find their rest.*
>
> *(from Vexilla Regis – tr. JMN)*

Only Christ, the true eternal High Priest, can reconcile God and man.

Hallow our fasts, O Lord, and forgive our faults.
> *(from the Collect for Monday after Passion Sunday)*

Dominica in Palmis
Palm Sunday

Glory and praise and honour to thee, O King, Christ and Redeemer.

Proper of the Day:	*Blessing and Procession of Palms*
	Gospel: Matthew 21:1–9
	Introit: Psalm 21:20, 22, 2
	Epistle: Philippians 2:5–11
	Gradual: Psalm 72:24, 1–3
	Tract: Psalm 21:2–9, 18, 19, 22, 24, 32
	The Passion: Matthew 26:36–75; 27:1–60
	Offertory: 68:21, 22
	Communion: Matthew 26:42

✠

'factus obediens usque ad mortem,
*mortem autem crucis'**

For the first three centuries of Christian history, the cross was not depicted in religious art. Even when, after the

---

* Philippians 2:8: 'becoming obedient unto death, even to the death of the cross'.

conversion of Constantine and the discovery of the True Cross by his mother, St Helena, the cross became the principal symbol of the faith, it was not generally a realistic crucifix that was made, but a triumphal cross covered with jewels and decoration. It is easy to see why the depiction of Our Lord's death should have been avoided: until Constantine's time, crucifixion was a common method of execution in the Roman Empire; the cross was then as shocking and distasteful as a hangman's noose or an electric chair might be to us today. Yet Our Lord did not die just any death: *'becoming obedient unto death, even to the death of the cross'*.

The whole saving purpose of the Crucifixion depends upon that obedience. Christ was obedient in every detail to his Father – as the Gospel accounts show us whenever they say that something happened to fulfil a prophecy from the Scriptures. There were many occasions during his thirty-three years when Our Lord might have died: when Herod sought to murder him as an infant, when the townspeople tried to throw him off the cliff top at Nazareth, or when they picked up stones to throw at him in the Temple. None of these occasions was yet 'his hour' and though God might have chosen to save us in any way he willed, the cross was the most costly way possible. This is not only because of the brutal, physical pain that was inflicted there. Men with cruel imaginations could certainly devise still worse, longer-lasting pain. It was the voluntary obedience and complete submission that alone was able to make an acceptable offering to the Father and undo the consequences of the first Adam's disobedience. For Christ to die without first offering himself would have made no difference. Death has no value on its own. It was his oblation in the upper room and in the Garden of Gethsemane that gave the sacrifice of Calvary its meaning. At the Last Supper he said, *'this is my body ... this is my blood'*, and so committed his life entirely into the Father's hands: *'not as I will, but as thou wilt'*.

Blessed John Henry Newman says that it is the mental sufferings of Christ which make the Crucifixion the greatest agony that the world has ever seen. Whereas we are able, when in pain, to shut off our minds, to a certain extent, from what the body is undergoing, the Son of God could not do this, since all knowledge is present to him. St Matthew tells us that when he had tasted the wine mixed with gall he would not drink it. There was to be no shirking the full punishment for sin which he bore for us. Physical pains, however terrible, have a limit, but there is no limit to the love which God bears towards humanity. As he hung upon the cross, Our Lord was fully conscious of every sin committed by every human being from the creation of the world until its end. Every time we sin, we reject God's love. Every act of spite and selfishness wounds the heart of him who was spat upon by the very creatures whom he had freely made as an act of pure, gratuitous love.

It is for this reason that we listen to the account of the Passion during this Holy Week. We are meant to realize that this is not simply a story about other people long ago: it is about us and the price that our Saviour paid to forgive us. Bishop Fulton Sheen said that every time a priest gives absolution in the sacrament of Confession, his hand, raised in forgiveness, is dripping with the blood of Christ. This death is for me: these sufferings he underwent, for you. What can we do but love him? How can we squander the forgiveness he has won? How can we treat lightly the precious, infinite graces offered us in the sacraments?

It is the extravagance of our love that is demanded by this extravagant emptying out of Jesus Christ. During Holy Week, our best companion in walking with the Cross is the one human being whose obedience matched that of her Son. Our Blessed Lady first knew the agony of separation when she lost the child Jesus in the Temple. This was a foretaste of her sorrow at his Passion. She had already promised that she would accept from God's hand whatever his will should be, and she knew that her heart would be pierced by a sword. First, she had to see her Son depart from her to carry out his public ministry, and then she had the intense pain of witnessing his death. Her total self-giving meant that she was able to share fully in all that the Lord went through. Blessed John Henry Newman says that when Christ was carrying his cross, there was only one person who could possibly comfort him, and that was his Mother: '*Mary would rather have had all the sufferings herself, could that have been, than not to know what they were by ceasing to be near him. He, too, gained a refreshment as from some soothing and grateful breath of air, to see her sad smile amid the sights and noises which were about him.*'

Everyone else was the cause of the disfigurement which Jesus bore in his body; only Mary was truly able to comfort and sympathize. To hold her Son lifeless in her arms was the path to life of this kindest and sweetest of all mothers. In imitating her maternal heart this Holy Week, may we follow him who emptied himself and became obedient unto death, even death on a cross.

✠

For further reflection:

> *The Cross doth chase all evil,*
> *Before it darkness flieth;*
> *That soul abideth steadfast*
> *Which on this sign relieth.*
>
> *(from Cultor Dei Memento)*

At the Last Supper he said, 'This is my body . . . this is my blood', and so committed his life entirely into the Father's hands.

Grant, O merciful God, that we who fail through weakness, may be relieved through the Passion of thy Son.

(from the Collect for Monday after Palm Sunday)

In Cœna Domini
The Lord's Supper

*'May God have mercy on us and bless us: may he cause the light of his countenance to shine upon us.'**

Proper of the Day: Introit: *Galatians 6:14; Psalm 66:2*
                              Epistle: *1 Corinthians 11:20–32*
                              Gradual: *Philippians 2:8, 9*
                              Gospel: *John 13:1–15*
                              Offertory: *Psalm 117:16, 17*
                              Communion: *John 13:12, 13, 15*

✠

'cum dilexisset suos, qui errant in mundo, in finem dilexit eos'†

Today, Our Lord sat at table with his disciples and he gave them two gifts beyond all understanding. First, he entrusted to them the sacrament of Holy Orders in all its fullness. The gift of the sacred priesthood in the Church today stems from those first Apostles, through the two-thousand-year succession of the laying on of hands. This gift of ordination is what enables Christ to be present now in the second gift of today – the greatest of all God's gifts – the most Holy Eucharist. The Eucharist is Our Lord's gift of himself; it is the source and summit of the Christian life, the certain pledge of future glory, the Bread of Life and the sacrament of eternal salvation. Today, we priests, in particular, ask you to pray for our faithfulness to the sacred ministry, that we may become truly conformed to Christ, who uses our hands and voices to make himself present in the world. Pray too, that many others will hear his call to labour in his

---

* Psalm 66:2.

† John 13:1b: 'having loved his own who were in the world, he loved them unto the end'.

vineyard. The Blessed Sacrament is what makes the Church the Body of Christ – there can be no Church without priests.

Yet, as we contemplate the wonder of the Eucharist and the self-giving love of the One who makes himself weak and fragile in the forms of bread and wine, we are also struck by the tragic indifference of human beings to God's love. Judas Iscariot was one of the Lord's closest companions – he witnessed his miracles, he heard his words first-hand. Judas was chosen to be a herald of the Good News to the nations, to be a foundation stone of the Church, and yet his heart became coarsened. At first, he retained some of the money destined for the poor, but gradually he forgot altogether the bright promises of eternal life and became entirely worldly, embittered and self-seeking. He is a terrible example of how sin can come to dominate us so that we become incapable of loving God and even incapable of receiving his love. Judas is a warning glimpse of Hell to each one of us. At the Last Supper, he had his feet washed by the Lord, but he still betrayed him with a kiss.

What is most remarkable is Our Lord's response. He knew that Judas had betrayed him, and yet he gave himself in Holy Communion. He knew that Judas cared more for thirty pieces of silver than for his dearest friend, but when he met him in the Garden, we read that Jesus still called Judas *'my friend'*. This infinite generosity and mercy is also given to us. Our Lord knew all our sins in all their banal details as he was nailed to the cross. Nevertheless, he said: *'Father, forgive them for they know not what they do.'* He knows now our selfishness and our malice, but still he entrusts himself to us and he makes himself vulnerable to our betrayal. He says, *'this is my body'*, not in spite of but because of our sins. He washes his disciples' feet, St John tells us, precisely because he knew that one of them was a traitor.

Why does Our Lord do this? It is because in the heart of God there is a deep longing, a yearning for us. He does not wait for us to reach out to him, but he empties himself out for us and comes to earth to seek our love in the great Sacrament of his Love. In March 2007, our Holy Father Pope Benedict published his exhortation, *Sacramentum Caritatis* – the Sacrament of Charity, of Love. The Pope urges all of us to be transformed by the Eucharist and to respond with love to the infinite love shown in this sacramental presence. We do this first by making sure that our celebration of the Liturgy is as beautiful as it can possibly be. Our churches should be true houses of God – places where we are silent and reverent. Those who decorate, or beautify, or clean the church and the sacred vessels of the altar are truly performing a noble act of love for Christ in the Blessed Sacrament.

The clergy are exhorted by the Holy Father to express their devotion by their obedience to the rite – whether ordinary or extraordinary – by not imposing their own personality upon the worship of the Church. The music used for the Liturgy should be noble, prayerful and elevating. '*We cannot say*', says Pope Benedict, '*that one song is as good as another.*' The Liturgy should be for everyone a true participation in Christ's own love, and so we should take the greatest care, especially at Sunday Mass, to arrive in good time, to prepare carefully and to make a good thanksgiving after receiving Holy Communion. It is by these little actions that we keep alive the love of God in our hearts, to prevent that love from going cold as it did in Judas Iscariot. In particular, the Holy Father urges us to receive Holy Communion frequently, and to remember that if we do so, we ought frequently to receive the Sacrament of Penance in Confession.

We are encouraged, all of us, to foster our love for the Blessed Sacrament by prayer before the tabernacle, by coming to Exposition and Benediction and by taking part in Eucharistic processions. It is by using all of these tremendous means at our disposal that we can be transformed by the Sacrament of Charity. If Christ loves us, this demands that we love one another, as he commanded us on this day. The Holy Eucharist challenges us to commit ourselves to social justice, to care for the poor and the sick and to live at peace. That great act of service and self-giving which was offered on this holy night was fulfilled in the sacrifice of the Cross tomorrow. In the Mass, we become true participants in these saving mysteries. We must allow ourselves to be loved by God so that we too can love. In the Blessed Sacrament of the altar, we are given the proof that he has loved us to the end.

For further reflection:

> *Thee we adore, O hidden Saviour, thee,*
> *Who in thy Sacrament art pleased to be;*
> *Both flesh and spirit in thy presence fail,*
> *Yet here thy Presence we devoutly hail.*
>
> *(from Adoro te – tr. JRW)*

He knows now our selfishness and our malice, but still he entrusts himself to us and makes himself vulnerable to our betrayal.

O God from whom the thief received the reward of his confession; grant unto us the full fruit of thy clemency.

(from the Collect of the Day)

Dominica Resurrectionis
Easter Sunday

'I arose, and am still with thee, Alleluia.'*

Proper of the Day: *Introit: Psalm 138:18, 5, 6, 1, 2*
                               Epistle: 1 Corinthians 5:7, 8
                               Gradual: Psalm 117:24, 1
                               Alleluia: 1 Corinthians 5:7
                               Sequence: Victimae Paschali
                               Gospel: Mark 16:1–7
                               Offertory: Psalm 75:9, 10
                               Communion: 1 Corinthians 5:7, 8

✠

'Haec dies quam fecit Dominus.'†

The night is over at last, dawn breaks, the eastern sky brightens, soon it will be day. Long shadows still slant across the garden, and the first touch of gold gleams on the entrance to the sepulchre. Like the women who came to the tomb, we are awake in the twilight, young in the growing radiance, full of promise of the splendour that is to come.

The women come to the tomb, their hearts too full of grief to speak. They bear bitter spices, for they know that Our Lord is dead, they saw him die. For years these women had been caring for him, supporting him from their own resources, sometimes welcoming him into their homes, sometimes following him as he walked the lanes of Galilee and the hard roads of Judea. They can do nothing for him now except to bury him with dignity that haste prevented on the day of his death. The spices are the tokens of their love, the alabaster jar of ointment Mary Magdalen had already poured over his feet, the evidence of her repentance and her tears. They grieve for him, but they grieve also for themselves and for their children, bearing the heavy

---

* Psalm 138:18.

† Psalm 117:24: 'This is the day which the Lord hath made.'

jars of myrrh, which weigh them down with sorrow for past sin, for repentance still incomplete.

But now they speak, in hushed whispers, anxious about the burden of the stone; how can they roll it away? For it is so great, this burden that keeps them from the Lord. But it has been taken away already, that heavy weight that neither man nor woman can bear, already lifted from them. The earth has trembled, and now it is still, the stone is gone. What is this stone? The stone represents the Old Law, the *'burden too heavy to bear'*, which the Pharisees and scribes would bind upon our backs. It is the *'old leaven, the leaven of malice and iniquity'*, the Law of condemnation. No one can claim to be righteous in the eyes of the Law, for it binds in so many ways, that all must acknowledge they have fallen short, failed to observe it in its majesty and perfection. *'If thou, O Lord, wilt mark iniquities, Lord who shall stand it?'* The Lord knows us better than we know ourselves: *'thou hast searched me out and known me'*.* But it is precisely because he knows and understands us that he can wipe away our guilt and lift our burdens from us. The Lord does not mark our iniquities, for he himself has taken the weight upon himself, bearing it away, for he became subject to the Law so that we can be free from that Law.

And now the women see a young man, on the right-hand side, who proclaims to them the consummation of the Gospel: *'He is risen; he is not here.'* The message is one of forgiveness, of hope: *'Tell the disciples, yes, even Peter, even the one who denied his master three times, tell them that he is going before you into the Galilee of the nations, into all the nations of the world.'* Sin is no more, we need not carry that burden still, for in him all sin is washed away. Sins that are past have no more power to harm us, once we have embraced that forgiveness which Christ won for us on the Cross. Even though our sins be as mean and cowardly as Peter's denial, the message of hope is for us. Though we have allowed seven devils to ravage heart and soul, we receive the liberation offered to St Mary

---

* Psalm 138:1.

Magdalen. We are free from the malice of the enemy, emancipated from slavery to sin, purged from the leaven of iniquity.

They do not see him yet, for it is not yet fully day, but there then they shall see him. Only when the sun has fully risen can they see him who is himself the Dayspring rising in the east. In the twilight they flee, and they say nothing, for they are afraid. But in the daylight they see him, in Jerusalem, in Galilee, in the upper room, by the lakeside.

The Gospel announces all of this for us too. This span of earthly life is still the twilight before the day. We know the sun has risen, we see the first shafts of light, for he rose from the dead two thousand years ago. But the Day of the Lord has not come yet, that final Sabbath which consummates all our expectations, banishes the night and fills us with radiance. That is the day the Lord has already made for us, now in anticipation we can rejoice and be glad in it.

The night is over, the night of sin and ignorance. Our lives were corrupted with the leaven of iniquity, we groaned under the weight of guilt. All that is now over, we can rid ourselves of the old leaven. We see the deacon on the right side of the sanctuary proclaiming to us the same message: 'He is risen.' No, we do not yet see him, not during this twilight existence of ours, waiting between the dawn and the daybreak, but we shall see him in the eternal Galilee when at last the Day has fully come.

We have become a new mixture of dough, unleavened, pure and true. It is in the unleavened Bread of the Eucharist that we find Our Risen Lord, and on his Eucharistic body we feast. He has become our Paschal sacrifice, the sacrifice of unleavened bread which we share – the pledge, the foretaste of the final banquet of the Lamb. We do not see him in his risen form, we perceive only the white disc elevated like the rising sun, and we can welcome him into our homes, under our roofs, for the healing of our lives. Our union with him in the Blessed Sacrament is as close and immediate as that of the women – closer indeed, for they could only see him at moments, in glimpses, whereas we can take him into our mouths, come to him every day for him to embrace us and incorporate us into his Body, the Church.

The story of the empty tomb, the stone rolled away, the shroud and grave-clothes resting, is the story of our hope and our joy, for he is alive, and he calls us to follow him into that Galilee where all sin and grief will be no more remembered. This is the Day which the Lord has made: let us rejoice and be glad in it.

✠

For further reflection:

> *Purge the old leaven out, that we*
> *May welcome with sincerity*
> *The Resurrection new;*
> *This is our hope's expected hour;*
> *Behold this day of mighty power.*
> *Break forth in triumph free;*
> *This is the day the Lord hath made,*
> *This day hath all our grief repaid,*
> *The day of jubilee.*
> *(from the Sarum Sequence for the Monday in Easter week)*

But in the daylight they see him, in Jerusalem, in Galilee, in the upper room, by the lakeside.

O God, who hast thrown open to us the gate of everlasting life, give effect to our desires, which thou dost anticipate and inspire.

(from the Collect of the Day)

Dominica in Albis
The Octave Day of Easter (Low Sunday)

'Who is he that overcometh the world, but he that believeth that Jesus is the Son of God.'*

Proper of the Day: Introit: 1 Peter 2:2; Psalm 80:2
                              Epistle: 1 John 5:4–10
                              Paschal Alleluia: Matthew 28:7
                              Alleluia: John 20:26
                              Gospel: John 20:19–31
                              Offertory: Matthew 28:2, 5, 6
                              Communion: John 20:27

✠

'Venit Jesus, et stetit in medio, et dixit eis:
"Pax vobis."'†

If we have ever experienced some shock or trauma in our life, such as an accident, assault or bereavement, it can be quite some time after the event before we can actually reflect on what happened in a dispassionate way. Then we begin to recall the circumstances, the character or characters involved, and somehow relive the awful experience. Such must have been the emotional state of the Apostles on that first Easter Sunday evening when all the excitement of the previous days had calmed. They were now feeling lonely, dejected and empty, trying to make sense of the events of Holy Week. We, therefore, only imagine their utter joy when they see Our Lord standing at the door of the room where they were concealed. He greets them in his familiar tone of voice with words of peace.

Not all the Apostles were present. Thomas was absent. St Gregory the Great comments: *'Surely you do not think that it was pure accident that this chosen disciple was missing; who*

---

* 1 John 5:5.

† John 20:19b: 'Jesus came, and stood in the midst and said to them: "Peace be to you."'

on his return was told about the appearance, and on hearing about it doubted; doubted, so that he might touch and believe by touching? It was not an accident; God arranged that it should happen. His clemency acted in this wonderful way so that through the doubting disciple's touching the wounds of his Master's body, our own wound of incredulity might be healed. And so, the disciple's doubting and touching was changed into a witness of the truth of the Resurrection.'

The reply of Thomas was not simply an exclamation but an act of faith in the divinity of Jesus: *'My Lord, and my God!'* These words have been an inspiration to countless generations of Christians, especially used to express faith in the Real Presence of Our Lord in the Blessed Sacrament at the moment of the consecration at Mass.

Thomas struggled to believe in the fullness of who Jesus is. He asked for proofs as sometimes we ask for signs. St Gregory goes on to say: *'It becomes clear that faith has to do with things that are not seen, for those things that are seen are no longer the object of faith but rather of experience.'*

Thomas saw one thing and believed another; we cannot yet *see* the divinity of Christ as God. Thomas saw the person of Jesus and recognized him as God by his great act of faith. It was a gift of faith, given by the same God, which aided him to see beyond the merely visible. So we can presume it is ourselves who are referred to when Our Lord spoke the words: *'Blessed are they that have not seen, and have believed.'* We live by faith, not by sight; faith is only faith when we live what we believe. Eastertide is the season of the liturgical year when we must renew our faith in our final goal: *'to seek the things that are above,'* as St Paul says, *'where Christ lives'*.

Blessed John Henry Newman said that there can be only two possible positions to adopt: atheism or Catholicism. So many intelligent people in our world have been duped by myths which have deflected them from the very core of revealed Truth. Somehow millions of souls have been manipulated by

---

* Homilies on the Gospel 26.

the various media without noticing or raising a cry of protest, not only in the name of Faith, but also of common sense and healthy reason. Perhaps it is a moment to hear again the words of Dante:

> *Christians, be serious in taking action:*
> *Do not be like a feather to every wind,*
> *Nor think that every water cleanses you.*
> *You have the New and Old Testament*
> *And the Shepherd of the Church to guide you;*
> *Let this be all you need for your salvation . . .*
> *Be men, do not be senseless sheep.**

We inhabit a world where the vast majority of our fellow men are more interested in novelty than in truth. This is why the essence of Eastertide continues to be faith and optimism. The Easter season invites us again to look to the person of Jesus, to the truth of his life and words, and to learn to live by this, rather than by fables and fashionable human theories. This truth is the most powerful and dynamic reality ever, and the truth which alone, if appropriated and lived, transforms any culture, philosophy or falsehood. It is expressed in the immortal words of St Thomas's act of faith: *'Dominus meus, et Deus meus.'*

During Eastertide, the Church loves to sing the joyful anthem to Our Lady – *Regina Caeli*. Here we not only exalt with her at the Glorious Resurrection of her Son, but also implore her: *'Ora pro nobis Deum, Alleluia.'*

✠

For further reflection:

> *Exult we on that day*
> *When Jesus rose again,*

---

* Paradiso V. 73–80.

And opened wide the living way
By which our life we gain,
Let stars and earth and heaven rejoice,
And all the quires on high
Upraise their glorifying voice,
To praise the Trinity.
(from the Sarum Sequence for the Octave of Easter)

He greets the Apostles in his familiar tone of voice with words of peace.

Grant us, Almighty God, the firm faith, that thine Apostle Thomas bids us.

✠

Dominica II Post Pascha
The Second Sunday after Easter

'*Rejoice in the Lord, O ye just; praise becometh the upright.*'*

Proper of the Day: Introit: Psalm 32:5, 6, 1
                      Epistle: 1 Peter 2:21–25
                      Paschal Alleluia: Luke 24:35
                      Alleluia: John 10:14
                      Gospel: John 10:11–16
                      Offertory: Psalm 62:2, 5
                      Communion: John 10:14

✠

'*Bonus pastor animam suam dat pro ovibus suis.*'†

This Sunday – the second after Easter – is known as Good Shepherd Sunday, based upon the texts of the Epistle and Gospel. This image of the Lord as the Good Shepherd is one

---

* Psalm 32:1.
† John 10:11: 'The Good Shepherd giveth his life for his sheep.'

which was extremely dear to our early Christian forefathers. After all, as we heard in the Gospel, the image was used by Our Lord himself to describe his sacred ministry; it was taken up by the Apostles (notably St Peter and St Paul) and so it comes to be found on the simple frescoes of the catacombs and in the mosaics of the early Christian churches.

This portrayal of Our Lord as a shepherd is probably familiar to us all. It depicts the Saviour as a young man, athletic and sometimes beardless. Across his shoulders he is carrying home the wandering sheep, representing the sinful human race which the Good Shepherd has sought out and rescued at such great cost. It is a beautiful and comforting image – and yet it is, perhaps, more complex than we realize. For the early Christians, familiar (as we are not) with the practices of shepherds in the ancient world, that simple picture would have carried another layer of meaning. In those days, if a sheep habitually wandered from the flock and lost itself upon the hillsides, the shepherd would sometimes be forced to take drastic measures to cure it of the habit. He would, we are told, break the front legs or otherwise disable the animal, and then, as in the image, carry it upon his shoulders. By the time the legs had healed, the sheep had grown so used to its master that it would always in future stay close to him, and never wander away and become lost.

That familiar image, then, of the Good Shepherd is a little more challenging than we often appreciate. It speaks to us not only of rescue and redemption, but also of suffering and sacrifice – a sacrifice in which we are called to share. A glimpse at the rich tapestry of texts used in the Mass today will show how these concepts are in fact interwoven in the history of salvation.

The Introit begins by recalling creation: *'By the word of the Lord the heavens were established.'* The Son of God, the eternal Word, through his Incarnation, came *'unto his own'*, as we recall at every Mass in the last Gospel. Yet, as we also recall, *'his own received him not'*. This divine humility – the Creator accepting rejection for the sake of his creatures – is alluded to in today's Collect: it was through humility that Christ raised up the fallen world and *'cause[s] us to rejoice in everlasting joys'*. But this humility was costly, and Our Lord's Passion is recalled by St Peter in the Epistle: *'Who did no sin, neither was guile found in his mouth. Who when he was reviled did not revile: when he suffered, he threatened not, but delivered himself to him that judged him unjustly.'* St Peter also explains the meaning of this suffering. First, and most important, the sufferings of Christ are undergone for our Redemption, to pay the price of our iniquity: *'Who his own self bore our sins in his body upon the tree.'* But, secondly, they are also given to us as an example that we *'should follow in his steps'*. Humility, mortification, and, yes, suffering, are all to be embraced by those who follow in the footsteps of the Crucified one. This explains the words of Our Lord in the Gospel, which are singled out for repetition in the Communion verse: *'I am the Good Shepherd; and I know my sheep and mine know me.'* The phrase speaks of a certain mutuality in our relationship with Christ. He knows us as friends because he sees in us a willingness to learn from his own divine humility. Specifically, those who truly know Christ will be willing even to suffer for him, in order to become more like the one they love. And this suffering, freely accepted, will be for the benefit not only of ourselves but of others, to whom Our Lord refers: *'other sheep I have, that are not of this fold'*. Precisely through our willingness to share in the Passion of our Saviour, the work of salvation is carried on, and the day becomes closer when *'there shall be one fold and one shepherd'*.

Even with our freely given co-operation, however, the work of Redemption is wholly dependent on divine grace, as the Secret reminds us: *'May this holy sacrifice accomplish in us what it signifies.'* The work is God's and its accomplishment lies with him. Only by sharing in this sacrifice, and in the Most Holy Eucharist, only by allowing ourselves to be fed by the hand of the Good Shepherd, can we grow in the strength needed to share in the work of the world's salvation. A challenge is set before us today, but it is a challenge made possible by the constant presence of the one whose loving call we follow. As we will pray in the Postcommunion: *'Grant, Almighty God . . . that we ever rejoice in thy gifts.'* Eastertide is the season for joy – the joy of knowing not only that we are redeemed, but that we are even called to share in the redeeming work of the one who saved us.

✠

For further reflection:

> *They stand, those halls of Sion,*
> *Conjubilant with song,*
> *And bright with many an Angel,*
> *And all the Martyr throng;*
> *The Prince is ever with them,*
> *The daylight is serene,*
> *The pastures of the blessed*
> *Are decked in glorious sheen.*
> *(from Urbs Sion aurea – tr. JMN)*

Only by allowing ourselves to be fed by the hand of the Good Shepherd, can we grow in the strength needed to share in the work of the world's salvation.

'The earth is full of the mercy of the Lord.'*
(from the Introit of the Day)

---

* Psalm 32:5.

Dominica III Post Pascha
The Third Sunday after Easter

'Sing ye a psalm to his name, Alleluia.'

Proper of the Day: Introit: Psalm 65:1, 2, 3
Epistle: 1 Peter 2:11–19
Paschal Alleluia: Psalm 110:9
Alleluia: Luke 24:46
Gospel: John 16:16–22
Offertory: Psalm 145:2
Communion: John 16:16

✠

'tanquam advenas et peregrinos'†

Our Lord warns his disciples that in a *'modicum'* ['a little while'] they will not see him, and again in a *'modicum'* they will see him. What, they wonder, does he mean by 'a little while'? Does he mean that after a little while, soon, they will not see him, and soon again they will? Or is it that they will not see him for a little while, and then will see him again for a little while?

As always, when Scripture can have two meanings, there is profit in both. It is true, historically, obvious in the context, that only a little while after he is speaking (for this is during the Last Supper) they will see him no more, for they will run and scatter, and only John will see him placed in the tomb. And again a little while, and it will be Easter, and they will see him, again in the upper room. They weep and lament, for they have seen him betrayed to death; but their sorrow is turned to joy. This is the last prophecy of the Passion and the Resurrection, within three days all will be fulfilled.

---

* Psalm 65:1.
† 1 Peter 2:11: 'as strangers and pilgrims'.

But maybe *modicum* refers to the duration of not seeing him. For only forty hours – *'a little while'* – he lay in the sepulchre. And then for *'a little while'* they do see him – a period of forty days during which he spoke with them in Jerusalem and Galilee, for he had *'not yet ascended to the Father'*. For the disciples, both interpretations are true.

Nor does it end there. After his Ascension, for yet another little while they lose sight of him, but it is only forty years, maybe, before again they see him, *'and that joy no man shall take from them'*.

It is this last interpretation that is most pertinent to us. We live in this world, for a little while, only forty years, or twice forty years, perhaps, and then we shall catch sight of him. The whole of our life on earth is but a moment, a flicker in the face of eternity. And it is a life of grief and distress, while the world rejoices around us. Our brief lives seem so long, but they pass like a shadow. Our earthly joys are so fragile and so transient, while the grief and the tears seem to endure. For so many of us who attempt to follow Our Lord, this world brings nothing but sorrow and frustration, while those who make no attempt to serve him appear to be joyful and triumphant. All this is but the beginning of the birth pangs; for once we are born into eternity it will all be forgotten in the joy of being, at last, truly human and truly alive.

It is in this context that we see the relevance of the Epistle. St Peter invites us to live in this world *'as strangers and pilgrims'*. Here is no abiding city, here is no continuing stay. We are citizens of Heaven; we do not really belong to this world. We should resist the temptation to try to live like those around us who do not know God. Surrounded by pagans, our way of life must be different, not only as a witness to them, but because only in this way can we prepare for the real life to come. *'I will praise the Lord ... as long as I shall be'*,* because it is in his service and in his praise that we wait for his face to be revealed again. Just as Christ had *'to rise again from the dead, and so*

---

* Psalm 145:2.

enter into his glory',* so do we suffer in this world – the injustice and cruelty of man, the ravages of disease and disaster. But as the woman rejoices in the birth of the child, so the Church rejoices in our rebirth to new life. That is why we mark the day on which a saint died; we call it his birthday – *natalitium* – for the new birth into the eternal day is the real beginning of life. All that we endure now is only a preparation, a little while of gestation until we begin to live.

St Peter invites us to put up with the world as we find it. We are not to waste our efforts in impossible struggles for justice and liberation in this world. Our life is brief enough. For those who first heard St Peter's words, the idea of converting or overthrowing the Emperor of Rome was inconceivable – it is the Emperor he means by *'honour the king'*. Yes, some hot-headed Judeans were conspiring to rise against the Empire, and only brought immense suffering on themselves and their people. In the same way it was utterly unrealistic for Christian slaves to rise against their masters in the name of justice – that would lead to more brutality and more deaths. In the first century there was nothing a Christian could do about social conditions, except to live peaceably, obey the laws, and placate their masters by cheerful obedience. The knowledge that we are free, with the true freedom of the children of God, does not mean that we do not have to submit to the same lack of freedom which bound Christ to the pillar and nailed him to the cross – but only for a little while.

Not that we are to be unconcerned about righteousness and justice on earth. Our Lord and his Apostles speak in many places about our duty to love our neighbour as ourselves: we are judged according to what we do to the least of our brethren.† We must live in this world, striving to do God's will and bring about his Kingdom *'on earth as it is in heaven'*. Our charity must of course be practical, within the limit of our means and our opportunities. We cannot right the wrongs of the entire

---

* Luke 24:46.
† Matthew 25.

world, or establish perfect governments in every land: what we can do is to treat those around us with the same self-giving love that Christ shows us, to improve whatever we can improve, and to endure whatever is beyond our power to change. In our practical benevolence and charitable action we demonstrate the love of Christ. In our endurance we share in his Passion.

St Peter is not talking about the end of the world here, although for a time it was fashionable to imagine that the Apostles were all obsessed with the end of time. He is talking about the span of our life on earth: brief enough, we need only suffer for a little while, and then we shall, each of us at our own moment, see the Lord face to face. That sight should be a moment of joy, the supreme gladness of seeing clearly the one who is only shown to us in symbol and sacrament: *'Then your hearts will rejoice, and that joy no one shall take from you.'* The date of the end of the world is utterly irrelevant: what matters to us is the end of our lives in the world. That will come, only in a little while more, when we stand in awe of his judgements, but if we have been faithful in praising his name in this life, then we shall rejoice in the Lord and sing psalms in his name.*

✠

For further reflection:

> *Enlighten, Lord, and set on fire*
> *Our spirits with thy love,*
> *That, dead to earth, they may aspire*
> *And live to joys above.*
>
> *That, when the judgement seat on high*
> *Shall fix the sinner's doom,*
> *And to the just a glad voice cry,*
> *Come to your destined home;*

---

* Cf Psalm 65:1, 2, 3.

Safe from the black and yawning lake
Of restless, endless pain,
We may the face of God partake,
The bliss of heaven attain.

(from Verbum supernum prodiens – tr. JHN)

We need only suffer for a little while, and then we shall, each of us at our own moment, see the Lord face to face.

Grant that all those enrolled in the Christian faith may follow after what is fitting to it.

(from the Collect of the Day)

Dominica IV Post Pascha
The Fourth Sunday after Easter

'Sing ye to the Lord a new canticle, Alleliua, for the Lord hath done wonderful things.'*

Proper of the Day: Introit: Psalm 97:1, 2
Epistle: James 1:17–21
Paschal Alleluia: Psalm 117:16
Alleluia: Romans 6:9
Gospel: John 16:5–14
Offertory: Psalm 65:1, 2, 16
Communion: John 16:8

'Cum autem venerit ille Spiritus veritatis, docebit vos omnem veritatem.'†

I t is surprising that one of the commonest complaints that children make against the judgements of their elders is the

---

* Psalm 97:1.

† John16:13: 'But when he, the Spirit of Truth, is come, he will teach you all truth.'

lack of fairness. How often have we heard the accusation, *'That's not fair'*, levelled at us by youngsters whose impression is that the case has gone against them or they have been dealt with unjustly. They are not always right in their conclusions but they often have a point. Phrases such as 'fair play' and 'fair and square' are proverbial in our language and we all know what they mean. No deception and no underhand treatment. Children often appear to have an innate sense of what is fair treatment and are very put out when it is not practised. Fairness is not just a vague idea. It is a real and necessary aspect of dealing with others and of ensuring that good practice governs our actions and our attitude. Fairness is linked to justice and is akin to it. It is a concept that is rooted in Divine Revelation. However things may look on the surface and however long it takes, God will see justice done. He will not permit it that those who have been the victims of unfair and unjust treatment will be left without redress or rescue. He has promised as much to those who are faithful even unto death, and announced it from ancient times that he will redeem them and do it unmistakably.

Still liturgically and spiritually in the afterglow of Easter, the Mass of today leads us to reflect upon this aspect of that victory – the justice of God. The Almighty not only rescues those who put their trust in him but also keeps his promises to them. This great truth, so much a part of ancient prophecies, is fulfilled personally with the coming of Christ and especially by his rising from the dead. What had looked like a total disaster for him, in human reckoning, was actually a triumph in disguise. A faithful few stood by him. Most of those who knew him either ran away or turned against him at the last. As man he was brought to the extremes of agony and of desolation on the cross. No other man had felt so abandoned because within his human identity as Jesus of Nazareth, there was in reality the perfection of the Second Person of the Most Holy Trinity, capable of the most intense sensitivity to pain and to suffering. He truly was the 'Holy One' upon whom all who gazed saw only defeat and broken humanity. Yet, unknown to most of them, he was in truth the instrument and agent of the justice of God, who looked death and Satan in the face and conquered both. That same justice raised him high and gave physical and visible definition to the prophecies of old which promised victory for the just man and reward for his fidelity.

Furthermore, there was another element to this victory for man which through the power of the Holy Trinity made possible the outpouring of the Holy Spirit to reveal this and other truths to those who are Christ's own. The Church is the continuity through time of the remembrance of her Lord and makes known in the world the insights which reveal his truth and his justice. As he promised the disciples before his death, that future gift would make deliberate unbelief like that of those who opposed him, a matter of serious culpability, and also grant to those who did believe, a certainty and a clarity of teaching that would confound his enemies. This promise and this gift is what the Church both leads us to recall and celebrate again each year. It is a hugely important and essential element of the Paschal Mystery because it confirms us in the faith and verifies that what the Church holds and teaches comes from the lips of her Divine Master. By his own words he promised us no less and, in the passage of time, he has confirmed it over and over again by the survival of the Church in so many places, against all the odds. We should all take courage, therefore, that what has been in the past will be in the future. We and all that is dear to us are in the hands of God, and he will see justice done, and truth prevail.

✠

For further reflection:

Triumphant in his glory now
His sceptre ruleth all,

Earth, heaven, and hell before him bow,
And at his footstool fall.

> *(from Chorus novae Jerusalem – tr. RC)*

This victory made possible the outpouring of the Holy Spirit.

May our hearts be fixed where true joys are to be found.

> *(from the Collect of the Day)*

Dominica V Post Pascha
The Fifth Sunday after Easter

'Shout with joy to God, all the earth, sing ye a psalm to his name.'*

Proper of the Day: Introit: Isaiah 48:20; Psalm 65:1, 2
Epistle: James 1:22–27
Paschal Alleluia: source unknown
Alleluia: John 16:28
Gospel: John 16:23–30
Offertory: Psalm 65:8, 9, 20
Communion: Psalm 95:2

'In illo die in nomine meo petetis.'†

'O Christian be aware of your nobility – it is God's own nature that you share: do not then, by an ignoble life, fall back into your former baseness.' These words from a sermon by Pope St Leo the Great, read at Matins on Christmas Day, urge us to consider the full consequences of the Incarnation for mankind, how the human being is ennobled by the Son's taking of our flesh. During Advent and Christmas we contemplate God's

---

* Psalm 65:1.
† John 16:26: 'In that day you shall ask in my name.'

coming *down* among us as man, living in the flesh and dwelling among us; over this Easter season – now coming to an end – we contemplate man's going *up* into God and his Kingdom. This upward movement began on Easter Sunday, with Our Lord, in the flesh, rising up from death to life. On Thursday and next Sunday, we celebrate its completion when Our Lord ascends, again in the flesh, to the very throne of God in Heaven. This flesh is our flesh: in Christ, man transcends all the choirs of Angels until he sits at God's right hand. '*O Christian, be aware of your nobility!*'

The Christian can only begin to become aware of his own dignity in Christ inasmuch as he contemplates the divinity of him who took our flesh and joined it eternally to his divine nature. The disciples, during Our Lord's earthly life before his Passion, were slow to come to such awareness. Indeed, during the Passion, they seemed to have abandoned all hope in whatever they had correctly understood about the Person of Christ when they fled from the Garden of Gethsemane, or later. In those three years of his public ministry, he is often addressed as Master, Teacher, even as a Prophet. He is clearly seen by the disciples to be a man of God. But did they really understand at that point exactly how he is *of* God?

Of course there were moments when his disciples became aware of Our Lord's divinity during those public years, but they were only moments – nothing permanent at that stage. There were the great theophanies at the Epiphany and the Baptism in the River Jordan; various miracles, particularly those physical miracles, which accompanied the forgiveness of sins and also manifested his divinity. Peter grasped it for a moment when he made his bold confession of faith at Caesarea Philippi. But perhaps what Our Lord meant most of all to the disciples as they travelled around the country was the fact that he was their intimate friend, their close companion and guide who always brought calm to chaos. His charismatic inner strength would have been a source of great consolation to those first disciples as he taught them about the Kingdom of his Father.

It is only with the Resurrection and the coming of the Holy Spirit that the divinity of Christ is made manifest to the hearts and minds of his followers. Only then can St Thomas the Apostle bow down to worship him with the words: '*My Lord and my God.*' Human bonds of love and affection are transfigured into the love and adoration of the Divine Majesty.

In this confession of faith, the unique sacerdotal mediation of Christ is at last comprehended. Our Lord can come to make all things new* precisely because the dynamic power of God's nature works in and through his humanity. This power is immense because it is the power of God himself which infinitely transcends the power of any mere mortal. Our Lord teaches in today's Gospel that merely by using his name can we obtain what we need – this is Jesus who, at the same time, is God the Son working with God the Holy Spirit to renew the face of the earth to the glory of God the Father.

But today's Gospel takes us a step farther. Our Lord invites us to consider our own dignity as being united to the Body of Christ himself. We are all called to participate in this unique mediation: '*In that day you shall ask in my name: and I say not to you that I will ask the Father for you: for the Father himself loveth you, because you have loved me and have believed that I came out from God.*' By having '*put on*'† Christ in Baptism and striving with God's grace to grow in the virtues, the Father can see the image of the Son himself in our souls. And God, in a certain sense, has already taken us up into himself. The dignity of our humanity comes not merely from the fact that we have the capacity to be spiritual, but rather because God calls to himself our whole being – including our bodies and our minds – and asks us to devote our whole lives to his glory, to his service and adoration.

✠

---

* Cf Apocalypse 21:5.
† Cf Galatians 3:7.

For further reflection:

> Hail! Name so precious to the ear,
> Sweet Jesu! Name which all revere,
> May naught on earth prevail to tear
> This title from our heart.
> By this let sin be done away,
> To this let each one homage pay,
> Through this in heavenly bliss we pray
> May we obtain a part.
>
> *(from the Sarum Sequence)*

Our Lord invites us to consider our own dignity as being united to the Body of Christ himself.

'Grant that we may think what is right and under thy guidance perform it.'

(from the Collect of the Day)

In Ascensione Domini
The Ascension of the Lord

'Why wonder you, looking up into heaven?'*

Proper of the Day: Introit: Acts 1:11; Psalm 46:2
Epistle: Acts 1:1–11
Paschal Alleluia: Psalm 46:6
Alleluia: Psalm 67:18, 19
Gospel: Mark 16:14–20
Offertory: Psalm 46:6
Communion: Psalm 67:33, 34

---

* Acts 1:11.

'Et Dominus quidem Jesus, postquam locutus est eis, assumptus est in caelum.'*

A scension Day is celebrated forty days after Easter. This is not merely the precept of the Church: it is based on the actions of Our Divine Saviour himself, as recorded faithfully by sacred Scripture. The Epistle of our Mass makes this very clear.

The question arises, however: why *forty* days? What does this number signify? And what was Our Lord doing during those forty days between his Resurrection and his return to his heavenly Father?

For an answer, we need to look at the sacred Scriptures. If we do so, we will find there that the number forty is regarded as a sacred number, and moreover, that it is invariably connected with a period of preparation. The paradigm for this is the forty years which the Israelites spent wandering in the desert, until such time as they had been made ready to enter the Promised Land prepared for them. A period of forty days was spent by Moses on the mountain, in the presence of God, before he was given the tablets of stone containing the Ten Commandments, a manifestation of God's loving concern for his people. The prophet Elijah, too, spent forty days journeying through the desert, until he reached the mountain of Horeb, where he too experienced a manifestation of God, in the *'still, small voice'* which spoke to him from outside the cave. Lastly, we remember that Our Lord himself spent forty days in the wilderness preparing for his public ministry – a period we recall each year with our observance of Lent.

The number forty invariably carries with it a sense of preparation: and if Our Lord spent forty days on earth between the Resurrection and Ascension, we are led to ask for what was he preparing us?

---

* Mark 16:19: 'And the Lord Jesus, after he had spoken to them, was taken up into heaven.'

The answer to that question lies in the close connection between today's Feast of the Ascension and the Feast of Pentecost, which falls next week. The forty days of Eastertide leading up to the Ascension are in fact a period of preparation for the birthday of the Church, which will be heralded by Pentecost. Our Lord spent those forty days personally instructing his Apostles in how they were to rule, guide and gather the Church, which was about to be born. He had already laid the foundations of the Church in his public ministry: he had chosen the Apostles, the first bishops, and he had selected Peter, the one who would govern the Church in his place. To these he had entrusted the Most Holy Sacrifice of the Eucharist. Now was the time for the final catechesis, before this new manifestation of God's love for the world.

We might like to ask, of course, what exactly did Our Lord say to his Apostles during those forty days of preparation? The simple answer must be that nothing in the Holy Bible tells us. The Church Fathers all agree that some of the instructions that Christ gave his Apostles were secret, and have never been written down. But the teaching of the Catholic Church has always been that revelation is contained not only in Scripture but also in Tradition, these two together containing everything necessary for our salvation.

And yet, while in some sense Our Lord's instructions remain for ever a secret, in another sense we know them clearly, for they are revealed openly in the life of the Church, which was born at Pentecost. It is, in fact, precisely *in* the life of the Catholic Church that all the teachings of the Lord are made manifest. In the Liturgy, in the Sacraments, in the interpretation of Sacred Scripture, in the doctrines of the Magisterium, in the Christian virtues and the moral life, and, above all, in the radiant holiness of the saints; in all these things the teachings of Christ become clear and are made known to us. Indeed, they are made known not merely as words or thought but as a reality.

Today's Feast of the Ascension, which marks the end of our Saviour's earthly ministry, is therefore inseparably connected to the ministry of his Church, which will begin on Pentecost Sunday. And we do well to remember that the Church's ministry is not something that happened in the past but continues across the years and down the centuries, and that our own lives of Christian discipleship are essential to that witness. Little wonder, then, that the Church spends the next nine days before Pentecost – the original Novena – in fervent prayer for the Church. May we, not only in our worship but in every aspect of our lives, make manifest the teachings Christ has left to his Church, and may we inherit the blessings he has promised to his disciples.

✠

For further reflection:

Sing we triumphant hymns of praise,
New hymns to heaven exulting raise:
Christ, by a road before untrod,
Ascendeth to the throne of God.

> *(from Hynmum canamus gloriae St Bede – tr. BW)*

Our Lord Christ sits now in glory at the right hand of the Father.

May we dwell in mind amid heavenly things.

> *(from the Collect of the Day)*

Dominica Pentecostes
Pentecost or Whitsunday

'The Spirit of the Lord hath filled the whole world.'

Proper of the Day: Introit: *Wisdom 1:7; Psalm 67:2*
                        Epistle: *Acts 2:1–11*
                        Paschal Alleluia: *Psalm 103:30*
                        Alleluia: *source unknown*
                        Sequence: *Veni Sancte Spiritus*
                        Gospel: *John 14:23–31*
                        Offertory: *Psalm 67:29, 30*
                        Communion: *Acts 2:2, 4*

✠

'Spiritus Domini replevit orbem terrarium.'[†]

'*The Spirit of the Lord fills the whole world.*' Thus begins the Introit for the Mass of Pentecost. The feast kept today marks the foundation of the Church and the beginning of her mission and ministry throughout the world. It also signifies her response to the mandate of Our Blessed Lord to preach the Gospel to the nations. Having been filled with the Holy Spirit, bestowed upon the Apostles by the Risen Lord on the evening of Easter and now confirmed in the Cenacle as they gathered there with Our Blessed Lady, the Church prepares to take the Truth of Jesus Christ to the ends of the earth.

The portion of Scripture appointed as the Epistle comes from the beginning of the second chapter of the Acts of the Apostles, and gives an account of that momentous day in Jerusalem. The Holy Spirit descends upon the followers of Our Lord, who had seen Jesus taken from their sight at the Ascension, and does so as tongues of flame. Together with the gift of being understood by people of many nations and of diverse languages, this phenomenon is a further sign of the universal mission of the

---

  * Wisdom 1:7.
  † Wisdom 1:7: 'The Spirit of the Lord hath filled the whole world.'

Church. The Apostles are strengthened and empowered by the Holy Spirit, being given courage to witness to their divine Lord; and it is the same Spirit who is the bond of unity among Christians.

These happenings on the Day of Pentecost in Jerusalem mark the fulfilment of the promises made by Jesus to the Twelve in his discourse after the Last Supper. The Gospel appointed for this feast, from the fourteenth chapter of St John, is taken from the same discourse and allows us to meditate upon Our Lord's teaching on the mission of the Holy Spirit and his promise of the same Spirit to his disciples as he instructed them before, and in preparation for, the great drama of his Passion, Death and Resurrection. We, like them, can now begin to glimpse the generosity of what Christ proposes, offers and guarantees. It is the Holy Spirit, the Third Person of the Blessed Trinity, that bond of love between the Father and the Son, who proceeds from both, whom the same Son now promises the Father will send on his account to those who love him and are thus true to his words. The Father and Son will come to dwell in them, making their continual abode in them.

The Spirit is described by Our Lord to his disciples as the one who will befriend them and who *'will teach ... [them] all things, and bring all things to ... [their] mind[s] whatsoever I shall have said to you'*. Jesus then bequeaths his gift of peace, a unique peace, which the world cannot bestow. He will utter the same words on the evening of the Day of Resurrection: *'Let not your heart be troubled, nor let it be afraid.'* The one promised by Our Lord is the Paraclete, or Advocate, or Comforter. In the words of the Sequence, *'Veni Sancte Spiritus'*, which is sung or recited immediately before the Gospel, the Holy Spirit is *'Consolator optime'* ['Thou of comforters the best']. To be comforted means to be given strength, not a human strength but a strength and peace that God alone can grant. The mission of the Paraclete is to remain with the disciples after his return to the Father and to deepen within them Christ's teaching, thereby filling them with that unique strength. Equally, the Holy Spirit stands as the witness to the truth of that teaching, so that the Church in turn may bring it to the whole of mankind.

The Church, which throughout her long history has often been troubled, persecuted, intimidated, or mocked, and still suffers the same today in many places, nevertheless has the sure promise of the continuing presence of her Master in this world through his gift of the Holy Spirit. It is to the Holy Spirit that we must turn in a special way on this feast, imploring his strength and a renewal of grace so that we, and the whole Church, may be cleansed, strengthened and thus sanctified, ready to fulfil the mission entrusted to us, each according to his or her own particular vocation.

✠

For further reflection:

> *Now let the sacred quire,*
> *With holy symphony,*
> *The promised joys sound forth*
> *In fullness sent from heaven.*
> *Assembled in one place,*
> *The Apostolic band*
> *Awaits the glorious gifts.*
> *Forthwith a voice divine*
> *Filling their hearts with power,*
> *Attests the Comforter.*

(from the Sequence for Monday after Pentecost,
Sarum Missal)

The Holy Spirit is the one who strengthens us to fulfil our particular vocations.

'May the infusion of the Holy Spirit cleanse our hearts and render them fruitful.'

(from the Postcommunion Collect of the Day)

In Festo Sanctissimae Trinitatis
The Feast of the Most Holy Trinity

'Blessed be the Holy Trinity and undivided Unity.'*

Proper of the Day: Introit: *Tobit 12:6 etc.; Psalm 8:2*
                            Epistle: *Romans 11:33–36*
                            Gradual: *Daniel 3:55, 56*
                            Alleluia: *Daniel 3:52*
                            Gospel: *Matthew 28:18–20*
                            Offertory: *Tobit 12:6 etc.*
                            Communion: *Tobit 12:6*

✠

'Ex ipso, et Per ipsum et in ipso sunt omnia.'†

The readings for the Feast of the Most Holy Trinity present us – appropriately enough – with three themes: the depth of the mystery of God, in the Epistle; and in the Gospel, the challenge of the apostolate and the consolation of God's abiding presence with us. We might see here something of the life of God himself, the awe-inspiring majesty of the Father; the apostolic example of his only Son, Our Lord; and the indwelling of the Holy Spirit in the Church.

St Paul's awe is clear in his words when he describes the mystery of God: 'O *the depth of the riches of the wisdom and of the knowledge of God! How incomprehensible are his judgements, and how unsearchable his ways.'*‡ *'Ex ipso, et per ipsum et in ipso sunt omnia'* ['For of him and by him and in him are all things']. And so, in the earliest documents of the Church, we find the doctrine of the Holy Trinity expressed: from the Father, by the Son and in the Holy Spirit. Again and again we find his threefold pattern in creation, in the Church and in our own prayer. It is the very reflection of the image of God in his

---

* Tobit 12:6 etc.
† Romans 11:36: 'Of him, and by him, and in him, are all things.'
‡ Romans 11:33.

{ 127 }

own creation. We are created, we fall, we are redeemed. The prayers of the rosary reflect God's gift to us – Joyful Mysteries; his Son's life among us – Sorrowful and Luminous Mysteries; and our return to him in the Holy Spirit – Glorious Mysteries. St Thomas Aquinas, in his *Summa Theologica* treats its subject matter in a Trinitarian form: God's own life, his gifts to us, and our return to him in the Spirit. Whether in the simplicity of St Patrick's shamrock, or in the complexities of mathematics, the number three is ever present in nature and speaks to us of mystery and eternity.

We shall never fail to find inspiration and consolation in our contemplation of the life of God. And so our apostolic lives should be inspired by the desire to bring others to that same consolation we ourselves have received. Our Christian lives began in baptism when we were reborn to a new life in God, dying in the waters of the font to our old lives, and rising from the water (as with Christ from the tomb) to a new life that will never end. This new life is lived out in a variety of different ways in the Church, but all of us have a calling from God – a vocation. And to some degree for all of us it is a vocation to teach others *'to observe all things whatsoever I have com-manded you'*.* In some cases this will be quite literally to teach – as parents, priests or teachers. For others, it will be a matter of living the Christian life as exactingly as possible so as to give a good example to others. But to all of us is given that com-mand to go out to the whole world and make disciples of all nations.

All this can seem overwhelming and challenging – under-standing the Mystery, spreading the faith. We are constantly made aware of our own weakness, intellectually, physically, morally. But in all this we have the consolation of the abid-ing presence of the Holy Spirit, who comes to help us in our weakness. When we do not know how to pray or what to say, how to live our lives, the Spirit is there with us. In fact, nothing comes from us, but all from the depth of God's love which he

---

* Matthew 28:20.

gives to us so that we can give it back to him in return, directly in our prayer, indirectly in our love for others. This is what it is to live with the life of God; not ourselves living, but God living in us, through us. The doctrine of the Blessed Trinity shows us God's inner life, a relationship of love between Father, Son and Holy Spirit. The more we contemplate this life, the more we can see how it is reflected in our own Christian lives.

Trinity Sunday is balanced in the liturgical year between the celebration of the events of the life of Our Lord in the Christmas and Easter Cycles, and in the celebration of the living out of that faith in the rest of the Church's year; for God himself is both the beginning and the end of our life, its inspiration and its goal. *'For of him, and by him, and in him, are all things: to him be glory for ever. Amen.'*

✠

For further reflection:

> *Blest be the Holy Trinity,*
> *Eternal Godhead Thou;*
> *Father, Son, Holy Ghost, one God*
> *To whom all creatures bow.*
> *Three persons in one Godhead dwell,*
> *One will have all three in perfect harmony.*
> *Godhead in Unity consists,*
> *Three Gods there cannot be;*
> *The right faith by Christ set forth*
> *Confesses steadfastly.*
>
> > *(from the Sequence for Trinity Sunday, Sarum Missal)*

We never fail to find inspiration and consolation in our contemplation of the life of God.

Let praise-giving resound in all men's mouths to the Father and the begotten Son; to the Holy Spirit also let like praise sound forth.

> *(Antiphon of First Vespers)*

In Festo Corporis Christi
The Feast of Corpus Christi

'He fed them with the fat of corn.'*

Proper of the Day: *Introit: Psalm 80:17, 2*
                        Epistle: 1 Corinthians 11:23–29
                        Gradual: Psalm 144:15, 16
                        Alleluia: John 6:56, 57
                        Sequence: Lauda, Sion
                        Gospel: John 6:56–59
                        Offertory: Leviticus 21:6
                        Communion: 1 Corinthians 11:26, 27

✠

'Caro mea vere est cibus.'†

Etched into our very genes is the propensity to sin, to put ourselves in place of God. This inclination is inherited from our forebears; given to us through the legacy of Adam and Eve. For as soon as man chose himself instead of God, chose his own pride and self-esteem in place of God, the die was cast. Every selfish pursuit that was placed on man's altars and worshipped blotted out the natural lines of communication with God. But that was man's free choice. However, when the Word – the *Logos* – with the Father before all worlds, entered humanity at the Incarnation; when the Divine Intention was announced to Mary; when the Word, the Concept, took flesh, man would soon be redeemed and forgiven. When Jesus gurgled in a manger; when Our Lord lived as man, and died on the Cross not before he had spoken the words, *'Father, forgive them'*, this was the life of the Son of God, of God made man, given up as a ransom for everyone's wrongdoing. Now, mankind was saved and relieved of the stain and guilt of carrying the legacy of Adam – what we term 'original sin' – which salvation and relief

---

* Psalm 80:17.

† John 6:56: 'For my flesh is meat indeed.'

would be confirmed by the sign and through the accompanying grace of Baptism. We have been given a clean slate, as it were; but even though this is the case, we constantly prefer the state of sin and revert to our old selfish ways: the legacy of Adam is potent, and we have to be rescued time and again through confession, penance and absolution. What can help sustain us in a state of grace? Keeping our focus on Christ, is the answer.

That is more easily said than done. But by infinite generosity Our Lord instituted the Mass at the Last Supper, and there gave us the Sacrament of his Body and Blood. This is curiously foreshadowed in today's Gospel when Jesus informs the astonished, surprised and, perhaps, outraged Jews, followers and bystanders that his own flesh is sufficient for the purposes of sustaining them. Indeed, only a few verses before today's Gospel, Jesus had said: '*I am the living bread which came down from heaven.*' In the light of the Glorious Resurrection, these utterances begin to make sense. Jesus was giving his hearers a Truth that would be fully revealed a little later. He was telling them that he was all that they required: he was their Salvation through the Redeeming power of his sacrifice upon the Cross. He was their Hope. And all this he tells us. Then, at the Last Supper, he gives them and us his body, not only within the Church to be born as he dies upon the Cross, but in the tangible form of bread and wine. The Mystery, at once fathomable and unfathomable, that is the Incarnation, helps us grasp something of the Mystery and miracle of the Blessed Sacrament. As Jesus brings God to earth – God veiled in flesh, the Incarnation of the Divine Intention, the Word, the *Logos* – so Jesus now takes on the veil of bread and wine at the Mass, so that his Real Presence may be imparted to us, for the good of our souls. The bread and the wine now become his true Body and Blood. This mysterious substantial Body of Christ is there on the altar for us to receive at Mass, and at other times when there is urgent need, and to adore in the Tabernacle, at Benediction, in the Holy Hour and during the Forty Hours. There in the Blessed Sacrament is the dual nature of Christ, the man and the Divine; there is the new-born babe, the Christ of the Beatitudes, the Christ of the Last Supper, there the Christ of Emmaus. There is the Christ, who earths himself in his most wonderful Sacrament – a God-charged fragment of substance now Christ's Body and Blood; by wonderful grace, a daily miracle of the Life, Death and Glorious Resurrection of our Saviour. Words can but prompt and nudge us towards the infinite vocabulary of contemplation.

The miracle of the Blessed Sacrament is as astonishing and extraordinary as the words delivered to Jesus' disciples and followers in today's Gospel. Perhaps we understand the words but we can only *begin* to comprehend the vastness of the generosity of the great gift that is the Blessed Sacrament.

For further reflection:

> *Here what Holy Church maintaineth*
> *That the bread its substance changeth*
> *Into flesh, the wine to blood;*
> *Doth it pass thy comprehending?*
> *Faith, the law of sight transcending,*
> *Leaps to things not understood.*
>
> *(from the Sequence)*

Words can but prompt and nudge us towards the infinite vocabulary of contemplation.

May we ever feel within us the fruit of thy Redemption.
(from the Collect of the Day)

Dominica III Post Pentecosten
The Third Sunday after Pentecost

'Look thou upon me, O Lord, and have mercy on me.'*

Proper of the Day: Introit: Psalm 24:16–18, 1, 2
       Epistle: 1 Peter 5:6–11
       Gradual: Psalm 54:23, 17, 19
       Alleluia: Psalm 7:12
       Gospel: Luke 15:1–10
       Offertory: Psalm 9:11–13
       Communion: Luke 15:10

☩

'Ita dico vobis: gaudium erit coram Angelis Dei super uno peccatore poenitentiam agente.'†

There is an old Spanish proverb: *'Tell me whom you live with and I shall tell you who you are.'* If there is any truth in this, where does it leave Our Lord, who seemed to favour the company of publicans and sinners – on the very fringe of polite Jewish society, not quite with the lepers, but almost we might think? Would it have troubled Our Lord? Not at all, since, according to his own understanding, he had come to seek out the *'lost sheep of Israel'*, among whom were to be found publicans and prostitutes and those on the margins.

Throughout the Gospel we see demonstrated quite plainly Our Lord's *'preferential option'* for those souls who were generally excluded by society. And if he showed real concern for them, they in their turn found him irresistible, for while he in no way condoned their behaviour or their profession, neither did he condemn them. Instead he *'welcomed them and ate with them'*, and in this way he won many over to a new life; offering them a fresh start, leading to a glorious eternity. This

---

* Psalm 24:16.

† Luke 15:10: 'So I say to you, there shall be joy before the Angels of God upon one sinner doing penance.'

he did, not by belabouring them with threats or unkind words, but with a gentleness and understanding many of them would not have expected, or ever known before.

Our Lord's way with sinners has remained the way of the saints. The famous dictum of St Francis de Sales is perfectly true: *'You catch more flies with a spoonful of honey than with a barrelful of vinegar.'*

Padre Pio would often comfort a penitent with the beautiful assurance that God's mercy is infinitely greater than their sin; and it is told of St Philip Neri, how, when consoling a woman who was convinced she was going to Hell, he asked her gently: *'Tell me, for whom did Christ die?' 'For sinners, Father,'* she replied. *'And what are you, my child?'* he asked. *'A sinner, Father.' 'Well, then,'* he exclaimed cheerfully, *'rejoice, because Paradise is yours!'* In that way her scruples were cured.

This gentle way with those who had transgressed the Law of the Lord was one of the things that so infuriated the Pharisees and Scribes, who were always on the look-out for ways by which they could trick him into giving them some pretext for removing him. So, when they expressed their surprise and out-rage at his choice of company, he did not bother to argue with them or try to justify his actions. Instead he told them three parables, two of which we have just heard: the story of the shepherd who left his ninety-nine sheep to go in search of the one who had wandered off, and that of the woman who turned her house inside out in an attempt to find her missing drachma. You might have thought that both shepherd and housewife would have been satisfied with what they had left – ninety-nine sheep safely grazing and nine drachmae – but no, the errant sheep and the lost coin were of equal value to their owners and well worth the effort involved in their recovery, something which our 'disposable' society, where even human life is cheap, might find hard to understand.

The third parable and the longest, which we did not hear, is the one which really brings the lesson home to us: it is that of the Prodigal Son. Here Our Lord is not talking about sheep or cash, but about a human soul, one lost in degradation, whose dignity is restored by a loving and forgiving father, overjoyed at the return of his boy. Together, the three parables offer us tremendous hope, because we are all of us sinners in need of God's mercy; and no matter how 'lost' we may sometimes feel or indeed actually be, the Lord is as assiduous in his search for us as the woman anxious to find her coin; as determined as the shepherd seeking out his silly sheep; and as patient and generous as the father of the feckless lad.

In his preaching and all his actions, Our Lord communicated the tremendous quality of his Father's just and merciful love for his people. It was a saint, Therese of Lisieux, who wrote: *'If my conscience were burdened with all the sins it is possible to commit, I would still go and throw myself into Our Lord's arms, my heart all broken up with contrition. I know what tenderness he has for any prodigal child of his that comes back to him.'* And it was one such prodigal son, the French writer, Charles Peguy, who spoke of himself as having re-entered *'his Father's house, having taken the roundabout path of a good sinner'*. And the same Peguy made the heartening observation that *'the sinner is at the heart of Christianity . . . no one is as competent as the sinner in Christian affairs . . . no one, except the saint'*.

Why should this be? Well, obviously someone at the heart of Christianity must be someone who loves Christ. The saints, those who are justified, orientate their whole lives towards him, seeking to imitate the one they love in everything, whether paying their tribute of suffering or simply in their goodness towards others. Yet, the repentant sinner – the lost sheep who now rides on the shoulders of the shepherd – can love Christ every bit as much as the greatest saint, precisely because he knows in the depths of his being what a price has been paid for him. Inexplicably, amazingly, he knows he has been prized as high as the rest of the flock put together. A single drachma has been transformed, in the divine economy, into something valued at ten times its apparent worth. For God does not reckon as the world reckons. To have experienced this dramatic turn-about, the entering of divine love into the darkest corners of our house, to have been retrieved so thoroughly from the waste-heap, should inspire in us an unshakeable love and trust in our Redeemer. This is why St Peter says in his Epistle that we should cast *'all your care upon him, for he hath care of you'*. On this basis, when we feel lost, isolated, in despair, we should nonetheless outface our enemy, stand up to the evil one, because if the Lord is coming for us, and we are willing to be found, the ravening predator cannot prevail.

If the sinner is indeed at the heart of our religion, it is not so that he may remain lost in sin, but that he may be found, reconciled and restored. Our Lord tells us repeatedly that when this happens it causes rejoicing. Not just in the heart of the Shepherd, but also among the Angels and saints. This is the meaning of the salvation Christ has won for us: that we may ourselves taste that joy, the joy that is the Communion of Saints, the forgiveness of sins, life everlasting. A life lived in the mystery of Love – the Blessed Trinity. *'Tell me whom you live with and I shall tell you who you are.'*

✠

For further reflection:

> No *sinful word, nor deed of wrong,*
> Nor *thoughts that idly rove;*
> But *simple truth be on our tongue,*
> And *in our hearts be love.*
>
> (from *Jam lucis orto sidere* – tr. JHN)

There will be joy before the Angels of God.

May we pass through things temporal and lose not those things eternal.

(from the Collect of the Day)

Dominica IV Post Pentecosten
The Fourth Sunday after Pentecost

'The Lord is my light and salvation, whom shall I fear?'*

Proper of the Day: Introit: Psalm 26:1, 2, 3
Epistle: Romans 8:18–23
Gradual: Psalm 78:9, 10
Alleluia: Psalm 9:5, 10
Gospel: Luke 5:1–11
Offertory: Psalm 12:4, 5
Communion: Psalm 17:3

✠

'In verbo autem tuo laxabo rete.'†

In the portion of the Gospel appointed for this Sunday, we read St Luke's vivid account of the call of Peter, James and John, which tells us what it means to have a sense of vocation. Compare this with the account of the call of St Matthew (Levi), which is told in a much more matter-of-fact way. The Lord called; and Matthew, touched by grace, got up and followed him. In contrast, Luke's account of the call of Peter, along with his colleagues, James and John, is much more personal. In the case of Peter, we can see that grace already at work. He had heard Christ preach, many times perhaps. Again, since it was his boat in which Our Lord was sitting, Peter might even have been in the boat beside him, listening intently to this preacher's astonishing words. Luke tells us that when he had finished speaking, Our Lord told Peter: *'Launch out into the deep, and let down your nets for a draught.'* It was clearly an order, yet one which Peter might well have refused to obey. He was, after all, an experienced fisherman, so he could have been forgiven had he questioned the wisdom of this Nazarine

---

* Psalm 26:1.

† Luke 5:5: 'But at thy word I will let down the net.'

carpenter's fishing tips. What would he know about it? Instead, Peter explained the situation: *'Master, we have laboured all night and have taken nothing.'* There must have been many nights like the past one, when the nets were hauled up empty. Yet Our Lord spoke with authority – even his opponents constantly recognized as much – and in a defining moment, Peter chose to obey the man he called Master. *'At thy word I will let down the net.'* What Peter had done every working night of his life, he now did simply because the Master had told him to. And, of course, his obedience was rewarded. Luke tells us that the haul was so great that the nets were at breaking point. Peter's crew had to ask their comrades to come and help bring in the mammoth catch. Furthermore, we are told, the boats were so heavily laden that they began to sink.

It was then that Peter understood who it was beside him in the boat, hauling the nets. All at once, he was overcome by the sense of his utter unworthiness in the presence of God, and this brought him to his knees: *'Depart from me for I am a sinful man, O Lord.'* That moment of recognition, which must have seemed so annihilating, was really a grace: transforming, humbling and healing, opening the way for conversion to new life. Because is that not what Our Lord offered Peter – a new life? From the moment he had willingly let down the nets, something he had done all his life, he now did at the behest of Christ. Peter had found his vocation. *'At thy word, I will ...'* How many echoes of the Annunciation there are in Peter's responses! Think too of the response of Thérèse of Lisieux to her vocation, how she determined to infuse every little thing she did each day with the urgency of her desire to serve and please God. The English metaphysical poet, George Herbert, puts it well: *'Teach me, my God and king, in all things thee to see; And what I do in anything, To do it as for thee.'* Here is enshrined the idea of doing what one does in a new way, with a sense of vocation.

It is in this moment of wondrous acquiescence on the part of their future leader that Christ gave his first promise to his new disciples: *'from henceforth thou shalt catch men'*. That last great haul of fish was nothing compared with what God had in store for Peter and his friends. They knew that things were different now, and so they followed him willingly, little knowing at that time quite where he was leading them, or what he had in store for them.

In the preceding verses, Our Lord had stated to the people that he *'must preach the Kingdom of God: for therefore am I sent'*. This was to be the work of the Apostles; and remains so to this day. The Lord is still calling disciples to be 'fishers of men' and 'good shepherds' after his own heart, and co-workers of his in the harvest. The men he calls to serve him and the Church as priests today are, like the first disciples of Christ, 'sinful men' and unworthy of so great a commission. They are nonetheless called to fulfil their part as members of the Body of Christ, continuing the ministry of Christ through their celebration of the Sacraments, their prayer and preaching, and their pastoral care of God's faithful people.

However, we should never forget that the Lord has called each and every one of us to his service; and even though our experience of that calling may not have been as dramatic or devastating as those of Peter and Paul or the Prophet Isaiah, our calling is nonetheless real. We are called to do God's work wherever we are, even if we judge ourselves to be unworthy to do so; besides, who could ever be unworthy of obedience to the law of charity: *'Bear ye one another's burdens and so ye shall fulfil the law of Christ'*?*

No, all the baptized, priests or laity, are servants of the living God, who says to us: *'You have not chosen me: but I have chosen you.'*† And he calls us, first, in order to transform us and to forgive our sins, so that we can then *'be made worthy of the promises of Christ'*. What are these promises? Eternal life? Yes, certainly. But if we look again at the fifth chapter of St Matthew's Gospel, and re-read the Beatitudes, we find

---

* Galatians 6:2.

† John 15: 16.

there our Christian vocation outlined – to be merciful, peace-making, pure in heart, meek, and so on. And attached to each command, we find the promise of beatitude that Christ makes to us: *'Blessed are the clean of heart, for they shall see God; Blessed are the merciful, for they shall obtain mercy.'**

Like Peter, we may fall at Our Lord's feet and plead sinfulness, knowing all too well our weakness, past failures and general unsatisfactoriness: but Our Lord bridges the gulf between God's holiness and our sin, telling us not to be afraid. His grace is indeed sufficient for us, so why waste time arguing and panicking, when all that is required is a simple act of obedience? *'But at thy word I will let down the net.'* *'And having brought their ships to land, leaving all things, they followed him.'*

✠

For further reflection:

And grant that to Thine honour, Lord,
Our daily toil may tend;
That we begin it at thy word,
And in thy favour end.

(from Jam lucis orto sidere – tr. JHN)

We should never forget that the Lord has called each and every one of us to his service.

May our rebel wills be turned to the Lord.

(from the Secret of the Day)

✠

---

* Matthew 5:8, 7.

Dominica V Post Pentecosten
The Fifth Sunday after Pentecost

*'One thing I have asked of the Lord, this will I seek after: that I
may dwell in the house of the Lord all the days of my life.'**

Proper of the Day: Introit: Psalm 26:7–9, 1
                         Epistle: 1 Peter 3:8–15
                         Gradual: Psalm 83:10, 9
                         Alleluia: Psalm 20:1
                         Gospel: Matthew 5:20–24
                         Offertory: Psalm 15:7, 8
                         Communion: Psalm 26:4

✠

*'Et vade prius reconciliari fratri tuo; et tunc veniens
offeres munus tuum.'†*

This long sequence of Sundays after Pentecost – the 'green'
Sundays of the year, as it were – are intended to help us
grow in understanding of the fundamental mysteries of our
faith. Thus Our Lord in the Gospel today reminds us of the
most basic tenets of our belief. First, the Lord makes a state-
ment which emphasizes the truth of his own Divinity: *'You
have heard that it was said to them of old . . . but I say to you
. . .'* No man would dare to oppose his own opinion to that of
Moses, the Lawgiver, the greatest of the prophets, unless that
man were himself something greater than the prophets – the
Incarnate Word, the Son of God. Secondly, Our Lord goes on
to remind us of the reality of judgement. This is a doctrine
which he himself taught on many occasions, and which we profess week by week in the recitation of the Creed: *'venturus est
cum Gloria iudicare vivos et mortuos'.‡* Yet today, in a society

---

   * Psalm 26:4.

   † Matthew 5:24: 'Go first to be reconciled to thy brother; and then coming
thou shalt offer thy gift.'

   ‡ 'He will come again in glory to judge the living and the dead.'

dominated by relativism, we often find the concept of divine judgement an uncomfortable one. We do well then, hearing our Saviour's words today, to remind ourselves that we shall one day have to account for our deeds before the one who can never be deceived, and that our moral choices, good and evil, do indeed have eternal consequences. Paradise awaits those who lovingly correspond with grace, while Hell – as Our Lord makes clear – is a terrifying possibility for those who refuse the divine invitation.

These are just some of the simple truths our Gospel today should bring to mind. But the most fundamental of all its teachings is perhaps the most important of all – it is the commandment of brotherly love, which forms the theme not only of the Gospel but of the Epistle from St Peter as well.

The Apostle encourages us to be *'lovers of the brotherhood ... merciful, modest, humble'*. These words chime with the message of the Gospel. We should note, however, that Our Lord places his commandment of fraternal charity in a particular context – namely, the context of worship and sacrifice. *'If, therefore, thou offer thy gift at the altar, and there thou remember that thy brother has anything against thee; leave there thy offering before the altar, and go first to be reconciled to thy brother: and then coming thou shalt offer thy gift.'* Why does Our Lord insist on this act of reconciliation prior to the offering of our gifts? Perhaps we need to ask in the first place, what are the 'gifts' which our faith causes us to place before the altar? Are the offerings referred to simply the bread and wine and water which the acolytes will present to the priest on behalf of the congregation? In some sense, yes, these things are our gifts, but the *true* gift each of us is called to bring to Mass is something even more fundamental. The gift, quite simply, which each of us is called to present before the altar is nothing less than our very selves, body and soul. Everything we are, everything we have, or do, or could ever be, all of this we are called to offer to God at Mass, along with the perfect Sacrifice of Calvary made present through the ministry of the priest.

For the Christian, in fact, true worship demands self-sacrifice.

And this is implicit in the Epistle as well. Speaking there of the fraternal love to which we are called, St Peter concludes with the command: '*Sanctify the Lord Christ in your hearts.*' What does this mean? Surely nothing less than the consecration of our very selves to Christ; for everything we have belongs to the Lord, and everything we do is for him.

That helps us understand why reconciliation is given such importance in today's Gospel, and why it is placed in the context of worship. For if, at this Mass, we bring before the Lord in sacrifice the gift of ourselves, and yet our minds and hearts are tainted with resentment, bitterness, hatred of others – what sort of offering is that to bring before the Lord? The Old Testament is clear that those who offer the Lord an unworthy sacrifice bring down judgement upon themselves. How wise, then, is the Church, in insisting on beginning every Mass with the *Confiteor*! First, the priest confesses, so that he may be worthy to offer the Sacrifice of Christ upon the altar. And then the people also confess, in order that they may be ready to offer their own spiritual sacrifices along with that of Christ to the Eternal Father.

These 'green' Sundays are given to teach us the most important lessons of our faith. Today, we have been reminded of the divinity of Christ, of the reality of judgement, of mercy of God and of our own call to self-sacrificial charity. Let us show, both in this church and outside, that we have learned those lessons well.

✠

For further reflection:

> *Extinguish thou each sinful fire,*
> *And banish every ill desire;*
> *And while thou keep'st the body whole,*
> *Shed forth thy peace upon the soul.*
>
> *(from Rector potens verax Deus – tr. JMN)*

Paradise awaits those who lovingly correspond with grace, while Hell is a terrifying possibility for those who refuse the divine invitation.

Pour into our hearts, O Lord, such love towards thee that we, loving thee in all things and above all things, may obtain thy promises.

(from the Collect of the Day)

Dominica VI Post Pentecosten
The Sixth Sunday after Pentecost

'Graft in our hearts the love of thy name, and grant us an increase of religion.'*

Proper of the Day: *Introit: Psalm 27:8, 9, 1*
                    Epistle: Romans 6:3–11
                    Gradual: Psalm 89:13, 1
                    Alleluia: Psalm 30:2, 3
                    Gospel: Mark 8:1–9
                    Offertory: Psalm 16:5, 6, 7
                    Communion: Psalm 26:6

✠

'Dominus fortitudo plebes suae.'†

One of the great benefits of life in the twenty-first century is the use we can make of so many different technologies which make life not only easier but more enjoyable. Virtually any information we require can be obtained with a few clicks on the computer; and we now view again and again not only our favourite photographs, videos and music, but also television programmes. However amazing this may seem, we are

---

* From the Collect of the Day.

† Psalm 27:8: 'The Lord is the strength of his people.'

only viewing something that has already occurred; information technology cannot make it possible to travel back or forth in time. Yet the Church does make this possible! Each and every time we come to Holy Mass we are actually present again at the Last Supper, at Calvary and at a meeting with the Risen Christ. All this is made possible by the power of the Holy Spirit acting in and through the Church, Christ's body. So when the action of the Mass begins, and when we hear the Scriptures read, all this is happening now, and we are brought into God's eternal *now* by the action of the sacred Liturgy.

The miracle of the loaves and fishes is a figure of the Holy Eucharist: Our Lord performed this as a preparation for his teaching about this Sacrament, and the Fathers of the Church have always interpreted it as such. We can see, in this act of Jesus, his solicitude for those who had human bodily needs. We understand, above all, that in this way the Lord is indeed *'fortitudo plebes suae'*, as the Introit of this Mass proclaims. Our Lord has continued to nourish and strengthen his Church through the centuries, and has ensured that we are always given priests, sufficient in number, to bring us the Body of Christ.

St Thomas Aquinas expresses this profound belief in his timeless sequence, *'Lauda Sion'*, for the Feast of Corpus Christi. *'Sumit unus, summunt mille'* ['Whether single or in union, few or thousands at Communion, every soul receives the Lord']. But, St Thomas continues: *'And the good and bad receive him, those who doubt and who believe him, but with what a different end: To the worthy soul salvation, To the impenitent damnation . . .'*

The Church takes great care to remind us to prepare properly for Mass and especially for Holy Communion. If we are intending to receive, it is because God has invited us. The requirements on our part are that we be in a state of grace, having made a sacramental confession beforehand if need be. Also, that we have fasted for at least one hour and that we are exteriorly modest and recollected.

At the end of the miracle, after they had all been fed, Jesus instructs his disciples to collect what remains of the bread. For those who believe, this is an expression of the extreme care we should take in everything we do with the Eucharistic species. No attention, however lavish, that we manifest towards the Blessed Sacrament is ever exaggerated. Christ is present in his Body, Blood, Soul and Divinity in the Blessed Eucharist, and this is further beautifully expressed by St Thomas in his hymn 'Tantum esse sub fragmento . . .'

> Though the Sacrament ye sever
> Into fragments, fear ye never
> In each part contains for ever
> What the whole contained before.

We can imagine that those present at the multiplication of the loaves and the fishes would have been awe-struck. It is this similar sense of wonder that the Church asks us to cultivate whenever we approach the Person of Jesus in the Eucharist. Pope John Paul II liked to use the phrase 'Eucharistic amazement' to capture the mood true believers should have when at Mass or at Eucharistic adoration.

Blessed Mother Teresa of Calcutta had a little sign placed in all the sacristies of her convents: 'This Mass, as my first Mass, as my last Mass, as my only Mass.' It is a reminder to the priest who celebrates, to approach the mysteries that he handles with all the Eucharistic amazement he can muster; otherwise, boredom, the feeling of routine, and lukewarmth can overcome.

In this Sacrament, Christ gives himself to us who are travellers on the road to Heaven, often exhausted by the roughness of the journey. With this viaticum, this food for our journey, we are given the strength to stay on the road and persevere. Our Blessed Lady is there to accompany us, as the Woman of the Eucharist who encourages us to strive for the fulfilment of the Eucharistic banquet in Heaven.

✠

For further reflection:

> *Approach ye then with faithful hearts sincere,*
> *And take the safeguard of salvation here.*
> *He that in this world rules his saints and shields,*
> *To all believers life eternal yields.*
> *(from Sancti, venite, Christi Corpus sumite – tr. JMN)*

Let us approach the Mass in Eucharistic amazement.

May we be cleansed by the effect of thy gifts and defended by their aid.

> *(from the Postcommunion Collect of the Day)*

Dominica VII Post Pentecosten
The Seventh Sunday after Pentecost

'A good tree cannot bring forth evil fruit, neither can an evil tree bring forth good fruit.'*

Proper of the Day: Introit: Psalm 46:2, 3
Epistle: Romans 6:19–23
Gradual: Psalm 33:12, 6
Alleluia: Psalm 46:2
Gospel: Matthew 7:15–21
Offertory: Daniel 3:40
Communion: Psalm 30:3

✠

'Attendite a falsis prophetis.'†

'*B*eware of false prophets,' says the Lord, in today's Gospel. The Holy Bible often has much to say on the subject of

---

* Matthew 7:18.
† Matthew 7:15: 'Beware of false prophets.'

{ 147 }

true and false prophets; let us therefore consider, as precisely as we can, what a prophet is.

A prophet is not someone who simply foretells the future, although that may well be an aspect of his prophecy. He is not a fortune-teller, although he may well sketch the consequences for you of certain action or inaction. Rather, a prophet is someone who claims to speak on behalf of God, to communicate some special message; and, as evidence that the message is true and genuine, or to show his credentials, one who might work a miracle of some sort. But it is the point of the message and the point of the sign rather than the magnificence of the sign which are the important features in any prophecy. For instance, considered as a prophet, Our Lord gives many teachings and instructions, and also works many great signs, which are confirmation that his words are true. One example is his teaching concerning the Blessed Sacrament, which we find in the sixth chapter of St John's Gospel. There, Our Lord presents a teaching – concerning the Real Presence in the Eucharist – which many found difficult, not just at that time, but as we know, in our own time as well. Our Lord realizes that this is something difficult to grasp, and supports the teaching with a great miracle: the feeding of the five thousand. The miracle underlines the message. Our Lord is saying: *'Listen, this is very important.'*

It is true to say that the various great works that we read of in the Gospels, and indeed in the Holy Bible generally, the healings, the walking on water etc., are not intended as ends in themselves – they are valuable teaching; in some cases acted parables. Their purpose is to direct our thoughts and our attentions towards the message or point that accompanies them. It was entirely within the power of Our Lord to heal not just a leper here and a cripple there, but rather to heal all lepers and cripples. But he did not do so. This is because it is Our Lord's priority that we are freed from a much more crippling disease – that of sin. Spiritual crippling is the really frightening sickness that Our Lord wants to free us from, and the only remedy for this is his own death on the Cross, and our participation in this death, which is, of course, the inner meaning of the Mass.

So, Our Lord exhorts us to be on the look-out for false prophets: those who claim to speak on his behalf, but cannot show evidence for this in their lives. They come in all shapes and sizes and will often appeal to our baser instincts and to our self-esteem. We see many examples of this throughout the world, whether in the cults and different heresies that abound in the twenty-first century, or those who profess to have the real answer to the Church's problems, which is often to ignore her teachings or re-interpret them in a more attractive way – in a way that might particularly appeal to our pride.

We need to bear in mind that that which brings greater comfort and earthly happiness is not necessarily what we need or what God wants for us. We know that it is sometimes important to forbid things that a child desires because we know better than the child what is likely to bring harm. It would be an irresponsible father who hands a penknife to his toddling son. In the same way, those who would seek to make us happy in this world by overturning the teachings of Our Lord and of his Church, are in the end doing us no service whatsoever. They claim to speak for the Lord: they speak only for themselves. Undoubtedly, our faith is not the easiest thing to live, but it remains true today as it was in the time of Our Lord, and those who say that it is not are the false prophets. These are they who feed people ice cream and trifle instead of the good healthy food necessary to sustain the spiritual life and bring us to Heaven. We must remember that the purpose of salvation is to save us from this world and its values. This is why Our Lady said to St Bernadette at Lourdes: '*I cannot promise to make you happy in this world.*' That is precisely the point. Our happiness derives entirely from doing the will of God.

Our Lord chillingly reminds us that even seemingly pious people may well not be those who speak for him. '*Not every one that saith to me: "Lord, Lord" shall enter into the Kingdom of Heaven; but he that doeth the will of my Father who is in*

Heaven, he shall enter into the Kingdom of Heaven.'* Who speaks for the Kingdom of Heaven and who speaks for the kingdom of this world? Again, we have the constant teaching of the Church to perpetuate the truth in our own age, and those who differ from it are the false prophets, who attempt to accommodate the whims and fancies of the age within that truth.

Those who seek to maintain the truth in integrity are under much pressure these days, and need our prayers, and our own faithfulness to the truth. Stand firm, take heart, and trust in the Lord, who promised that the gates of Hell themselves cannot stand against the Church, Christ's Bride.

✠

For further reflection:

> *And I hold in veneration,*
> *For the love of him alone,*
> *Holy Church as his creation,*
> *And her teachings as his own.*

(from Firmly I believe – JHN)

The purpose of salvation is to save us from this world and its values.

Put from us all that might be harmful and give us all that will be profitable.

(from the Collect of the Day)

✠

---

* Matthew 7:21.

Dominica VIII Post Pentecosten
The Eighth Sunday after Pentecost

*'Thou wilt save the humble people, O Lord, and wilt bring down the eyes of the proud.'**

Proper of the Day: Introit: *Psalm 47:10, 11, 2*
                        Epistle: *Romans 8:12–17*
                        Gradual: *Psalm 30:3; 70:1*
                        Alleluia: *Psalm 47:2*
                        Gospel: *Luke 16:1–9*
                        Offertory: *Psalm 27:32*
                        Communion: *Psalm 33:9*

✠

'Quia filii hujus saeculi prudentiores filiis lucis in generatione sua sunt.'†

Today's Gospel comes into the category of what we might call the difficult sayings of Our Lord. He seems to be suggesting that dishonesty and bribery can sometimes be the best policy. It is certain that he cannot be so saying: we must look carefully to ascertain what precisely he does mean.

Our Lord makes the observation, *'the children of this world are wiser in their generation than the children of light'*, immediately after the parable has been told. Even this observation requires a little thought. It demands our attention. Our Lord is saying that we should be as eager for the gospel, for the Faith, as those without faith are for their own prosperity. In a sense, we should be shamed by the example of those who dedicate all their efforts, their intelligence, their skills, their time and energy, to becoming richer for the few years until they die; we, after all, have all eternity to lose or gain, and if our faith is something that is a Sunday nuisance, then we ought to consider

---

   * Psalm 17:28.
   † Luke 16:8b: 'For the children of this world are wiser in their generation than the children of light.'

ourselves very foolish indeed, perhaps on a par with those who get themselves into debt or into one feckless pickle or another entirely through neglect of their finances. To build an earthly fortune takes hard work and dedication; can we expect to do anything less for eternity? God does not *owe* us salvation, any more than the state owes us a living. A character in Bruce Marshall's *All Glorious Within* announces quite astutely that no one will wake up in heaven wondering how on earth he got there. Grace is certainly given us – and grace in abundance – but we must co-operate with it. We cannot be saved despite ourselves, whatever Luther said to the contrary.

Does Our Lord further suggest that we use tainted money to buy ourselves friends who will welcome us into the tents of eternity? Does Our Lord actually suggest that we buy ourselves into Heaven? In fact, it is a comment on how we are to use our earthly wealth. Those who will welcome us into eternity are, of course, not our fellow human beings whose goodwill we purchase, but Our Lord himself, Our Lady and all the saints. If we want to purchase their favour, it must be by giving to the poor, those from whom we do not expect a return. And in those poor and sick we see the Lord and – and this is more important – the Lord sees us, because we know that whenever we do anything for the poor and the sick, Christ himself will be gazing lovingly from their eyes at us. Perhaps, as one writer has said, our true wealth will be known on the last day not by what we have but by what we have given away. However, to possess wealth is not in itself wrong – though poverty is, of course, an evangelical counsel – but it carries with it onerous responsibilities, as, indeed, do the God-given talents and skills we possess. The Christian has a duty to make proper use of all these gifts if he hopes to be welcomed into the tents of eternity. We should never lose the opportunity to carry out acts of mercy and charity throughout our lives; it is, quite simply, a part of the Christian's vocation.

'For the children of this world are wiser in their generation than the children of light.'

For further reflection:

> From all the sorrows of their bed
> The sick in torment cry aloud;
> The poor so anxious to be fed
> Oft trampled by the madding crowd;
> And there lies Christ, forlorn and sad.

To build an earthly fortune takes hard work and dedication; can we expect anything less for eternity?

'We have received thy mercy, O God . . . Thy right hand is full of Justice.'*

(from the Introit of the Day)

Dominica IX Post Pentecosten
The Ninth Sunday after Pentecost

'For thy magnificence is elevated above the heavens.'†

Proper of the Day: Introit: Psalm 53:6, 7, 3
Epistle: 1 Corinthians 10:6–13
Gradual: Psalm 8:2
Alleluia: Psalm 52:8
Gospel: Luke 19:41–47
Offertory: Psalm 18:9–12
Communion: John 6:57

'Videns civitatem, flevit super illam.'‡

Jerusalem, it has been said, is the most fought-over city of all time. In ages past, the very name of that city evoked

---

* Psalm 47:10, 2.
† Psalm 8:2.
‡ Luke 19:41: 'Seeing the city, he wept over it.'

passionate and powerful urges of devotion and desire and conquest. Hundreds of thousands of Europeans, over several centuries, marched out on crusade to capture it. Many more pilgrims have gone there peacefully to walk in the footsteps of Our Blessed Lord. It is truly a city that can never be spoken of without arousing some religious feeling. Its name is synonymous with the place of eternal glory and – as we read in today's Gospel – with punishment of those who reject Christ. Today it is also a divided and uneasy city. It is as though the prophecies of Our Lord which told of its destruction in AD 70 somehow have continued to our own day. Coming to terms with its own past and its future destiny has been a dolorous procession of circumstances over which few have any control or immediate solution. Indeed, it is in some ways a symbol of the human condition of so many of our contemporaries, at war within themselves and uncertain about everything except the possibility of destruction.

Faithlessness is not regarded today as a particularly serious offence. Many of our fellow Christians and many more of those who have no belief at all consider it a matter of personal choice. Religion is something that one might adopt as a useful support to cope with life's problems. Belief is something else. Religion and belief are not necessarily the same things. The Devil believes, but he is not religious. What distinguishes false religion from true belief are the added virtues of hope and charity – or, as we call it, love. The one who believes centres that faith on the Person of Our Lord and of his Church, which is inseparable from him and what he taught. No one can pretend otherwise. Belief which is focused on personal gain, immediate satisfaction and indulgence is utterly false, as the Epistle today tells us. It brings only bitter disappointment and futile expectation. It compares typically with the lack of respect, and of the hostility shown to Our Lord by those who knew and saw him in the city of Jerusalem. There dwelt the curious, the comfortable, the conceited, the self-important and the contemptuous. Many of them felt neither the need nor the slightest inclination to look or listen or learn from his words and deeds. He was either a threat or a nuisance, and they would have none of it. But Our Lord wept over them because he saw what was coming and was heartbroken about it, loving the city as one of its own in religion, and knowing how much he, as God, had done for it.

There are words of warning here for us too. We can become so complacent and at ease with our sins that we do not see what is not too far ahead. Our Lord's warning to Jerusalem is a warning for us too, if we fail to take note of where we are heading. How many times does Our Blessed Lord weep for us? He does not want to see us waste and squander his gifts and all that we are capable of, but he will not force us to be good. What he does want is our loving response and our hearts open to receive forgiveness and healing. Shall we then, like the people of that holy city, reject his offer and refuse to acknowledge that we have sinned and lost our way? No. Rather, let us think carefully what it is that is at stake, even if we cannot bring ourselves to weep with him for our ingratitude and disdain. The city could have changed its ways and welcomed him as his disciples did. But the city chose not to do so. Let us not make the same mistake. Let us raise our eyes up to where he hangs upon the cross and then down again to where he dwells in the tabernacle of our Church. Rather than lose him and all that has any value in our lives, let us rest our weary limbs in his company and let him take us by the hand and lead us to a place of rest within the walls of the Heavenly Jerusalem.

✠

For further reflection:

O sweet and blessed country,
Shall I ever see thy face?
O sweet and blessed country,
Shall I ever win thy grace?

Exult, O dust and ashes!
The Lord shall be the part:
His only, his for ever,
Thou shalt be, and thou art.

(from Urbs Sion aurea – tr. JMN)

But Our Lord wept over the city because he saw what was coming, and was heartbroken about it.

'My house is the house of prayer for all nations; but you have made it a den of thieves.'*

Dominica X Post Pentecosten
The Tenth Sunday after Pentecost

'Hear, O God, my prayer, and despise not my supplication.'[†]

Proper of the Day: *Introit: Psalm 54:17, 18, 20, 23, 2*
                                    Epistle: 1 Corinthians 12:2–11
                                    Gradual: Psalm 16:8, 2
                                    Alleluia: Psalm 64:2
                                    Gospel: Luke 18:9–14
                                    Offertory: Psalm 24:1, 3
                                    Communion: Psalm 50:51, 21

'et qui se humiliat, exaltabitur'[‡]

It would appear that today's Epistle and Gospel are particularly appropriate to the times in which we live. In the Epistle, we hear St Paul on a favourite theme – that the Church on earth is the Mystical Body of Christ. It is a simple and clear,

---

* Luke 19:46.
† Psalm 54:2.
‡ Luke 18:14: 'and he that humbleth himself shall be exalted'.

but wonderfully rich analogy. The Church is to be understood as the continuation of the physical presence of Christ on earth. In other words, since he has ascended into Heaven, he uses the hands and voices and bodies of those within the Church – namely, us. St Teresa of Avila says that on earth Christ has no hands but ours and no voice but ours. So, Christ is the head and we the limbs, and so on. St Paul uses this analogy to underline the fact that members of this mystical body ought not to be fighting among themselves. After all, if a physical body has different members for different purposes, so the Church. Some people are excellent at visiting the sick, some are excellent administrators, some Marthas, some Marys. The foot, after all, can never see as clearly as the eye.

The key lies in the Gospel. Everyone who exalts himself will be humbled, and everyone who humbles himself will be exalted. This implies a proper use of the virtue of humility. Humility is not decrying all that one does, being a malcontent, but having a realistic appreciation of one's gifts, and doing the best with those gifts. Our talents are gifts from God to assist in the vocations to which we have been called. To envy the talent or job or the function of others, or, conversely, to be glad that we are so much superior to the cleaner or the cook both in talent and position, is to fail in humility in each case.

The Pharisee was a proud man and upright in all respects. He was grateful to God that he held the position he held, and that in every aspect of his life he was infinitely superior to most people and to this publican in particular, standing not far away.

The publican simply struck his breast, too overcome with shame to look up, and said: 'O God, be merciful to me a sinner.'

✠

For further reflection:

> *So the day's account shall stand,*
> *Guileless tongue and holy hand,*
> *Steadfast eyes and unbeguiled,*
> *'Flesh as of a little child.'*
>
> *(from Lux ecce surgit aurea – tr. JHN)*

We must struggle for that crucial, and sometimes elusive, virtue of humility.

'Let thine eyes behold the thing that is equitable.'*

Dominica XI Post Pentecosten
The Eleventh Sunday after Pentecost

'Let God arise and let his enemies be scattered: and let them that hate him flee from before his face.'†

Proper of the Day:	Introit: Psalm 67:6, 7, 36, 2
	Epistle: 1 Corinthians 15:1–10
	Gradual: Psalm 27:7, 1
	Alleluia: Psalm 80:2, 3
	Gospel: Mark 7:31–37
	Offertory: Psalm 29:2, 3
	Communion: Proverbs 3:9, 10

'Et apprehendens eum de turba seorsum . . .'‡

S t Mark makes a point of telling us that Our Lord was in the
Decapolis, a region straddling the Jordan east of Galilee,
and like Galilee inhabited by a mixed population of pagans

---

* Psalm 16:2.
† Psalm 67:2.
‡ Mark 7:33: 'And taking him from the multitude, apart . . .'

and half-breed Jews. The respectable thoroughbred inhabitants of Jerusalem, and the Pharisees who came from Jerusalem and Judea, dismissed these northerners as half-breeds and mud-bloods. Demons are most often encountered in these territories where pagans lived alongside the Jews, for the area was only half-converted, on the very fringes of the Holy Land. But it is in the north that Our Lord preaches most, and it is among this mixed population that he works most of his miracles. It was in the Decapolis that Our Lord had healed the demoniac whose demons fled into a herd of swine.

Now he is presented with a man who is deaf and dumb, invited to cure this merely medical complaint. There is a crowd of local onlookers, but Our Lord leads him aside to somewhere more private, in the presence only of the Apostles, and perhaps the friends or relations who had brought the man. He heals him in seclusion, and tells them not to speak of it to anyone – in strange contrast to his orders to the man whose evil spirits were sent into the swine, who was told to proclaim the Gospel throughout the Decapolis.*

This seclusion, this desire for secrecy, is most characteristic of Our Lord's ministry. In this he is giving us an example, not to have our good deeds trumpeted before us, not to seek pub-licity. It is the Kingdom of God we should proclaim, the works of God, not our own. Our Lord never does anything publicly to impress the crowds – that was the second temptation in the desert† – but despite his commands, the story is told, and '*all were astonished*'.

St Paul tells us in his Epistle that his primary message is about the Resurrection of Our Lord, and he gives us a list of the times when he was seen by the Apostles and disciples – by Peter, by the Eleven, by five hundred brethren, by James, by all the Apostles again, and at last by Paul, in a rather different manner. It is, incidentally, a proof of the Tradition that St Paul's list is not the same as that in the Gospels, which all differ slightly

---

* Mark 5:19, 20.
† Matthew 4:6.

from each other: there are independent traditions, different in irrelevant detail, but all agreeing on the essential facts. Thus there are five separate witnesses to the reality that Christ rose from the dead in the human body, none of them dependent on any other and therefore all the more credible.

One of the essential facts that St Paul and all the Gospel writers tell us is that Our Lord never showed himself to the crowds: he appeared only to those who already loved him, who already believed in him, with the significant exception of Paul himself. Here again is his love of seclusion, his refusal to force men to believe. He worked miracles because he loved people: he rose from the dead because our faith is to be in God, who is not of the dead but of the living.*

It is in humility that God's power is strongest. He whose name is to be exalted above every other name† gives us an example of lowliness, diverting attention away from himself to his Father, working in secret as our Father works in secret.‡ Yet humility always precedes glory, as St Jerome says.§ A city on a hill-top cannot be hidden; the works and words of the Son of God cannot be concealed. The message that St Paul received privately, on the road to Damascus, that he was told in seclusion by Ananias in Straight Street,¶ must now be proclaimed from the housetops, preached throughout the world.

Our Lord shows his humanity, his compassion with all suffering mankind, when he groaned or sighed. He shows his divinity in the effortless cure. He shows that he is truly flesh by touching the man, even to the use of spittle. He demonstrates that he is the Word of God by that single word of command, *eph-phetha!* Thus is the essential message demonstrated to this little group of Galileans and half-pagans. This Jesus of Nazareth is truly human, the Son of Man, and at the same time he is truly divine, the Son of God. He is the 'God in his holy place', who

* Mark 12:27.
† Philippians 2:9.
‡ Matthew 6:4.
§ Cantena Aurea.
¶ Acts 9.

comes to those who are *'of one mind ... in a house'*.* This is the Lord who has lifted us up, the Son of Man to whom *'I cried ... and thou hast healed me.'*†

The man from the Decapolis is bound by disease of some kind. We are bound by sin, unable to hear the Word of God clearly, incapable of proclaiming it as we should. The cure for us is the same as it was for him: the presence of the living God among us. The Decapolis reminds us, perhaps, of the Decalogue, the Ten Commandments by which both pagans and Jews must live. The touch of Our Lord on the tongue is a prophecy of the gift of himself in Communion so that our *'barns shall be filled with abundance, and ... presses shall run over with wine'*.‡ Through word and Sacrament we hear the message; our tongues are loosened, we sing his praise.

We have received that message in an unbroken line from the Apostles, the message St Paul handed over to us as he received it, *'Tradidi enim vobis in primus quod et accepi.'*§ This is the true meaning of Tradition, the continuous succession of preachers passing on the message from generation to generation. It is for us in turn to pass on that Tradition, unchanged, to those who come after us. But we need, and they need, the touch of the Son of Man, the sound of the Word of God, to loosen the ligaments of our tongues and unblock our ears. We must not be exalted and proud of having the true faith, like the Pharisees from Jerusalem; the best of us are only half-breeds and mud-bloods, half-converted inhabitants of the Decapolis, on the edge of the wild. Here we shall see demons put to flight; here we shall see miracles. If we have the humility to acknowledge that we are less than the 'least of the Apostles' then we shall be given the courage to recognize that by the grace of God we too are able to continue the great work of calling all God's people to faith and salvation.

---

* Introt of the Day.

† Offertory of the Day.

‡ Communion of the Day.

§ Epistle of the Day: 'For I delivered unto you first of all, which I also received.'

For further reflection:

Lord, on the Cross thine arms were stretched
To draw the nations nigh;
O grant us then that Cross to love,
And in those arms to die.

(from Labente jam solis rota – tr. JC)

The man from the Decapolis is bound by disease of some kind:
we are bound by sin.

Forgive us aught whereof our conscience is afraid, and grant us
all we dare not ask in prayer.

(from the Collect of the Day)

Dominica XII Post Pentecosten
The Twelfth Sunday after Pentecost

'O God, come to my assistance; O Lord make haste to help
me.'*

Proper of the Day: Introit: Psalm 69:2, 3, 4
Epistle: 2 Corinthians 3:4–9
Gradual: Psalm 33:2, 3
Alleluia: Psalm 87:2
Gospel: Luke 10:23–37
Offertory: Exodus 32:11, 13, 14
Communion: Psalm 103:13, 14, 15

✠

'Deus, in adjutorium meum intende.'†

Seven times during the day, and once during the night, does
the Church daily cry out to her Lord and Saviour with these

---

* Psalm 69:2.

† Psalm 69:2: 'O God, come to my assistance.'

words from Psalm 69, at the beginning of each canonical hour of the Divine Office. Though she calls out so often, she fears not that she will remain unheard. Rather, she pleas with sure faith that her Lord will act, and in the certain hope that her members will be saved if they fully co-operate with God's grace. Though beset by many real perils in this world, she has confidence in the promise Our Lord made to Peter that *'the gates of hell shall not prevail against it'.**

Man is constantly in need of God's help. Without it, failure is guaranteed. In Adam's Fall, all mankind lost what are called the 'preternatural gifts' – infused knowledge, immortality and integrity. If that was not bad enough, man was at the same time cut off from God's grace through the first sin. In Adam, man is seen to be heavily paralysed and enfeebled in comparison with what God had intended him to be in the beginning. Man cannot restore his own nature. It requires something rather higher than humanity, something far greater than any created order: the help of God himself. We recall Christ's words in St John's Gospel concerning the vine: *'without me you can do nothing'.*†

Turning to our Gospel for today, the ancient Fathers of the Church often saw in the man fallen among robbers, Adam himself, or, at least, everyman. The robbers are the Devil and his demons who stripped man of his preternatural gifts and virtues through temptation so readily accepted. Man is wounded by being cut off from God's grace. He is left half dead. Note, however, that man is not entirely obliterated – there remains some good in him. He is gravely weak but is still able to reach out to God if so inclined. Nevertheless, he is powerless to restore his relationship with God.

'Many prophets and kings have desired to see the things that you see, and have not seen them; and to hear the things that you hear, and have not heard them.' It is Jesus Christ, the Son of God and the Lord of all Creation, for whom mankind

---

* Matthew 16:18.

† John 15:5.

– and, perhaps, the whole of creation – has been longing since the beginning of the world. The sacrifices and laws of the Old Covenant were only a preparation for Christ's coming; he completes and perfects them. Thus, the priest and the Levite pass by. They can assess and confirm the man's condition, just as St Paul tells us that the Law can convince us of sin but cannot cure it. That Our Lord has the Samaritan treat the man and cure him is a rebuke to the Jewish leaders. Remember that it is a lawyer – and an *expert* in the Law, no less – whose question prompts Jesus to tell the story. This lawyer is intent upon showing his own skill, rather than learning the truth from Our Lord. He is typical of the leaders of the day who prided themselves in knowing the letter of the Law without actually implementing it in a spirit of love and service. The lawyer is *'willing to justify himself'*. The Jewish people were in danger of looking in on themselves as if they already had all things necessary for salvation. But only Christ can make one just, and those whom he ordains to continue his ministry, the ministry that St Paul refers to in the Epistle as *'the ministration of justice'*.

If the ancient Fathers of the Church saw the man fallen among robbers to be everyman, they saw the Samaritan to be Jesus himself. Samaritans were viewed by the Jews as foreigners because, among other things, they did not practise the fullness of the Jewish faith. Nevertheless, Samaritans did recognize the Pentateuch as Sacred Scripture. So, in addition to the intended rebuke of the lawyer, it was fitting that Christ should be the Samaritan in this parable because, in Christ, the Jews and the pagans become one people.

The Samaritan tends the wounds, pouring in oil and wine. In this the sacraments are indicated, and the grace which touches and transforms our lives. The inn serves as the Church. *'Whatsoever thou shalt spend over and above, I, at my return, will repay thee.'* There is no limit to the Lord's tender love and mercy. *'Of his fullness we all have received; and grace for grace.'**

---

* John 1:1.

This story is a comment on social awareness – identifying and defining the neighbour, who is, of course, both the Samaritan and the man abused and broken. Before the Samaritan can help, the injured man must accept the help offered. However, we miss so much of its teaching if we do not encounter the supernatural within it. Christ's teaching goes deeper than loving thy neighbour as thyself. We love and serve one another out of gratitude for all that God has done for us, and that gratitude grows in proportion to how much we reflect upon our being raised from the dust of the road to the newness of life in him. *'Love one another as I have loved you.'**

'Deus, in adjutorium meum intende.'

For *further reflection:*

Father, whose promise binds thee still
To heal the suppliant throng,
Grant us to mourn the deeds of ill
That banish us so long.
                    (from *Te laeta mundi Conditor* – tr. *JMN*)

There is no limit to the Lord's tender love and mercy.

Grant that we may run without stumbling towards the attainment of thy promises.
                    (from the Collect of the Day)

* John 13:24.

Dominica XIII Post Pentecosten
The Thirteenth Sunday after Pentecost

'To Abraham were the promises made, and to his seed.'*

Proper of the Day: Introit: *Psalm 73:20, 19, 23, 1*
                            Epistle: *Galatians 3:16–22*
                            Gradual: *Psalm 73:20, 19, 22*
                            Alleluia: *Psalm 89:1*
                            Gospel: *Luke 17:11–19*
                            Offertory: *Psalm 30:15, 16*
                            Communion: *Wisdom 16:20*

☩

'Surge, vade: quia fides tua te salvum fecit.'†

Leprosy was one of the most feared diseases of the ancient world. Indeed, it was regarded in horror for many centuries, well into modern times. While today our western world is mercifully free from this affliction, we do well to remember those elsewhere who still have cause to dread this terrible disease.

Precisely because leprosy was so feared, lepers themselves were forced to live apart from the rest of the community, and this involuntary isolation became a secondary cause of their suffering. Wandering from place to place, restless, homeless, severed from all the normal human bonds of friendship and kindred, cut off too from their past and with little or no hope for their future, the life of one suffering from leprosy was a truly miserable existence.

St Augustine, commenting on the passage from St Luke which forms our Gospel today, compares the unhappy lot of the leper to the unfortunate state of one who is guilty of heresy or schism. Heresy, or false belief, afflicts and corrupts the true faith as a disease afflicts the body, while schism is a wilful

---

* Galatians 3:16.

† Luke 17:19: 'Arise, go thy way: for thy faith hath made thee whole.'

separation from the communion of the Church, which isolates those guilty just as lepers found themselves isolated at the time of Our Lord's ministry. That St Augustine should use such a powerful analogy ought to make us realize – more forcibly, perhaps, than is often the case – just how seriously the Fathers of the Church viewed the sins of heresy and schism. Today, the modern world celebrates the right of every person to live by his own belief, no matter how dangerous or absurd, and the questioning of these concepts tends to be met with, at best, a shiver of polite disdain. Not so for our forefathers in the faith. For them, heresy and schism were powerful and sinister realities, only to be adequately described by comparison to such terrible afflictions as leprosy or any plague.

Even if, in our modern times, we tend to be less comfortable with such analogies, they still convey a certain truth from which we can learn. Interestingly, a Cardinal of the Roman Curia recently drew precisely such a parallel between spiritual and physical ailments. *'Much is spoken today of diseases like Alzheimer's and Parkinson's. By analogy, their symptoms can, at times, be found even in our own Christian communities. For example, when we live myopically in the fleeting present, oblivious of our past heritage and apostolic traditions, we could well be suffering from a spiritual form of Alzheimer's. And when we behave in a disorderly manner, going whimsically on our own way without any co-ordination with the head or with the other members of our community, it could be ecclesial Parkinson's.'**

The examples which the Cardinal uses demonstrate how heresy and schism can afflict us spiritually just as cruelly as leprosy affects the body. These spiritual diseases weaken our faith, and separate us from the living communion of the Church. Truly, if we deny those traditions faithfully passed on by the unbroken witness of the Church, and deriving from Our Blessed Lord and his Apostles, or if we are so led astray by pride that we actually dare to oppose our own ideas and opinions to the authoritative teaching of the Magisterium, then indeed we

---

* Ivan Cardinal Dias speaking at Lambeth Conference in Canterbury, 2008.

are in the wretched state of those ten men in the Gospel today – sick, wandering and likely to expire.

What remedy can there be for those who find themselves in such an unhappy state; surely only that proposed by Our Lord himself – the remedy of obedience? *'Go, show yourselves to the priests.'* Christ himself, God Incarnate, was obedient to the Old Law so long as its writ prevailed – how much more should we be to the living Law of grace and truth which he has committed to his Holy Catholic Church? And obedient to the priests of that Church, especially to the Pope, the Vicar of Christ, whom the Lord chose in a particular way to share in his own authority.

Of those ten men we saw healed in the Gospel, only one turned back to give thanks, and that man was a Samaritan, the very one we might have thought least likely – due to his own religious background – to return and pay homage. That man, the Samaritan, received kind words from Our Lord, and an additional blessing. A reminder, then, if we needed one, that while we may be called to hate heresy, we are most certainly commanded to love heretics, to pray for them and to draw them back to the Church with open arms. That generosity, which Our Lord demonstrates, was shown at its fullest extent on the Cross at Calvary, when no human being was excluded from the possibility of forgiveness and grace. Remembering our own sins and the healing they require, let us never be so foolish as to judge or condemn our fellow creatures, but do our best to lead them all to the merciful Redeemer.

✠

For further reflection:

Faith of our fathers! We will love
Both friend and foe in all our strife;
And preach thee too, as love knows how,
By kindly words and virtuous life.

(from Faith of our Fathers)

Let us never be so foolish as to judge or condemn our fellow creatures.

Give to us an increase of Faith, Hope and Charity.
(from the Collect of the Day)

Dominica XIV Post Pentecosten
The Fourteenth Sunday after Pentecost

*'Behold, O God, our protector, and look on the face of thy Christ.'**

Proper of the Day: Introit: Psalm 83:10, 11, 2
Epistle: Galatians 5:16–24
Gradual: Psalm 117:8, 9
Alleluia: Psalm 96:1
Gospel: Matthew 6:24–33
Offertory: Psalm 33:8, 9
Communion: Matthew 6:33

✠

'Ne solliciti sitis animae vestrae quid manducetis, neque corpori vestro quid induamini . . . Quaerite ergo primum regnum Dei.'†

It is now almost impossible to open any one of the weekend newspapers or colour supplements without finding a plethora of advertisements that promise you the possibility of effortless rejuvenation, beauty and a physique that will qualify you for instant fame and success in the world. One of the fastest growing and largest profit-making industries in the United Kingdom

---

* Psalm 83:10.

† Matthew 6:25, 33: 'Be not solicitous for your life, what you shall eat, nor for your body, what you shall put on . . . Seek ye therefore first the Kingdom of God.'

today is that of cosmetics. Hot on the heels of this, is the glossy journalism that exalts youthfulness, good looks and glamour. We can forget all the previous prohibitions of what to eat, and what not to eat, for good health, since the new commandment of our generation is: *Thou shalt not grow old gracefully!* The twenty-first-century philosophy of life is that anyone has the right to do what he or she likes with his or her own body.

The Christian vision of the body, on the other hand, is a vision which is based on interior beauty and inner youthfulness: something we can only discover in the soul, since our immortal soul does not age. The liturgy of this Sunday exhorts us to long *'for the courts [dwelling place] of the Lord'*,* and to shun *'the lusts of the flesh'.*† We are told: *'Be not solicitous for your life . . . nor for your body'*,‡ or how we clothe and feed them.

This is really good news, the liberating news, of our holy religion. The outward form of things may be what is initially attractive, but with the passing of time and the tarnishing of the human façade, it is the inner beauty of soul and spirit which improves, and which is of more vital concern.

Much of the Pontificate of Pope John Paul II was spent in expounding an integrated vision of the person – body, soul and spirit. This is his *theology of the body.* As he explains, the physical human body has a specific meaning and is capable of revealing answers regarding fundamental questions about us and our lives: is there a real purpose to life and, if so, what is it? Why were we created male and female? Does it really matter if we are one sex or another? Why were man and woman called to communion from the beginning? What does the marital union of a man and woman say to us about God and his plan for our lives? What is the purpose of married and celibate vocations? What exactly is love? Is it truly possible to be pure of heart? All these questions and many more find answers in the treasury of writing bequeathed to us by that great Pontiff.

---

* Psalm 83:2.
† Galatians 5:16.
‡ Matthew 6:25.

The Church continues to teach a revolutionary and life-transforming message of hope that counteracts societal trends which urge us to view the body as an object of pleasure or as a machine for manipulation. Our Catholic belief about life and the body is that of reverence for the gift of our being with all its wonderful faculties, and challenges us to live it in a way worthy of our great dignity as human persons. This vision, or theology, is not only for young people or married couples, or for those who have grown old, but for all ages and vocations since it sums up the true meaning of the human personas created by our loving Father God.

One of the key words that we can associate with the understanding of who we are, and how we are to live, comes powerfully through the life and teaching of Pope John Paul II – it is the word *purification*. If we wish to glorify God in our lives, if we wish the face of Christ and his Church to be visible and radiant, then we must constantly purify ourselves. If not, we very quickly become the servants of this world and of mammon. We are called upon by Jesus to purify ourselves of anything that does not speak of God and what his Church professes. The saints are the people who, in the history of the Church, have made a difference. The heretics have cried: *'Let us change the Church!'* The saints have said: *'Yes, let us change the Church, but by beginning with* us – *with me!'* There is much to purify in the Church today, as in former times, but we must begin with ourselves.

The spirit of the world affects all of us; it can make us selfish and reduce our propensity to give ourselves unselfishly in love to others. The desire to possess more and more, to look more attractive, to control others, is encouraged everywhere we look. *'For after all these things do the heathen seek . . . Seek ye first the Kingdom of God.'*

May the most pure and Immaculate Virgin Mother of God obtain for us the graces we need to live in this world as God's children, so that at the end she will, as we have so often prayed: *'Et Jesum, benedictum fructum ventris tui, nobis post exsilium ostende'* ['And after this, our exile, show us the fruit of your womb, Jesus'].

For further reflection:

> *That God would keep our conscience pure;*
> *Our souls from folly would secure;*
> *Would bid us check the pride of sense*
> *With due and holy abstinence.*
>   *(from Jam lucis orto sidere – tr. JMN)*

There is much to purify in the Church today, as in former times, and we must begin with ourselves.

May the Church be ever free from harm and guided in good.
>   *(from the Collect of the Day)*

Dominica XV Post Pentecosten
The Fifteenth Sunday after Pentecost

'Incline thy ear, O Lord, to me and hear me: save thy servant, O my God.'*

Proper of the Day: Introit: Psalm 85:1–4
                      Epistle: Galatians 5:25, 26; 6:1–10
                      Gradual: Psalm 91:2, 3
                      Alleluia: Psalm 94:3
                      Gospel: Luke 7:11–16
                      Offertory: Psalm 39:2, 3, 4
                      Communion: John 6:52

---

* Psalm 85:1.

'Non efficiamur inanis gloriae cupidi.'*

Humility is for cowards, and charity for the weak. In our world, Christian virtue has become synonymous with weakness. In today's Epistle, St Paul reminds us of the true nature of humility and charity and, particularly, of pride: *'For if any man think himself to be something, whereas he is nothing, he deceiveth himself.'* Of course, we know that pride is always a deception. It all began with Eve's being duped by the serpent into believing that if she ate the fruit, she would become like God. Satan, in the guise of the serpent, tricked her into believing that she was something other than that she was. Pride is always a deception. In her desire to become like God, Eve forgot that she was merely a creature of God: she realized the truth too late. Pride is clearly a mimicry of God – and a poor one; pride conceals from us the reality of who we are. Pride is, therefore, a deception and it is Satan who deceives many into believing that they can be their own God. And so, contraception, abortion and euthanasia all spring from the root of this self-centred pride. If pride is deception, humility is truth and reality.

The word 'humility' has its roots in the earth and soil – *humus* – and is a reminder of whence we came and where we go. St John Chrysostom tells us that the grave is the school where we learn humility, but how can we practise humility before it comes to that? First, we listen – perhaps to our neighbour; we might actually learn something. We might not know better than our neighbour. In the second place, we ought to take pleasure when our neighbour is praised for his good qualities. We tend to look upon everyone as a rival to be outdone, rather than a brother to be loved. St Paul warns us about jealousy and envy. We must remember that the Blood of Christ was shed for each one of us – not just for *me*. We are all members of the same spiritual family and we can all share in the fruits of one another's talents and gifts.

---

* Galatians 5:26: 'Let us not be made desirous of vainglory.'

In the third place, we must take correction humbly. If it is intended to be helpful, it can bring us face to face with who we really are and with what we should be. And in the fourth place, we should, by the same token, exercise compassion for the weaknesses of others and to help our neighbour rise above them. Pride makes us insensitive to others: humility makes us reach out to others.

In today's Gospel the humble heart of Jesus is moved to pity and compassion upon the sufferings of others. In his mercy, he cures them and makes them better. A humble man is not surprised at the faults and limitations of others – rather, he shows compassion. Humility is patient and blossoms into charity. And we must be patient with ourselves in our striving for humility. As St Francis de Sales tells us, the thought of the many benefits bestowed on us must inevitably make us humble before God. Let us consider over and over again the many good things lavished on us and let us remember that God is the source of all our gifts and talents. The more we appreciate his blessings, the more we are humbled by them and appalled by past sins. As soon as we receive Our Lord in the Blessed Sacrament, let us ask him to transform our hearts.

> 'Let us not be made desirous of vainglory. And in doing good, let us not fail; for in due time we shall reap, not failing.'

✠

For further reflection:

> *In heaven thine endless joys bestow,*
> *And grant thy gifts of grace below;*
> *From chains of strife our souls release,*
> *Bind fast the gentle bands of peace.*
>   *(from Hominis superne Conditor)*

And we must be patient with ourselves in our striving for humility.

May thy Sacraments ever guard us against the assaults of the devil.

(from the Secret of the Day)

Dominica XVI Post Pentecosten
The Sixteenth Sunday after Pentecost

'Have mercy on me, O Lord, for I have cried to thee all the day.'*

Proper of the Day:	Introit: Psalm 85:3, 5, 1
	Epistle: Ephesians 3:13–21
	Gradual: Psalm 101:16, 17
	Alleluia: Psalm 97:1
	Gospel: Luke 14:1–11
	Offertory: Psalm 39:14, 15
	Communion: Psalm 70:16–18

✠

'Et qui se humiliat, exaltabitur.'†

We like to be invited to special events; and the greater the occasion, the more and the better we prepare ourselves. We mark our calendars and look forward to the day. Then we dress up in our smartest clothes and take a gift as a sign of friendship.

Now God is inviting each and every one of us his children to a sumptuous banquet, to receive his Body and Blood in Holy Communion. But to receive the many graces of this banquet, we must prepare ourselves and practise humility. As the man with the withered hand in today's Gospel, we must humbly approach Jesus to be cured of the disease of sin. If we fall into mortal sin, of course we must receive the Sacrament of Penance

---

* Psalm 85:3.

† Luke 14:11: 'And he that humbleth himself, shall be exalted.'

before arriving at the Communion rail. However, if we are not conscious of mortal sin, then it is not required to go to confession before receiving Holy Communion. But, even if we do not fall into mortal sin, we should come to confession regularly so that our Holy Communions can be as spiritually fruitful as possible. In Holy Communion, Our Lord wants to flood our souls with his grace; but through our impatience, our vanity, our jealousy, through our attachment to our own ways and opinions, and so on, we ourselves close the tap and receive only a few drops.

Confession helps us benefit more and more from our Communions because it is a powerful means to humility. There are three acts in a good confession. First of all, we ask Our Lord for the grace to make a good confession and then we confess our sins in kind and in number or frequency. In the second place, we must be contrite, and the perfect contrition is the sincere regret of having offended the Sacred Heart of Jesus. In the third place we have to do penance because this penance helps repair the damage done by our sins and restore the order and harmony which should exist in our souls. But why do we confess through a priest? In this sacrament, the priest is the instrument, the spiritual doctor through which Jesus Christ heals our souls. When we kneel in the confessional, we kneel before Jesus crucified on Calvary, and his most Precious Blood cleanses our souls. Humility is the key to a blessed eternity.

It is a great joy for a priest to welcome souls to confession, because he sees the beauty of God's grace at work. He has a great respect and profound esteem for those who come to confession, for he is happy to serve the penitent. And so, we should approach the confessional with great confidence in God's mercy, and even with a certain joy, because, in the confessional, Jesus Christ himself welcomes us with open arms. Our beloved Jesus is greatly consoled by our sincerity and humility in confession.

If we are humble on earth, we shall be for ever happy in the eternal Banquet in Heaven. Humility is the key to a blessed eternity. *'And he that humbleth himself, shall be exalted.'*

For further reflection:

> *Monarch of all things, fit us for thy mansions;*
> *Banish our weakness, health and wholeness sending;*
> *Bring us to heaven, where thy Saints united joy without*
>   *ending.*

(from Nocte surgentes – tr. PD)

In the confessional, Jesus himself welcomes us with open arms.

'When thou art invited to a wedding, sit down in the lowest place, that he who invited thee may say to thee: "Friend, go up higher."'

(from the Antiphon for the Magnificat at Vespers)

Dominica XVII Post Pentecosten
The Seventeenth Sunday after Pentecost

May our vices be healed and eternal remedies be made available to us.

Proper of the Day: Introit: Psalm 118:137, 124, 1
                     Epistle: Ephesians 4:1–6
                     Gradual: Psalm 32:12, 16
                     Alleluia: Psalm 101:2
                     Gospel: Matthew 22:34–46
                     Offertory: Daniel 9:4, 17–19
                     Communion: Psalm 75:12–13

*'Diliges Dominum Deum tuum ex toto corde tuo . . .'**

Technology has largely replaced our former dependence upon memory. There was a time when people committed to memory many more things than they do nowadays. Its decline

---

* Matthew 22:37: 'Thou shalt love the Lord thy God with all thy heart . . .'

has led some people to believe that it is impossible for us to recall more than a few sentences of text. That may be because we have lost the facility to do so. More primitive societies can still memorize a great deal. Shakespearean actors in our own time also need good memories. In the time of Our Blessed Lord's life on earth it was common for scholars of Scripture to commit long tracts of it to memory and to be able to quote freely from it. The first and most important phrase that a Jewish child learnt from early childhood was called the *shema*. It is one of the verses Our Lord quotes today in the Gospel: *'Thou shalt love the Lord thy God with all thy heart, and with thy whole soul, and with thy mind.'* This verse from the book of Deuteronomy* was at the very heart of the Old Testament religion and was basic to it. In his reply to the Pharisee, Our Lord adds a text from Leviticus: *'Thou shalt love thy neighbour as thyself.'†* They are his own summary of everything written in the Law and the Prophets.

Love of God is linked to love of neighbour. But love of God must come first. One of the great deceptions that have gained widespread acceptance is the notion that we can be charitable and unselfish towards our neighbour without any reference to God. In fact, for some people, it makes more sense. For them we cannot benefit God and he can do little for us. So religion for them is purely a matter of live and let live, with no strings attached. We do not have to be as wise as Solomon to come to the realization that when love of God is removed from consideration, love of neighbour ceases to be an obligation but easily becomes an option I may choose, if it is not too inconvenient. If I am answerable to no one but myself, I may do what I please, if it suits me. There is nothing to persuade me that I should love the unlovable people around me if God's law does not command me to do so. Why do we think that love is commanded by God and not merely suggested? Because it is an unlikely manner in which to behave without some compelling reason

---

* Deuteronomy 6:5.
† Leviticus 19:18.

to do so. As with many other aspects of human relations, it is because God commands it that we learn to act accordingly, not relying solely on human instinct to guide us.

When God is absent from the equation, immoral and unethical solutions to solve people's problems are quickly sought: euthanasia for the weak and helpless considered too unhappy to live; abortion for the child thought to be unloved by its prospective parents. Such things are now considered compassionate. Loving our neighbour means, for some, helping them to end their lives. It is a travesty of love and totally against what God's commands. We need much more than human sentiment to guide our actions in the right way, because, of ourselves, we can do no lasting good nor sustain a life of virtue. We must be first enabled to perform any good work by the grace of God. This is the prerequisite to every selfless deed and to the formation of habits and an outlook that places God before all else and our neighbour as next in line as a consequence of loving God. Reliance on God is the bedrock of any genuine spiritual life that is worthy of the name. How is that best expressed? By accepting through prayer and worship the dominion of the Almighty over us, we reach beyond this world to appreciate God's love for us; we are dignified as beings made in his image and likeness, and we are enabled to recognize the same dignity in others. 'Thou shalt love the Lord thy God with all thy heart . . .'

✠

For further reflection:

Thee all the armies of the sky
Adore, and laud, and magnify;
And Nature, in her triple frame,
For ever sanctifies thy name.

And we, too, thanks and homage pay,
Thine own adoring flock today;

O join to that celestial song
The praises of our supplicant throng.

(from Adesto, sancta Trinitas – tr. JMN)

Reliance on God is the bedrock of any genuine spiritual life.

'Blessed are the undefiled in the way: who walk in the law of the Lord.'

(from the Introit of the Day)

Dominica XVIII Post Pentecosten
The Eighteenth Sunday after Pentecost

'Let peace be in thy strength, and abundance in thy towers.'*

Proper of the Day: Introit: Ecclesiasticus 36:18; Psalm 121:1
Epistle: 1 Corinthians 1:4–8
Gradual: Psalm 121:1, 7
Alleluia: Psalm 101:16
Gospel: Matthew 9:1–8
Offertory: Exodus 24:4, 5
Communion: Psalm 95:8, 9

'Da pacem Domine.'†

In today's Mass the Church prays for peace from God. But in the Gospel we do not find peace. We find, rather, the beginning of Our Lord's disputes with the scribes that will lead in the end to his arrest and to his Passion and death. Peace will come only at a price – the price of courage and the price of truth.

---

* Psalm 121:7.
† Ecclesiasticus 36:18: 'Give peace, O Lord.'

The Gospel finds Our Lord at the height of his popularity. His fame as a healer has spread. But the clouds are gathering. St Matthew places this event in the middle of a whole series of other healing miracles by which he wants to show that Our Lord does indeed have divine power – power over things, power over spirits, power over souls for the remission of sins. It is interesting to compare the different emphases given to this event by St Mark and St Matthew in their Gospels. In St Mark we find the detail of the stretcher-bearers taking off the roof to lower the sick man down in their anxiety to get him to Jesus. In St Matthew we find it placed in a series of miracles that not only show his power but also beget rumour and reputation that in the end bring suspicion upon him. And at the end of the series of miracles Our Lord shares his power, so much feared by the authorities, with his disciples.

There is, of course, no necessary connection between sickness and sin. Perhaps in his own conscience the paralytic was able to see a connection implied by Our Lord's words to him. It is important that the sickness is the opportunity for God's power to be made visible.

The very fact of the forgiveness of sin implies the action of a divine power. Who but God can penetrate to the human soul and there recognize and remove a spiritual wound? Who may take a debt owed to God and, putting himself in God's place, declare that debt written off; surely only one who claims to be God? No wonder the scribes began to murmur to themselves: '*He blasphemeth.*' But just as he could see into the soul of the paralysed man, so also he could read the minds of the scribes: '*Why do you think evil in your hearts?*'

Which indeed is easier to say: '*Arise and walk*' or '*Thy sins are forgiven thee*'? Both are the actions of divine power, but with this difference, that the one is visible and the other invisible. The sensible evidence of the one gives credence to the other. The physical miracle becomes the witness to and guarantee of the spiritual. The scribes were clever enough to know that something had taken place that shook their own religion to its foundations. From now on, conflict was inevitable. The crowd meanwhile continued to grow and to follow him; they continued to do so right up to his entry into Jerusalem. This too was inflammatory. It had to be controlled, and was controlled, as the events leading to Jesus' trial were to prove.

Today's Mass texts – as opposed to the Epistle and Gospel – relate to the Dedication of a church. Certainly they speak of rejoicing when we come into the house of the Lord; of Moses' consecrating an altar to the Lord; of worshipping the Lord in the holy Temple. Quite rightly we hope for peace from our churches. We want them to be places of peace, and to promote peace in the world. We want them to lead us to peace in the next life. They can be and are all these things. As we find in the Gospel, Our Lord shared his power of healing and forgiving sins with his Apostles, and later on gave them the power of making him present in the Eucharist. But our churches must also be places that inspire us and fire us up for the challenge of the Christian life, that heal us and nourish us for a struggle. The challenge faced by Our Lord in the Gospel shows us that our faith will be challenged. But the truth alone will lead us to true peace, though we have to fight for it. We cannot come to the joy of the Resurrection without passing through Calvary. The Mass texts pray for peace and celebrate the Church. The Gospel shows Our Lord at the beginning of the trials that were to be his in the earthly Jerusalem, the City of Peace. May we faithfully follow through them with him to the heavenly Jerusalem where that peace will last for ever.

✠

For further reflection:

To pray for mercy when we sin,
For cleansing and release,
For ghostly safety, and within
For everlasting peace.

                                    (from Ecce jam noctis – tr. JHN)

May we follow him faithfully to the heavenly Jerusalem where
that peace will last for ever.

*'Let peace be in thy strength and abundance in thy towers.'**
(from the Gradual of the Day)

Dominica XIX Post Pentecosten
The Nineteenth Sunday after Pentecost

'Attend, O my people, to my law; incline your ears to the words
of my mouth.'†

Proper of the Day: Introit: *From an unknown source and Psalm 77:1*
Epistle: *Ephesians 4:23–28*
Gradual: *Psalm 140:2*
Alleluia: *Psalm 104:1*
Gospel: *Matthew 22:1–14*
Offertory: *Psalm 137:7*
Communion: *Psalm 118:4, 5*

'Et induite novum hominem.'‡

It is not enough to be called and chosen by grace, we must
respond to that call with faith and hope and charity. Just as
Our Lady – chosen before the creation began – had to give her
consent, *'be it done to me according to thy word'*, so we must
respond to God's grace if our justification is to be crowned by
sanctification.

The parable of the wedding feast in St Matthew's Gospel
differs from the similar one in St Luke's,§ in that it speaks of
the Church in this world, rather than the Church triumphant in

---

* Psalm 121:7.
† Psalm 77:1.
‡ Ephesians 4:24: 'And put on the new man.'
§ Luke 14:16–24.

the next. In the first instance we can understand it in relation to the unbelievers among God's own people. The first messengers sent to them were Moses and the former prophets Elijah and Elisha, but they would not listen. Then came the later prophets, and these they persecuted, until the King of Babylon came as a scourge of God and burnt their city. A remnant remained, the poor, the country people, the beggars, and they were gathered together to restore Jerusalem under Ezra and Nehemiah. That much the Pharisees would recognize and appreciate. But of course there is a second interpretation: the later wave of servants is the Apostles, and these the chief priests and Pharisees were to persecute, until the Romans came and burnt their city.

Nor should we imagine that the parable cannot be applied to us too: we may have been invited to enter the Kingdom of Heaven, but we may be so choked by the affairs of the world – the farm in the country, the trading – that we refuse to come to the banquet Christ has prepared for us. We are invited Sunday by Sunday, feast after feast, to partake of the Banquet of the Lamb, but any excuse will do. Business affairs demand attention more than the affairs of God; many are quite prepared to insult and attack those who try to call them back to their faith. And that is why our churches are filled with the outcasts, the poor, those, perhaps, unwanted by the commercial world.

Even so, the King found a man not wearing a wedding garment. Now, such garments were provided by the host and given to each guest as he arrived: this is a man who has refused to put on his host's free gift. Certainly that is so in the application of the parable, for the garment is the clothing of righteousness: 'the whole armour of God . . . the breastplate of justice . . . the shield of faith . . . the helmet of salvation'.* In today's Epistle, St Paul bids us put off the old nature and put on the new.

The wedding garment is, above all, charity. God's free gift to us is charity, without which faith is worthless, as St Paul tells us in another place.† Charity – love – must flow both from God to

---

* Ephesians 6:13–17.
† I Corinthians 12:2.

us and from us to God, for just as we are assured of how much he loves us, so we are commended to love him: *'Thou shalt love the Lord thy God with thy whole heart, and with thy whole soul, and with thy whole mind.'** That love, in turn, must bear fruit in the love of our neighbour: *'If any man say "I love God" and hateth his brother, he is a liar.'†* The fruit of charity is listed by St Paul: *'charity, joy, peace, patience, benignity, goodness',‡* etc. These form the wedding garment without which we cannot remain in God's Church, the Kingdom of Heaven on earth, nor enter eternal life.

We are called, then, by God's grace, and our justification depends on him alone, as the Council of Trent teaches us. We can do nothing to earn our invitation to the banquet, but once we have accepted that initial invitation, the dialogue continues. God offers us his love, that charity which is to bear fruit in our lives. We cannot refuse that gift of charity, presuming that our invitation alone will suffice. It is not enough to have been justified by grace, we must allow that grace to be fruitful in good works, to clothe us in that new nature which responds freely to God's grace. (A point poor Dr Luther never quite grasped!) As the Psalmist says: *'Thou hast commanded thy commandments to be kept most diligently: O that my ways may be directed to keep thy justifications.'§* If we wish to preserve that justification which God has given us, we must respond to his commandments, to love God and to love our neighbour.

If we think that the call alone is sufficient, and do not concern ourselves to put on the wedding garment that Christ offers us every day, then we have no excuse, we can only be silent, if we find ourselves cast out into the outer darkness. The Fathers of the Church teach that this means heresy, the outermost darkness of those who have once known the truth and have lost it.¶ It is true that those who refuse the working of grace in their

---

* Matthew 22:37.
† 1 John 4:20.
‡ Galatians 5:22, 23.
§ Psalm 118:4, 5.
¶ St John Chrysostom Catena Aurea ad loc.

hearts very easily lose even that degree of faith they had pos-
sessed. Yet we are still talking about the Church in this world
– as long as this world lasts, there is the chance of repentance,
of returning, of being welcomed again by the King with the call
*'friend'. 'If I shall walk in the midst of tribulation, thou wilt
quicken me, O Lord'*,* and from *'whatever tribulation they
shall cry to me, I will hear them'.*† Only at the end will darkness
become everlasting for those who refuse the light.

St Paul's teaching, therefore, is in complete accord with
the Gospel: we must put off the old man, and put on the new
*'putting away lying, speak ye the truth ... Give not place to
the devil'.* Those who have formerly lived in the darkness of
error, or who have been outcast from God's people, have now
been called into the Church, where each one should work *'with
his hands the thing which is good'.* Justification, the call to the
Kingdom of Heaven, is always to be followed by sanctification,
the work which God's grace does through our hands. Thus
again we must say with Our Lady, *'I am the handmaid of the
Lord, be it done unto me according to thy word.'*

✠

For further reflection:

Begotten of no human will,
But of the Spirit, thou art still
The Word of God in flesh arrayed,
The promised fruit to man displayed.
The virgin womb that burden gained
With virgin honour all unstained;
The banners there of virtue glow;
God in his temple dwells below.
                    (from Veni Redemptor gentium – tr. JMN)

---

* Psalm 137:7.
† Introit of the Day.

We must respond to that call with Faith, Hope and Charity.

Remove everything that might hinder us, O God, so that we may be freed in body and soul to seek thy will.

(from the Collect of the Day)

Dominica XX Post Pentecosten
The Twentieth Sunday after Pentecost

'Blessed are the undefiled in the way, who walk in the law of the Lord.'*

Proper of the Day: Introit: *Daniel 3:31, 29, 35; Psalm 118:1*
                      Epistle: *Ephesians 5:15–21*
                      Gradual: *Psalm 144:15, 16*
                      Alleluia: *Psalm 107:2*
                      Gospel: *John 4:46–53*
                      Offertory: *Psalm 136:1*
                      Communion: *Psalm 118:49, 50*

✠

'Credidit homo sermoni, quem dixit ei Jesus.'†

'O My God, I firmly believe in all that thy holy Catholic and apostolic Church approves and teaches, since it is thou, the infallible truth, who revealed it to thy Church.' Thus runs the prayer published as an Act of Faith in many of our devotional books. We can never have enough faith, and should pray daily for its increase. *'I do believe, Lord! Help my unbelief.'‡* Thus exclaims the man in St Mark's Gospel who wishes his son to be freed from a dumb spirit.

---

* Psalm 118:1.
† John 4:50: 'The man believed the word which Jesus said to him.'
‡ Mark 9:23.

Today's Gospel concerning the healing of the ruler's son at Capharnaum teaches us this lesson. But before we proceed to examine it, let us first be clear as to the identity of this man. Sts Matthew and Luke record a similar episode taking place in Capharnaum. However, those evangelists record not a ruler and his son, but a centurion and his servant.* Some editions of the Holy Bible contain cross-references connecting all three passages. There is no reason to suppose that, due to the similarity of the stories, they tell only of one episode. The synoptic evangelists clearly do tell of one miracle: the healing by Our Lord of the servant of a Roman centurion, who, St Luke adds, was fond of the Jewish people. But John writes of a ruler and his son. The word 'ruler' in this case is probably a high-ranking official of the King (or Tetrarch) Herod Antipas.

Proceeding now to the narrative of the healing, it appears to be a straightforward account of a man's faith in Our Lord being rewarded by the healing of his son. *'The man believed the word which Jesus said to him.'* In other words, the man's faith is such that only a word from Our Lord is necessary, rather than the physical act of the laying-on of hands. But when we consult the Fathers on this text, the ruler comes under close scrutiny and his faith found to be deficient in some way. It is noted, for example, that twice the text records that the ruler *'prayed him to come down, and heal his son'*. So, say the Fathers, the ruler first thought that Our Lord could not cure the boy unless he was personally present. *'And mark his earthly mind'*, continues St John Chrysostom, *'shown in hurrying Christ along with him; as if Our Lord could not raise his son after death.'* Chrysostom even suggests that the ruler probably came to Our Lord as a last resort when all else had failed. Clearly, the man's faith grows as the text continues, since, as we have noted, *'The man believed the word which Jesus said to him.'* But why do the ancient Fathers of the Church seem to treat this man so harshly?

---

* Matthew 8:5–13; Luke 7:2–10.

The answer is precisely because of the existence of the similar account of the Roman centurion and his servant in the Gospels of Matthew and Luke. Comparing the differences in the two narratives with that of St John's account shows that the centurion has greater faith than the ruler. The ruler invites Our Lord to his house for the healing, but in the case of the centurion, it is Our Lord who suggests he go to the centurion's house. That provides the centurion with the opportunity to make his astonishing declaration of faith that Our Lord need *'only say the word, and my servant shall be healed'*. On the other hand, the ruler asked his servants *'the hour wherein'* his son *'grew better'*. Only as a result of the answer given, did the ruler know *'that it was at the same hour that Jesus said to him "thy son liveth"'*. Only then he *'himself believed, and his whole house'*. In contrast, the centurion makes no such enquiry. The words from Jesus are sufficient for him readily to attribute any sudden recovery of his servant to Our Lord's spoken decree.

That the ruler's faith is, perhaps, weaker than that of the centurion does not mean that the ruler's faith is worth nothing. We all have small beginnings and advance at different rates. God is pleased with our efforts, no matter how small the results may seem, so long as he sees that we are trying and co-operating with the grace he gives us. What is displeasing to him is our complacency when we feel we are doing well and coast along without really trying. Our Lord worked two similar miracles in Capharnaum, inter alia, for the very purpose of our being able to compare them. If we only had a measure of the ruler's faith we should be satisfied, perhaps. Nevertheless, the greater example of the centurion urges us to press on and never to think that we have enough faith.

✠

For further reflection:

Let faith discern the eternal light
Beyond the darkness of the night,

And through the mists of falsehood see
The path of truth revealed by thee.

(from Immense caeli Conditor – tr. GG)

'The man believed the word which Jesus said to him.'

Bestow on thy faithful pardon and peace, letting them feel
secure in thy service.

(from the Collect of the Day)

Dominica XXI Post Pentecosten
The Twenty-First Sunday after Pentecost

'All things are in thy will, O Lord; and there is none that can
resist thy will.'*

Proper of the Day: Introit: Esther 13:9, 10, 11; Psalm 118:1
                     Epistle: Ephesians 6:10–17
                     Gradual: Psalm 89:1, 2
                     Alleluia: Psalm 113:1
                     Gospel: Matthew 18:23–35
                     Offertory: Job 1
                     Communion: Psalm 118:81, 84, 86

'Carnem quoque ejus gravi ulcere vulneravit.'†

As we begin to approach the end of the Church's year and realize that Advent is looming, the Church throws up before us thoughts of the next world and the Four Last Things. The prayers and readings of today's Mass are indeed particularly solemn and grave.

One of the most striking prayers of today's Mass is the unusually long and vivid Offertory passage. This tells of the

---

* Esther 13:9.

† Adapted from Job 1: '[Satan] wounded his flesh also with a grievous ulcer.'

Old Testament figure of Job, *'simple and upright and fearing God'*, and yet tempted to the extreme by Satan: his property and children were attacked and *'Carnem quoque ejus gravi ulcere vulneravit'*. Originally, the text was even longer and included Job's passionate cry for happiness which is the great desire of every man's heart and which God alone can provide. Job was focused on the joys of Heaven despite the misery he faced in the world.

The Gospel contains the well-known parable of the servant who owes his master ten thousand talents, and receives forgiveness, but lacks compassion towards his fellow-servant who owes him a small debt of one hundred pence. The unmerciful servant is ultimately punished and delivered to the torturers. The passage reminds us that we need to be constantly aware that the choices we make in this life have eternal consequences.

St Augustine called eternity a *magna cogitatio* [a great thought] standing at the very heart of our life as Christians. Many of the saints, for example, were more aware of eternity than of the present, despite often holding positions of great responsibility. St John Fisher, Bishop of Rochester and martyr, ate his meals in the presence of a skull, to remind him of the shortness of this life. St Thomas More, the former Lord Chancellor, was visited in prison by his wife, who tried to persuade him to compromise his principles and thus be freed and enjoy perhaps twenty more years of earthly life. *'O foolish woman,'* the condemned man exclaimed, *'do you want me to condemn my soul to an eternity of torments for twenty years of life?'*

We are, indeed, made for eternity with God, and yet, so distracted are we by the concerns of everyday life, that it is very easy to forget all about it. The day will come however – perhaps sooner than we like to think – when we will reach the threshold of eternity and be called to account for our lives. At the moment of our death, we will be like the tree mentioned in Ecclesiastes: *'If the tree fall to the south or to the north, in what place soever it shall fall there shall it lie.'** A tree falls on

---

* Ecclesiastes 11:3.

the side to which it inclines and at death we shall go the way that we are inclined; either towards God or away from him, to Heaven (even if we are in need of extensive purification) or to Hell.

Modern Catholics are often nervous in thinking about such things. The reality of death, judgement and Hell, which formed the staple diet of reflection for previous generations, now seems too final, too negative. But these considerations should not make us morbid or lead us to despair. Rather, they challenge us to examine our lives, to make the most of God's grace and continual mercy, and to strive for holiness.

When we come to Mass and receive Holy Communion, we are given all the graces that we need to make the right choices. We are presented, if you like, with our spiritual weaponry for the coming week – what St Paul refers to in today's Epistle as *'the armour of God ... of truth ... the breastplate of justice ... the shield of faith ... the helmet of salvation ... the sword of the spirit'*. Let us then make the petitions of the Collect our own, as we continue this spiritual warfare: may the Lord protect us from the wiles of the Devil, and may we be given the gift of devotion by which the mind is drawn towards the service of God, the practice of good works and the thought of eternity.

✠

For further reflection:

> *I can no more; for now it comes again,*
> *That sense of ruin, which is worse than pain,*
> *That masterful negation and collapse*
> *Of all that makes me man; as though I bent*
> *Over the dizzy brink*
> *Of some sheer infinite descent;*
> *Or worse, as though*
> *Down, down for ever I was falling through*
> *The solid framework of created things,*

And needs must sink and sink
Into the vast abyss.
(from the Dream of Gerontius – JHM)

Modern Catholics are often nervous about thinking of the Four
Last Things.

*'My soul is in thy salvation, and in thy word have I hoped.'**
(from the Communion of the Day)

Dominica XXII Post Pentecosten
The Twenty-Second Sunday after Pentecost

*'Remember me, O Lord, thou who rulest above all power; and
give a well-ordered speech in my mouth.'* †

Proper of the Day: Introit: Psalm 129:3, 4, 1
Epistle: Philippians 1:6–11
Gradual: Psalm 132:1, 2
Alleluia: Psalm 113:11
Gospel: Matthew 22:15–21
Offertory: Esther 14:12, 13
Communion: Psalm 16:6

✠

*'Reddite ergo quae sunt Caesaris, Caesari: et quae
sunt Dei, Deo.'*‡

In the course of his public ministry Christ encounters two
types of enquirers: those who questioned him in order to
seek and find the truth; and those who set out to trick him

---

* Psalm 118:81.
† Esther 14:12.
‡ Matthew 22:21: 'Render therefore to Caesar the things that are Caesar's,
and to God the things that are God's.'

and thereby to compromise his mission. The first group of questioners wanted to live and breathe the saving truths which Jesus alone brings; the other type of questioner had an altogether different motive. The questioning of Our Lord by the Pharisees in today's Gospel clearly falls into this second category. Jesus is thus rightly and righteously angered by the Pharisees' blatant hypocrisy, particularly so since those who had been charged with teaching men in regard to their duty towards God are now using their position to undermine those very obligations. They ought to have known better.

And so it is that the brilliant answer given by Our Lord, 'Render therefore to Caesar the things that are Caesar's, and to God the things that are God's', cuts clean through his opponents' ploy: no human obligation can stand in the way of the fulfilment of what rightly and firstly pertains to God. In other words, our responsibilities in this world and our responsibilities to our fellows, important as they are, cannot and must not dilute or override our duty to our Maker. These duties may often be in harmony, but equally, there are times when they are distinctly at odds owing to man-made laws that militate against the Divine Law. This principle has been courageously upheld by Christians through the centuries, the martyrs of the Church bearing particular testimony to the integrity demanded of those who follow Our Lord.

Liturgically speaking, as we draw close to the end of the Church's year, and given the ever-strengthening theme of the return of the Lord, it is important to understand today's Gospel in the light of the call to await his return at the close of the age. How are we to await his coming? The answer is given in the Epistle. Standing ready for the Second Coming, the Church must continue her task of making the Word of God known throughout the earth. It is the preaching of the Gospel that brings joy, charity, contentment and peace. Again, however, we are reminded of our dependence upon God and not our own strength in the Introit today: 'If thou, O Lord, shalt observe iniquities, Lord, who shall endure it? For with thee *there is merciful forgiveness.'* And before him we must come in humility and trust, confident that his promise to us in Christ will be fulfilled.

The rendering unto God and to Caesar thus becomes more starkly juxtaposed. Human ties and obligations are put into perspective. God has begun the work of sanctification in our souls; and he will not abandon us, provided we remain receptive to his grace.

For further reflection:

> *Grant us, when this short life is past,*
> *The glorious evening that shall last;*
> *That, by a holy death attained,*
> *Eternal glory may be gained.*
>
> *(from Rerus Deus tenax vigor – tr. JMN)*

It is the preaching of the Gospel that brings joy, charity, contentment and peace.

May we obtain in deed what we ask in faith.

(from the Collect of the Day)

Dominica XXIII Post Pentecosten
The Twenty-Third Sunday after Pentecost

'In God we will glory all the day long: and in thy name we will give praise for ever.'

Proper of the Day:	Introit: Jeremiah 29:11, 12, 14; Psalm 84:2
	Epistle: Philippians 3:17–21; 4:1–3
	Gradual: Psalm 43:8, 9
	Alleluia: Psalm 129:1, 2
	Gospel: Matthew 9:18–26
	Offertory: Psalm 129:1, 2
	Communion: Mark 11:24

✠

'Nostra autem conversatio in caelis est.'†

We are so involved in the activities of everyday life that we often lose heart; we forget what is essential; we forget that God is calling us to eternal happiness in Heaven; we forget that most things in life are but vanity except for those things destined for eternity.

In today's Epistle, St Paul invites us to look to Heaven, to that glorious place which God has reserved for each and every one of us. One day, after our earthly bodies have corrupted and wasted away, we shall rise again in the general resurrection of the dead. This body, which has shared our good works, will receive its reward. No longer troubled by weariness and disease, our bodies will be transformed and resemble the glorified body of the Risen Christ. They will shine as the sun; they will share in the soul's more perfect spiritual life, able to move in Heaven with the utmost ease and speed. One day, we shall rejoice in the company of our patron saints, who helped us by their prayers; we shall rejoice in the company of our guardian Angel, who was our faithful companion through all our hard-

---

* Psalm 129:2.
† Philippians 3:20: 'But our conversation is in heaven.'

ships. And what will be our joy when we shall see Our Blessed Mother; and when we see with our own eyes the glorified body of Our Risen Lord Jesus Christ? Like St Thomas, shall we put our hands into his pierced side; like St John, shall we lean our head upon his Sacred Heart?

But the recipe for this victory is that our every thought, word and deed must be for eternity, for Heaven. St Paul warns us today of the enemies of the Cross of Christ, who are absorbed with earthly things, whose God is their appetites and whose end is unhappiness and destruction. We must not be blind to the danger: the Devil loves to enchain men in the bonds of sin and passion; he tricks them into a false sense of liberty and pleasure; but he controls them like marionettes on strings; he binds them as slaves to sin.

No, we are not of this world: we were made for Heaven; we were created to be holy. Holiness [*Kadosh* in Hebrew] embodies the idea of a spiritual separation between divine perfection and human imperfection. To separate the holy from the profane, we must be dead to sin and this world but alive in Christ. We must cut each one of those puppet strings with which the Devil tries to control us. Striving for holiness, however, does not mean that we cut ourselves off from society – it means that we have a great obligation to edify those around us. God has a mission for each and every one of us. He calls all of us to be missionaries in our own way. Our mission is to save souls and to do what we can to save the souls of those people we meet every day.

Despite our unworthiness, we are privileged souls; we have received a wealth of grace. And now, we must make use of the graces God has given us to edify, to elevate to God a world which is continually sinking into sin and unhappiness. We have a mission to give prayerful witness and to win souls of today's world by the power of good example. In our workplaces, we must encourage virtue. We win the hearts of others through kindness to them. And it is through charity that we overcome the power of darkness.

When we see the impure crudeness of today's world, we remember *Kadosh* [holiness]. We are not of this world, because God has made us for Heaven. When we feel anger and resentment and when we are the victims of ridicule, we remember *Kadosh*. Our every thought, word and deed must be for eternity.

'Rejoice and be glad, for your reward is great in Heaven.'

For further reflection:

O thou Light, most pure and blest,
Shine within the inmost breast
Of thy faithful company.
Where thou art not, man hath naught;
Every holy deed and thought
Comes from thy divinity.
                                    (from The Golden Sequence – tr. JMN)

We sometimes forget that God is calling us to eternal happiness in Heaven.

'If I shall touch only his garment, I shall be healed.'
                                    (from the Gospel of the Day)

Dominica Ultima Post Pentecosten
The Last Sunday after Pentecost

Stir up we beseech thee, O Lord, the will of thy faithful to seek more earnestly this fruit of the divine work.

[The Proper for the twenty-third Sunday is used for all further Sundays after Pentecost including the last except for the Collect, Epistle, Gospel, Secret and Postcommunion Collect. If there are more than twenty-four Sundays after Pentecost, the penultimate Sunday will use the Collect, Epistle, etc. from the Sixth Sunday after Epiphany; the pre-penultimate Sunday, the fifth after Epiphany, and so on until the third after Epiphany is used. There can be no more than twenty-eight Sundays after Pentecost.]

Proper of the Day: Epistle: Colossians 1:9–14
                      Gospel: Matthew 24:13–25

✠

'Caelum et terra transibunt, verba autem mea non praeteribunt.'*

There is much anxiety in our culture that centres on the end of the world – and you do not have to be a Christian to share it. In the Middle Ages, it was believed by many that the invention of the crossbow – the ultimate killing weapon – heralded the beginning of the end. We have come a long way from the crossbow; the dropping of the first atomic bombs in Japan gave us a new level of nervous anticipation as to what the future might bring. We have had, in recent years, the Cuban missile crisis, the hole in the ozone layer, the rise of rogue states, and now the fear of what zealous bigots can do with an aeroplane or an envelope of white powder. There is little doubt that we humans live rather precariously.

---

* Matthew 24:25: 'Heaven and earth shall pass away but my words shall not pass away.'

The existentialist philosophers used to think much about this fear, and they were not and are not the only ones. There have always been groups of people gathering together in the belief that they have particular knowledge about the end of the world or some coming disaster. There seems never to be any lack of enthusiastic adherents because, in the end, we are all living in the shadow of the same uncertainty about what the future holds.

We can see this even in the Gospels. Our Lord made a considerable number of predictions of the future, and many of them involve death and disaster. They fall roughly into two – the predictions of the destruction of Jerusalem, and the predictions concerning the end of the world. Jerusalem and its temple were indeed to be destroyed in AD 70 by the man who was to become shortly afterwards the Emperor Trajan. Often, however, in the Gospels we find predictions of the end of Jerusalem and the temple mixed up with predictions about the end of the world. Regarding the end of the world, Our Lord says that there will be many earthquakes, plagues, famines, wars; for these will inevitably occur. Well, this is not to be wondered at. Almost any age of the world that we can think of has had its ample share of these things.

It is not the end of the world that should concern us unduly but our own end. From the standpoint of our own death, what will we regard as having been really important in our lives? Probably not our careers or the state of our bank accounts but, probably, our families and those we have loved on earth; and maybe our own judgement – our faithfulness – will seem very important because for that we shall have to render an account to God. It will come down to the question, which we must constantly ask ourselves, whether God and our neighbour have been the principal concerns of our life. Holy Scripture constantly emphasizes this question. Remember Our Lord's summary of the Law and that in today's Gospel he tells us, '*my words shall not pass away*'.

What we have to console us, however, is that though death

is inevitable, Hell is not. We have been given all the great consolations of our holy faith and all the assistance possible to avoid that fate, and all we need to do is to use them regularly, above all confession and Holy Communion, as part of our trying to acquire virtue and good habits. If we are trying to live a good life, trying to put right those things that are wrong, then we have no need to fear the judgement of the one who loves us more than we deserve, and who came, as St Paul says, not to condemn the world, but so that through him the world – and that means us – might be saved.

✠

For further reflection:

> *Within our senses ever dwell,*
> *And worldly darkness thence expel;*
> *Long as the days of life endure,*
> *Preserve our souls devout and pure.*
>
> *(from Aeterna caeli gloria – tr. JMN)*

What we have to console us is that though death is inevitable, Hell is not.

Whatsoever is corrupt within our minds, may it be cleansed by the power of thy healing Sacraments.

(Cf Postcommunion Collect of the Day)

In Festo Immaculatae Conceptionis
The Immaculate Conception (8th December)

'Thou art fair, O Mary, and there is not a spot in thee.'*

Proper of the Day: Introit: Isaiah 61:10; Psalm 29:2
                           Epistle: Proverbs 8:22–35
                           Gradual: Judith 13:23; 15:10
                           Alleluia: Canticle of Canticles 4:7
                           Gospel: Luke 1:26–28
                           Offertory: Luke 1:28
                           Communion: ref. Magnificat

✠

'Ave Maria, gratia plena: Dominus tecum.'†

Pope Pius IX will be remembered – along with so much else in his 33-year reign – as the Supreme Pontiff who in 1854 solemnly defined the doctrine of the Immaculate Conception of the Blessed Virgin Mary. The ceremony took place in St Peter's Basilica in Rome in the presence of hundreds of bishops from all over the world as well as hundreds more priests and religious, and thousands of the Roman people. Like so many special events in honour of Our Lady, the decision of the Holy Father was immensely well received. It also enhanced popular devotion to Mary in the recognition of her singular honour. Within a few years, the Apparition of Our Lady to Bernadette at Lourdes, during which she referred to herself as The Immaculate Conception, led to another great shrine in the south of France which continues to draw millions of pilgrims each year. The Miraculous Medal connected with the devotion of the same name also depicts Mary as the sinless virgin. A similar image of Our Lady forms an essential part of the devo-

---

* Alleluia – Canticle of Canticles 4:7.
† Luke 1:28: 'Hail Mary full of grace, the Lord is with thee.'

tional material of the worldwide Legion of Mary, which has an apostolate to the lapsed and the forsaken in the faith.

Some people think that it was only in 1854 that the notion of Mary's unique privilege was discovered. This is entirely wrong. The belief is very old indeed and evidence of it can be found in many parts of the Middle East and Europe in the Middle Ages. It was particularly popular in England before the Reformation, and old festal Calendars indicate that the feast was kept by the monks in the Diocese of Winchester even before the Norman Conquest. However, at this time the doctrine as we know it had not been explained or defined as necessary to be believed by the whole Church. Only some places followed the tradition of the special Feast. These aspects of the story of our Redemption – like so many others – were discussed and written about by many great scholars. It is to a Franciscan scholar called John Duns Scotus* that we owe the best explanation which finally paved the way for the later definition. Our Lady was preserved from the stain or defect of original sin from the moment when her soul and body were fused at conception. In other words, she was never tainted in any way by sin but redeemed at that moment in advance of all the rest of mankind.

Two important details derive from this great dogma. The first is connected with the sanctity of all life from the moment of conception. Every conceived human being receives a soul directly from God and is a sacred fusion of the natural and the spiritual that must be protected at all costs. No one has any right to destroy directly what God has dignified with a soul and given the potential of heavenly glory. An unborn child may not come to term naturally, and that is sad but accidental. Where a child is conceived and able to be born it must be protected at every stage, and its right to live defended. The second aspect of Mary's privilege which engages our attention is that she has a unique relationship to her Divine Son. She was both redeemed by him before all others at her own conception and then, later, as a virgin conceived him who was her Redeemer.

_____
* c. 1270–1308.

Her conception paved the way for the coming of the Lord as a human child and as a Saviour of all who share his human nature, which is also hers. Everything human about him stems from her; his genealogy, his blood type, his features were all derived from Mary's own. This was all made possible by her sinless identity from the very moment of her conception, which made her a perfect choice for God. After Our Lord himself, no other person born on this earth has been so privileged or deserves such honour from all believers. 'O Mary, conceived without sin, pray for us who have recourse to thee.'

For further reflection:

> *The God whom earth, and sea, and sky*
> *Adore, and laud, and magnify;*
> *Who o'er their threefold fabric reigns,*
> *The virgin's spotless womb contains.*
> *The God whose will by moon and sun*
> *And all things in due course is done,*
> *Is borne upon a Maiden's breast,*
> *By fullest heav'nly grace possessed.*
>
> (from: Quem terra, Pontus, ethera)

She was both redeemed by him before all others at her own conception and then, later, as a virgin conceived him who was her Redeemer.

Grant that through Mary's intercession we may be cleansed from sin and come with pure hearts to thee.

(from the Collect of the Day)

In Festo Purificationis B. Mariae V.
The Purification of the Blessed Virgin Mary (Candlemas) (2nd February)

'An old man was carrying a Child but the Child was the old man's Lord.'*

Proper of the Day: Introit: Psalm 47:10, 11
                            Epistle: Malachi 3:1–4
                            Gradual: Psalm 47:10, 11, 9
                            Alleluia: from the writings of St Augustine
                            Tract (in place of the Alleluia after Septuagesima):
                            Luke 2:29, 30–32
                            Gospel: Luke 2:22–32
                            Offertory: Psalm 44:3
                            Communion: Luke 2:26

✠

'Lumen ad revelationem gentium et gloriam plebes tuae Israel.'†

Deep in the heart of Leviticus is the detail of the cleansing or purification of a woman after childbirth. It is a marriage of ritual and sensible precaution, of ceremony and, perhaps to a certain extent, misunderstanding. It is of its time, of course. However, the need for cleanliness and hygiene, rest and recuperation were probably behind the tradition. And in order to comply with this religious discipline, Our Lady dutifully visits the Temple to receive the priestly blessing and ritual purification; to give thanks that she has borne the child announced to her by the Angel of God, and to present and dedicate her male child to the Lord. Not a wealthy woman, Mary offers a turtle dove for sin and a turtle dove for sacrifice. What irony here, for the most perfect vessel has given birth to a boy in whose honour

---

* From the writings of St Augustine.

† Luke 2:32: 'A light to the revelation of the Gentiles, and the glory of thy people Israel.'

these ceremonies were devised and are being enacted. Soon, Mary and Joseph and the Babe prepare to leave the Temple; but there in the precinct is Simeon, an old man and well known in and around the Temple; someone who will be missed sorely by the layman and priest alike when eventually he dies.

St Luke tells us so much behind the words of this narrative. Simeon was a well-respected man, a devout man who meditated on the Scriptures. The Heavenly Father smiled on this his faithful servant, saying: *'You are an old man now, having dedicated your whole life to my service, a faithful worshipper and a good man. Before I take you from this world, you shall set your eyes upon the child I promised through the prophet Isaiah and many others; upon the child who will save mankind; the child who will be the glory of Israel and a light to the whole world.'* Simeon brimmed with this confidence. And how gently it is all revealed to us through the hand of St Luke, who, it is most likely, collected the episode from the tongue of Our Lady herself.

From her very Immaculate Conception Our Lady was free from the taint of original sin – the sin of Adam and Eve; the sin of pride, selfishness, of being so bound up in one's own desires and interests that they obscure one's lines of communication with the Heavenly Father. From us Baptism has removed that taint, but we, nonetheless, are free to fall into those same sins and constantly do so, being made whole again and again through the Holy Sacraments.

Jesus is presented in the Temple by the one who has already received the grace given in Baptism from her very conception. Jesus is presented in the Temple whose High Priest would be instrumental in his condemnation and death. Jesus is presented in the Temple by the one chosen to house this glorious light for Israel and the rest of mankind. The new Eve – for Mary was her very antithesis – presents the new Adam to the Heavenly Father. Adam's pride was Mary's humility; his selfishness was her selflessness; his unfaithfulness was her steadfastness; her interests and desires were those that centred on her Son, the

Son of the Heavenly Father. Nothing obstructed her lines of communication with God: she placed no idol between herself and God.

Through Simeon, God reveals the Light of the Gentiles so that we who now ponder these words can see again more clearly and understand. Jesus is the Word who enlightens every man. Simeon, half blind with age, recognizes the light of Christ on seeing Mary and Joseph prepare to leave the Temple. They walk towards him because he has positioned himself before them. He steps out and bars their way because quite suddenly he instinctively knows that in this child, God has fulfilled his magnificent promise to Israel and the whole world, and, indeed, his kindly and generous promise to Simeon.

Shakily, probably to the consternation of Mary and Joseph, the old man takes Jesus in his arms and is the first stranger with any glimmer of understanding, to thank God for sending a Saviour. He squints curiously at the child. With his aged eye he sees but dimly: in his mind, however, everything is now quite clear to him. '*Now thou dost dismiss thy servant, O Lord, according to thy word, in peace,*' he says, '*because mine eyes have seen thy salvation . . . a light to the revelation of the Gentiles, and the glory of thy people Israel.*' Before John the Baptist is able to point out the Lamb of God to his own disciples, Simeon is recognizing the Light of Christ.

This Feast is a feast of purity and light, of utter perfection. It is a Feast that draws attention to our origins, to the fall of man and to the promise of the Light, which came into the world as the Word made flesh, the Son of the Most High God.

'*A light to the revelation of the Gentiles, and the glory of thy people Israel.*'

✠

For further reflection:

The Angel-lights of Christmas morn,
Which shot across the sky,

Away they pass at Candlemas,
They sparkle and they die.

Comfort of earth is brief at best,
Although it be divine;
Like funeral lights for Christmas gone,
Old Simeon's tapers shine.

And while the sword in Mary's soul
Is driven home, we hide
In our own hearts, and count the wounds
Of passion and of pride.

(Candlemas – JHN)

Jesus is presented in the Temple whose High Priest would be instrumental in his condemnation and death.

May we be presented to thee, O God, with purified hearts.

(cf The Collect of the Day)

In Nativitate S Joannis Baptistae
The Nativity of St John the Baptist (24th June)

'Thou, child, shalt be called the Prophet of the Highest; thou shalt go before the Lord to prepare his ways.'*

Proper of the Day: Introit: Isaiah 49:1, 2; Psalm 91:2
                                Epistle: Isaiah 49:1–3, 5–7
                                Gradual: Jeremiah 1:5, 9
                                Alleluia: Luke 1:76
                                Gospel: Luke 1:57–68
                                Offertory: Psalm 91:13
                                Communion: Luke 1:76

---

* Luke 2:76.

'Joannes est nomen ejus.'*

It is certainly not the custom of the Church to celebrate natural birthdays – indeed, the only person in the Holy Bible who does so is King Herod, as John the Baptist was to discover to his cost – for we are born into a world of sin, stained by the inheritance of Adam, slaves to the Evil One, crying out for redemption. In most cases we prefer to commemorate the day of earthly death, a saint's new birth, his *natalitia*, into eternal life. Only twice in the year do we keep a merely human birthday as a feast, for Our Lady and for John the Baptist. Yet the date upon which we celebrate this birth points us directly towards the birth of God made man: *'He must increase,'* says John, *'but I must decrease.'*† From now on until Christmas the days will decrease, until the coming of the Daystar from on high.

The reason why Our Lady and St John are so privileged is not far to seek – they alone were born in no need of justification, already cleansed from original sin. Our Lady indeed was so from the moment of her conception; as was St John, as the Church has come to realize, from the time of the Visitation, when he leapt in his mother's womb for joy at the presence of the Lord.

The call of John the Baptist, already from his mother's womb, was foreshadowed in the call of the great prophets. Isaiah sang of how *'the Lord hath called me from the womb: from the bowels of my mother he hath been mindful of my name'.*‡ Jeremiah likewise heard the Lord say: *'Before I formed thee in the bowels of thy mother, I knew thee: and before thou camest forth out of the womb, I sanctified thee and made thee a prophet unto the nations.'*§

Both were chosen for the specific task of proclaiming the glory of God to his people, calling them back from sin, urging them towards loyalty and faithfulness, and preparing them for

---

* Luke 1:63: 'John is his name.'
† John 3:30.
‡ Isaiah 49:1.
§ Jeremiah 1:5.

the greater glory to come. Isaiah recalls: *'he said to me, thou art my servant Israel . . . that I may bring back Jacob unto him . . . that thou mightest say to them that are bound: Come forth, and to them that are in darkness: Show yourselves.'** Jeremiah knew what suffering his vocation would bring, but also how the Lord would protect him: *'be not afraid at their presence: for I am with thee to deliver thee, saith the Lord'.*† John the Baptist is to have a harsh and dangerous vocation *'like a sharp sword'*, and will witness to his message with his blood, but will also know the shielding protection of God: *'in his quiver he hath hidden me'.*‡

None of the prophets took the office of prophet upon themselves, indeed most were reluctant to accept it, but God chose them, he justified them, he sanctified them as they responded to his call: *'Lo. here am I, send me!'*§ The ancient prophets responded to God's call, but not until they were grown men: John the Baptist responded immediately. *'For, behold, as soon as the voice of thy salutation sounded in my ears, the infant in my womb leapt for joy.'*¶ The embryo prophet recognized his embryo Saviour, and rejoiced. So he was born, three months later, already sanctified for his mission. In the meditation of the Church, over many centuries, we have come to understand how this meant that he was born immaculate, without stain of original sin. It was this meditation, and meditation on the call of the prophets, that enabled the Church, at length, to understand Mary's own Immaculate Conception, for if the Precursor was to be privileged with justification before birth, how much more privileged must be the Mother of the Lord!

'How shall this be done?' The answer is concealed in the name which the child is given: *'He shall be called John.'* That name, in Hebrew, *Jokhanaan*, means 'the grace of God'. It is by grace, and grace alone, that all these things come to pass.

---

* Isaiah 49:3, 5, 9.
† Jeremiah 1:8.
‡ Isaiah 49:1, 2.
§ Isaiah 6:8.
¶ Luke 1:44.

There could be no question of any pre-existing merit, for the child was unborn, without name and without voice. The call, the choice, the conferred justification, was all the work of God, the initiative of God alone. Grace is God's free gift to us: he pours out his love upon us, yearning for us, for he calls us back to himself like a shepherd calling his sheep, *'to give knowledge of salvation to his people unto the remission of their sins'.**

Zachary bears witness to the primacy of God's grace in the words he wrote: *'John is his name.'* And he bears witness again in the first words that he uttered: *'Blessed be the Lord God of Israel; because he hath visited and wrought the redemption of his people.'* Was not this literally true? For three months, the Incarnate Lord, still in his Mother's womb, had been a visitor in the home of Elizabeth and Zachary. She recognized him at once, when he had been conceived only a few days, *'whence is this to me that the mother of my Lord should come to me?'.*†
Zachary can speak only now, but he too acknowledges that his visitor was none other than the Lord, the God of Israel, the creator of Heaven and earth.

It is through the Incarnation that God redeems his people. It is his work, his grace, his love. Not only John the Baptist, but both his parents are prophets, all united in acclaiming the identity of the child of Mary, who is true God and true man. For this reason, the name John has also been interpreted as meaning 'the one who points out' – *demonstrantem.*‡ It is to be his task to point out the Lamb of God, to prepare his people for his coming, to proclaim him when he came, to die for his truth. John is always the one who calls others to faith, himself called to *'raise up the tribes of Jacob and to convert the dregs of Israel'.*§ John has an important part to play in the work of salvation, for he must respond to the grace that is in him. He is *'called the prophet of the Highest; for thou shalt go before*

---

* Luke 1:77.
† Luke 1:43.
‡ Origen in Catena Aurea ad loc.
§ Isaiah 49:6.

*the face of the Lord to prepare his ways'.** He began that work three months before his birth; he continued it until his death.

In celebrating the birth of St John the Baptist, we celebrate the mystery of God's grace, the love by which he initiated our redemption, the means by which he achieved it. Our celebration points us all the more clearly to the essential mystery of our faith, that God has visited his people, and redeemed them.

For further reflection:

> *O what a splendour and a revelation*
> *Came to each mother, at thy joyful leaping,*
> *Greeting thy Monarch, King of every nation,*
> *In the womb sleeping.*
>
>

(from Ut queant laxis – tr. RER)

The call of John the Baptist, already from his mother's womb, was foreshadowed in the call of the great prophets.

'The Lord hath called me by my name from the womb of my mother.'†

(Introit of the Day)

<hr>

* Luke 1:76.
† Isaiah 49:1.

In Festo Sanctorum Apostolorum Petri et Pauli
The Holy Apostles Peter and Paul (29th June)

'Now I know in very deed, that the Lord hath sent his Angel.'*

Proper of the Day: Introit: Acts 12:11; Psalm 138:1, 2
                              Epistle: Acts 12:1–11
                              Gradual: Psalm 44:17, 18
                              Alleluia: Matthew 16:18
                              Gospel: Matthew 16:18
                              Offertory: Psalm 44:17, 18
                              Communion: Matthew 16:18

✠

'Tu es Christus, Filius Dei vivi.'†

These Princes of the Apostles are this day celebrated together – the rock and foundation, and the evangelist of the Gentiles. The disciplines of evangelism – teaching, working of miracles, preaching, and so on – spring from the Church's well-founded body. Saul was transformed from an ardent persecutor of those who followed 'the Way' on the road to Damascus, into a great apologist and tireless traveller and letter-writer. He had been every bit as fanatical and relentless as the most aggressive and enthusiastic atheists of our own day. Who knows *their* future? However, St Paul's conversion is more especially celebrated in the feast of that name and in tomorrow's feast, The Commemoration of St Paul. The Proper of this Mass is primarily concerned with St Peter. Before Sts Peter and Paul were given their respective commissions, they both were to declare, in one way or another, *'Thou art Christ!'*

---

* Acts 12:11.
† Matthew 16:16: 'Thou art Christ, the Son of the living God.'

If we agree that Paul was a surprising choice, was Peter any more likely a choice for the position of a firm and unswerving rock? Happily, Christ sees beyond the superficial evidence. Oh yes, Peter brimmed with bluster, impetuosity and the instant response. Perhaps this side of his character complemented and balanced the other – that of a patient fisherman. Fishermen, if they are good fishermen, are obliged to be patient whether or not they spear, net, or simply sit on a river bank puffing contentedly at a pipe after three hours without a bite. But the Prince of the fishers of men had to grow up with Christ in an apprenticeship, at times uncomfortable. At just the wrong moment and evidencing a complete lack of understanding, Peter declares on the Mount of Transfiguration: *'Let us make here three tabernacles, one for thee, and one for Moses, and one for Elias.'* And, as recorded in Matthew, a little after the passage from today's Gospel, we find Peter protesting that the Christ should not suffer. *'Go beyond me, Satan, thou art a scandal unto me!'* is the crushing reply. *'Get out of my sight; get away from me!'* Such was Peter's apprenticeship. Satan is the obstructer. We give him form and we place him on our own altars, between ourselves and God. We focus on him because he is made of our pride, our selfishness and our desires. Frequently corrected and shown up in front of others, Peter never gives up, never sulks. The others do not mock him. After all, he was a senior man in a thriving fishing business. Indeed, does he not put into words the thoughts that they had not the courage to utter? But Peter's supreme moment comes, and in a high point in his apprenticeship. *'Whom do men say that the Son of Man is?'* The usual nonsense comes out, usually the reincarnation of some unlikely people. *'Yes, but whom do you say that I am?'* Peter blurts out something he has been longing to say: *'Thou art Christ, the Son of the living God.'* It is simple and straightforward, and Jesus' answer is unequivocal: *'Peter . . . upon this rock I will build my Church.'*

Our Lord looks beyond what has happened and what will happen. He knows that his Bride, the Church, will be set on a sure foundation. Nevertheless, there are darker days to come, of course. The great confession and affirmation will soon, for a while, be negated and denied, retracted. *'Of course I do not know the man! Just because I am a Galilean, you think I must know him. Of course I don't.'* The words he spoke were much to that effect. Consider the self-loathing Peter must have felt. We know the feeling when we fall prey to our abiding and besetting sins. In falling prey to them, we say, *'I do not know the man'*, as surely as if we had used those very words, and so we give substance to Satan.

What passed between Peter and Our Lord as the cock crowed? We know that Jesus looked at Peter. We can but surmise, but would this not have passed between them? As he caught Jesus' eye, Peter, immediately ashamed, contrite, devastated, confessed and asked forgiveness in an exchange of glances. In the look Jesus gave Peter, Peter was forgiven, comforted and given strength for the future. Even so, who can doubt that Peter went away and buried his face in his hands. The after-shock of denying the Christ he had so fervently declared was devastating. It is a shock we know well as people already committed to Christ as Peter was. We are part of the Body of Christ's Bride, who is one with the Bridegroom built firmly on the rock of St Peter, whose life with Our Lord illustrates and reflects our own. We are all capable of that same denial in circumstances far less dire than those in which Peter found himself. But we turn again, and always shall because we have already declared: *'Thou art Christ, the Son of the living God!'*

✠

For further reflection:

> *Good Shepherd, Peter, unto whom the charge was given*
> *To close or open ways of pilgrimage to heaven,*
> *In sin's hard bondage held may we have grace to know*
> *The full remission thou wast granted to bestrow.*
>
> *(from Aurea luce – tr. TAL)*

What passed between Peter and Our Lord when the cock crowed? We know that Jesus looked at Peter.

'Thou shalt make them princes over all the earth: they shall remember thy name, O Lord, throughout all generations.'*
(from the Offertory of the Day)

Pretiosissimi Sanguinis D. N. Jesu Christi The Most Precious Blood of Our Lord Jesus Christ (1st July)

'Thou hast redeemed us, O Lord, in thy Blood.'†

Proper of the Day: *Introit: Apocalypse 5:9, 10; Psalm 88:2*
     Epistle: Hebrews 9:11–15
     Gradual: 1 John 5:6–9
     Alleluia: from an unknown source
     Gospel: John 19:30–35
     Offertory: 1 Corinthians 10:16
     Communion: Hebrews 9:28

✠

'quanto magis Sanguis Christi'‡

The nineteenth century was both a time of great trial for the Church and also of great expansion. It opened with the Napoleonic conflict in Europe and closed with the threat of another and even more destructive war. In between, there was persecution of the Church in parts of Europe and also in many mission lands. Yet the Church grew in numbers in the Americas and Australia, and was beginning to make gains in Africa and

---

* Psalm 45.16, 17.
† Apocalypse 5:9.
‡ Hebrews 9:14: 'how much more shall the Blood of Christ'.

Asia. New religious orders were founded to teach and evange-
lize at home and abroad. In Great Britain and Ireland, Catholics
gained religious freedom and increased hugely in numbers. The
Holy See presided over and promoted this universal growth and
from time to time drew the attention of Catholics everywhere
to a special aspect of doctrine upon which to focus their devotion. The great Feast which we celebrate this day was such a
gift. It reminds us that the Precious Blood of Christ, shed once
upon the Cross, is the price of our redemption and continues
through the Mass to be the effective remission of our sins until
the end of time. It is the continuous stream of God's mercy and
sacrificial love that pays the debt of our disobedience, washes
away the guilt of our shame and in sacramental form nourishes
our fidelity.

Today's Epistle provides us with a clear reference to the vital
connection between the priesthood of the Old Testament and
its expiatory blood offerings and the One Priesthood of Our
Lord. Previously, the rituals of the Temple had been carried on
by the ministry of the High Priest, with innumerable offerings
of animals and with scrupulous attention to detail. Christ's one
offering on the cross, in which he willingly allowed himself to
be the victim as well as the One effecting the offering, replaced
and converted into reality what had been until then the only
available and symbolic means of propitiation and worship.
Until the coming of the Son of Man, God had permitted the
former dispensation to make satisfaction in a certain manner
for the sins of his people. Now, by a supreme act of divine
condescension and self-sacrifice, the only possible offering of
impeccable character, namely that of the human life of Our
Lord, made perfect atonement in a way which none of the previous offerings could make up. His offering was of the highest
possible kind, being that of a perfect man who was also God,
offered freely and in supreme knowledge of divine glory set
aside in order to render that oblation total.

We live in an age when such profound realities seem to
count for little – sometimes even among many of our fellow

Catholics. Unless we regularly reflect and meditate upon them, our fervour receives little or poor nourishment and becomes less than lukewarm. We may be receiving Holy Communion weekly or even more often, but our awareness of the immensity of the mystery in which we are privileged to share can become vague and commonplace. There is nothing cheap about God's generosity. It cost him, in the person of his divine Son, everything that he had to give, to the very last drop of his human life-blood. Never let us be found wanting in our appreciation of this overwhelming gift. At the same time, as we enjoy the benefits of forgiveness in the Sacrament of Penance, and nourishment in the Most Holy Eucharist, may we always render thanks that God did not abandon us to the misery into which we might descend without his intervention, and for the sacrifice that gave us back our lost dignity.

'For if the blood of goats and of oxen . . . sanctify such as are defiled . . . how much more shall the blood of Christ.'

✠

For further reflection:

He endured the nail, the spitting,
Vinegar, and spear and reed;
From that holy Body broken
Blood and water forth proceed;
Earth, and stars, and sky, and ocean
By that flood from stain was freed.
(Lustra sex qui jam peracta – tr. JMN)

Never let us be found wanting in our appreciation of this overwhelming gift.

'The chalice of benediction which we bless, is it not the communion of the Blood of Christ?'
(from the Offertory of the Day)

In Transfiguratione D. N. Jesu Christi
The Transfiguration of Our Lord Jesus Christ
(4th August)

'Thy lightnings enlightened the world: the earth shook and trembled.'*

Proper of the Day: *Introit: Psalm 76:19; 82:2, 3*
                               Epistle: 2 Peter 1:16–19
                               Gradual: Psalm 44:3, 2
                               Alleluia: Wisdom 7:26
                               Gospel: Matthew 17:1–9
                               Offertory: Psalm 111:3
                               Communion: Matthew 17:9

✠

'Illuxerunt coruscationes tuae orbi terrae.'†

L ove them or hate them, storms are awe-inspiring things. It is easy to understand why thunder is so often thought of as the voice of God. Lightning is beautiful and terrifying all at once. Each burst gives an instant of strange vision among the darkness and clouds. It is one of David's favourite images in the psalms, and the Church takes up his words to introduce the glory and contradictions of today's feast. *'Illuxerunt coruscationes tuae orbi terrae'* ['Thy lightnings enlightened the world']. Just as lightning in a storm gives us a moment of vision in the gathering darkness, so the Transfiguration gave the disciples a vision of hope in the sufferings that were about to come upon them.

A great deal of our faith is puzzling: God is near us but far away; immanent but transcendent; like us but also wholly other. These contradictions are especially apparent in the Feast of the Transfiguration. The event takes place up a high

---

* Psalm 76:19.
† Psalm 76:19: 'Thy lightnings enlightened the world.'

mountain. In one sense the disciples are close to God; but then a cloud takes Christ from their sight. Then God seems remote and awe-inspiring to the disciples until, once again – and St Matthew alone gives us this detail – Our Lord returns to them, touches them to give them courage. These are the contradictions of our Christian life as well. In our prayer, God can sometimes seem remote and distant. Like the author of the *Cloud of Unknowing,* we have to fire off our arrows of prayer into the darkness of the cloud, trusting by faith that there is someone to receive them. At other times God seems close to us – we can almost hear his voice and feel his touch. One of the practical lessons of this feast is a lesson in prayer, of living with this difficulty and accepting his closeness or his distance as his will for us.

Peter, James and John, faithful Jews, would have been aware of the religious meaning of high places. Horeb, Sinai and Moriah, all were mountains where God had made himself known to his people. In Our Lord's life, mountains are places of significance. They are places of temptation, of preaching, of prayer. Above all, a mountain is the place of his suffering. Here again, the Transfiguration brings us face to face with another puzzle – the contrast between the glory of God and his suffering on the Cross.

From the very earliest times the link between the Cross and the glory of Our Lord was made explicit. St John speaks of the Cross as the exaltation of Jesus and St Paul, of the Cross as the power and wisdom of God. The Transfiguration brings these two together, and we have to see them together, difficult though this is, if we are to have the clearest image of God we can have this side of Heaven. On Mount Tabor, at the Transfiguration, Our Lord was seen in glory, clothed in garments *'white as snow'*. He is accompanied by Moses and Elijah. He is revealed by the voice of God himself as his beloved Son. By contrast, on Calvary, he is in agony on the cross, hung between two thieves. Far from wearing dazzling apparel, he is stripped of all his clothes and the sky turns black in the middle of the day. It is not the voice of God that declares him to be the Son of God, but the astonished words of a Gentile soldier.

Just as in our prayer, so also in our lives, God is in the sorrows and well as the joys, the highs and the lows. Our Lord asks us to take up our cross and follow him up the mountain. There will be suffering for us all, as there was for him. But today's feast shows us that up the mountain, beyond the suffering and through the clouds there is joy for all his faithful people.

✠

For further reflection:

More bright than day thy face did show,
Thy raiment white as fallen snow,
When on the hill to mortals blessed
Man's Maker wast thou manifest
(from O nata Lux de lymine)

The Transfiguration gives us a vision of hope amid the sufferings of this life.

'Grant, we beseech thee, almighty God, that we may grasp with purified minds this most holy mystery of the Transfiguration of thy Son.'
(from the Postcommunion Collect of the Day)

In Assumptione B. Mariae V.
The Assumption of the Blessed Virgin Mary (15th August)

'A great sign appeared in heaven: A woman clothed with the sun, and the moon under her feet.'*

Proper of the Day: Introit: *Apocalypse 12:1; Psalm 97:1*
                      Epistle: *Judith 13:22–25; 15:10*
                      Gradual: *Psalm 44:11, 12, 14*
                      Alleluia: *from an unknown source*
                      Gospel: *Luke 1:41–50*
                      Offertory: *Genesis 3:15*
                      Communion: *Luke 1:48, 49*

☩

'Benedicta tu inter mulieres . . .'†

The Assumption of Our Lady is surely one of the most lovely of all her feasts which, like that of the Ascension of Our Lord, turns our thoughts heavenward; the image of the Son receiving his Mother into the glory of Heaven is certainly one that captures the imagination. In his Assumption hymn, Father Faber paints the scene for us in words almost as richly as Tiepolo would have done on canvas:

> Ah happy Angels, look, how beautiful she is,
> See Jesus bears her up,
> Her hand locked in his!
> Oh, who can tell the height of that fair mother's bliss!

But it is precisely this exuberant vision, with its suggestion of cherubs and clouds and *'fields of starry light'* which causes some to stumble in their faith in this event. This is a dogma we seem to *'know more by the heart than the head'‡*. Seen through

---

* Apocalypse 12:1.
† Luke 1:42: 'Blessed art thou among women . . .'
‡ Mother Janet Stuart RSCJ.

the lens of our contemporary, scientific view of the universe, a bodily assumption seems so improbable. And yet, we are asked to hold it as an article of faith. In his book of essays *A Devil's Chaplain* Professor Dawkins – the well-known evangelist of atheism – singles out this doctrine as being a particular example of religious nonsense, setting up an Aunt Sally – the Blessed Virgin zooming improbably into the heavens – in order to knock it down as irrational. The fact that the doctrine was defined in the twentieth century is especially galling to Dawkins. Even at the time, Pope Pius XII had his critics. Why choose to define the doctrine at this time? Why define it at all? And why make belief in the Assumption of Mary *de fide* for Catholics? Yet God acts in and through his Church, and the deposit of Faith, while it may not be added to, has been unpacked for us as the Church has grown – and is growing – in its understanding of herself and her mission. She has had to speak to each generation in succession, finding ways in which to teach the Faith to people so that they will be able to grasp and understand.

The doctrine of the Assumption was defined by Pius XII in November 1950 – midway through the last century. It was indeed a timely event. Let us recall what had been happening during the first half of that century. Two World Wars, fought on an unprecedented scale, with millions of dead. Remember the appalling genocide which took place in Europe at the behest of Hitler, who intended – and very nearly effected – the extermination of the Jewish people. And now think of all that has been happening since that time, which has seen the growing culture of death; the frightening rise in the number of abortions; the inexorable push for the introduction of euthanasia; the almost universal use of contraception and all the other trappings of the sexual revolution. At the same time there has been an almost total loss of belief in the concept of the human soul. Where that happens, the de-spiritualized human body becomes paramount, even exalted – sex, a recreational activity; the gymnasium the new temple. But at the same time the body becomes something degraded and expendable. Nonetheless, above all this there stands the radiant figure of the Blessed Virgin, the woman clothed with the sun, adorned with the stars. Mary is the sign and pledge of the eternal life God has promised his children. In the Assumption, we see her glorified in both soul and body in Heaven, a beautiful reminder of the truth that human beings are redeemed – body and soul. Here is a wonderful expression of a vital truth of our faith, that God loves his creation and wants to save it.

Here is the crux of our reply to the cynics. Mankind is central to that creation, which God declares in the book of Genesis to be 'good'. What is more, he made us *in his own image*. What a mysterious destiny – midway between the angelic and the animal realms lies something which reflects the nature of God himself. And yet, we abused that destiny, wrecked the original unity between man, woman and God, and fell from grace. Mary is nothing more and nothing less than the answer that God gives to this self-inflicted mess. Mary is the prototype of a redeemed humanity, a humanity in which body and soul are no longer at war with one another and with God. The work of our restoration which the Lord began in Our Lady's Immaculate Conception was brought to perfection in her Assumption, when the Lord took his mother to himself. She fell asleep and awoke in the eternity prepared for her. And why not? Citing St John Damascene as an authority, the Pope stated that it was impossible to suppose that she who conceived Christ, bore him, fed him with her milk, held him in her arms and pressed him to her bosom, should after this earthly life be separated from him in either body or soul. Yes, *'it was fitting that she ... should look upon him as he sits with the Father. It was fitting that God's Mother should possess what belongs to her Son.'* We could say that the Ascension of Christ implies the Assumption of his Blessed Mother. We must stop worrying about the mechanics or the physics of the event: the Church does not. That this wonderful event happened is sufficient for our purposes.

Mary's Assumption is the fulfilment of the Lord's desire

expressed in his High Priestly prayer: *'Father, I will that where I am, they also whom thou hast given me may be with me; that they may see my glory which thou hast given me, because thou hast loved me before the creation of the world.'** So when we celebrate the Assumption of Our Blessed Lady, we are also celebrating the triumph of God's grace in redeemed mankind. The truth is, we are not cast down but lifted up, and the image and likeness of our God, once all but effaced by the sin of our first parents, has through the Second Adam and the New Eve, been lovingly restored in us. The Resurrection of Christ *'the first-fruits of them that sleep'* is truly the Resurrection of God; the Assumption of Mary is the sign of hope we all need, if we are to persevere in our quest for God, because in her, Mother and the image of the Church, we see the Body finally united with the Head who has gone before us.

In celebrating this joyful feast, we do not, as some may think, ascribe more glory to the Blessed Virgin than is her due. Rather, we give thanks to Almighty God for the fulfilment of the wonderful promises of Christ, in which, through Our Lady's prayers we may be worthy to share. Our hope is that when the time comes for us to die, the Lord will receive our souls into his care and that on the last day, the Risen Christ shall raise our bodies glorified as his body, and unite them to our souls in a Resurrection like his own.

✠

For further reflection:

> *Mother of God, accept our prayers this day,*
> *Whereon to heaven's portals thou wast borne.*
> *Dear to the Father, Jesus' Mother pure,*
> *The Holy Spirit's temple thou wast made.*
> *Fair spouse of God, thou Christ the King hast borne;*
> *Lady, thou art in heaven and on earth.*
> *(from the Sarum Sequence for the Feast of the Assumption)*

---

* John 17:24.

When we celebrate the Assumption of Our Blessed Lady, we are also celebrating the triumph of God's grace in redeemed mankind.

Through the prayer of the most Blessed Virgin, assumed by thee into heaven, may our hearts be set on fire with love and ever yearn for thee, O God.

(from the Secret of the Day)

In Exultatione S. Crucis
The Exaltation of the Holy Cross
(14th September)

'Christ became obedient for us unto death: even the death of the Cross.*

Proper of the Day:	Introit: Galatians 6:14; Psalm 66:2
	Epistle: Philippians 2:5–11
	Gradual: Philippians 2:8, 9
	Alleluia: Fortunatus
	Gospel: John 12:31–36
	Offertory: Prayer
	Communion: Prayer

'Et ego si exaltatus fuero a terra, omnia traham ad meipsum.'†

Today's feast celebrates the Cross in a way that would be inappropriate for Good Friday, just as Corpus Christi celebrates the Holy Eucharist in a way that would be inappro-

---

* Philippians 2:8.

† John 12:32: 'And I, if I be lifted up from the earth, will draw all things to myself.'

priate on Maundy Thursday. The Exaltation of the Holy Cross specifically recalls Emperor Heraclius' recapture of the relics of the True Cross in the year 629. These precious relics had been carried away by Chosroes, the King of Persia. The feast is also obviously related to the Invention of the Holy Cross in May, commemorating the discovery of the True Cross by St Helena early in the fourth century.

We do more than simply recall an historic event; today's feast gives us an opportunity to reflect on the mystery of the Cross in both the story of our redemption and our personal path to holiness. It is so easy to see a cross simply as a symbol of our faith or even as a pretty decoration, which we hang in our house or wear about our person. Very often the cross is a thing of great beauty, as we see in the countless depictions of the Crucifixion in churches and art galleries around the world. For the people of ancient times, however, the idea of a Feast of the Cross would have been a shocking paradox, akin to a modern celebration in honour of the gallows or electric chair. For them the cross was a terrible thing, a humiliating and painful way of death that has given the English language the word *excruciating*, literally meaning *out of crucifixion or crucifying*. Victims died of blood loss, dehydration or asphyxiation, and it could take several days to die, in some cases. Indeed, Pilate was surprised that Jesus only survived three hours, though given the brutality of his scourging and the carrying of the cross, it was hardly surprising. The cross was such an awful reality that the first Christians did not use it as a symbol.

Yet, this terrible instrument of death was the instrument of our salvation. Behind the pain of the Cross lay the joy of the Resurrection. That is what we celebrate today and that is why the Cross has become the great symbol of Christianity. St Augustine noted that *'the Cross, which was the gibbet of criminals, has made its way to the foreheads of emperors'*.

But how does the Cross feature in our own lives? At Baptism, we are marked with the sign of the Cross and we participate in the life and death of Jesus. We suffer with him. This gives suffering a special dignity – it is our participation in the Passion and constitutes a path of sanctification. It is not as if the Passion of Christ were insufficient for the Redemption of the world; rather, our sufferings, if borne out of love, are a share in Christ's once-and-for-all Passion, just as the Eucharist is the sacramental extension or renewal of that Sacrifice.

None of us can avoid carrying our cross. We do not have to look very far to find it or invent complicated penances – the cross can easily be found among our families and our workplaces and our acquaintances. There may be great crosses – bereavement, major disappointment, or serious illness. But the smaller crosses can be just as burdensome – an insult or criticism, the reappearance of an old wound, a continuing headache, whatever it might be. If there is nothing we can do about them, our great challenge is to accept these sufferings out of generosity maybe, and humility. The Curé d'Ars taught that *'our greatest cross is the fear of the cross'*:

> *On the Way of the Cross, you see, my children, only the first step is painful . . . Most men turn their backs upon crosses, and fly before them. The more they run, the more the cross pursues them, the more it strikes and crushes them with burdens . . . He who goes to meet the cross, goes in the opposite direction to the crosses; he meets them, perhaps, but he is pleased to meet them; he loves them; he carries them courageously. They unite him to Our Lord; they purify him; they detach him from this world; they remove all obstacles from his heart; they help him to pass through life, as a bridge helps us pass over water.*

How do we react to the inevitable suffering of this life? The story of the Passion gives us two possible ways – we can follow the example of the bad thief or the good thief. Both suffered in equal degree. Both were dying on their crosses. But one battled with suffering and blamed God: *'If thou be Christ, save thyself and us!'* The other accepted his suffering and his sentence, and prayed to God for help: *'we received the due reward of our deeds; but this man has done no evil ... Lord, remember me when thou shalt come into thy kingdom'*.

When we suffer, do we do so with love or with bitterness? When we meet the Cross, do we run away or do we embrace it, seeing it as – in the words of the Curé: *'the ladder to Heaven'*.

Let us be servants of the Cross, for therein shall lie our victory!

For further reflection:

> *The Cross let all its servants praise,*
> *By which new life and healthful days*
> *Upon them are bestowed;*
> *Let each and altogether cry,*
> *'Hail, Cross, the world's recovery,*
> *Salvation-bearing Rood!'*
>
> (from the Sarum Sequence)

When we suffer do we do so with love or with bitterness?

'Sweet the wood, sweet the nails, sweet the load that hangs on thee.'

(from the Alleluia of the Day)

In Dedicatione S. Michaelis Archangeli
The Dedication of St Michael the Archangel
(29th September)

'Bless the Lord, all ye his Angels: you that are mighty in strength, and execute his word, hearkening to the voice of his orders.'*

Proper of the Day: Introit: Psalm 102:20, 1
                                 Epistle: Apocalypse 1:1–5
                                 Gradual: Psalm 102:20, 1
                                 Alleluia: from a prayer to St Michael
                                 Gospel: Matthew 18:1–10
                                 Offertory: Apocalypse 8:3, 4
                                 Communion: Daniel 3:58

✠

'Dico enim vobis, quia Angeli eorum in caelis semper vident faciem Patris mei, qui in caelis est.'†

St Michael is often presented to us by the artist as a battle-ready champion armed with a lance or spear with which he is piercing – almost nonchalantly – a hapless green reptile. Sometimes, because of this, an illustration of this saint is almost indistinguishable from one of St George, save that St Michael, along with every Angel of every degree, is usually equipped with a fine pair of wings. These creatures of pure spirit, whose vocation includes the conveyance of the attributes of God and messages from God to mankind, are given wings by artists as metaphors of speed and immediacy. We begin to grasp these things a little better when a picture is painted for us, and this is, of course, the vocation of the artist.

---

* Psalm 102:20.

† Matthew 18:10: 'For I say to you, that their Angels in heaven always see the face of my Father, who is in heaven.'

When Christ, the Holy Lamb, triumphed on earth, there was rejoicing in Heaven because *'that old serpent called the devil and Satan'** had been crushed and confined to the deserts and wastelands of the earth, and had been cast aside as one now vulnerable and vanquishable. Clearly, no place could ever be found in Heaven for anything that would obstruct the will of God.

Satan, the opponent and obstructer of all that is good, is given life in man's weaknesses – in his pride and in his selfishness. Satan is able to place himself between us his victims and God, disguising himself as our favourite idol, whatever it is – our standing in society, our self-importance, our immodesty, our petty desires and pleasures, and so on. Michael, the Prince of the Angelic Host, is the one who reminds us of the vanquishing power and strength of the Lamb, and so encourages us to take up the necessary and appropriate arms.

It is apparent that each of the Angels of God has a special vocation in the same way each of us has his own special vocation. The Guardian Angels, for example, are spoken of unequivocally by Our Lord in today's Gospel, and their duty made clear to us in terms we cannot misconstrue. It is, on the face of it, a sobering thought that our worst and least moments are always known to God. More sobering still is the fact that we forget that that is the case; we can so easily put it from our mind. However, it is, is it not, a strengthening and comforting thought that the Heavenly Father, the God of Creation, is concerned with each individual in goodness and in sin?

There is no place in Heaven for pride and selfishness or anything that man places between himself and God. Our Lord makes this apparent when he declares that we are to become as little children, as innocents – those innocent of allowing their desires to stand between them and the Heavenly Father. The children, in this case, are the *'poor in spirit'*,† who dwell in the Kingdom of Heaven. They are also the *'little ones'*, the

---

* Apocalypse 12:7ff.
† Matthew 5:3.

ones who confess the faith and strive earnestly to resist, ignore and banish Satan from inhibiting their focus upon God. Selfish desires obstruct our way to God: the *poor in spirit, the little ones*, have the Kingdom of Heaven already established in their hearts; in other words, they live on earth as though they were in Heaven. If we are not poor in spirit, our lines of communication with God are therefore unclear. This is bad enough, but woe betide anyone who causes others to lose their innocence and to turn away from God; make no mistake, God will know, for the Guardian Angels, those Heavenly agents, have access to God and are in constant contact – their lines of communication are always clear and direct. *'See that you despise not one of these little ones, for I say to you, that their Angels in Heaven always see the face of my Father who is in Heaven.'* We ever strive to be numbered with these little ones, and it is a wonderful grace that lost innocence can indeed be restored by good confession, penance and absolution.

We give thanks for the intercession of St Michael and we give thanks that he defends us, shows us God's strength, and shows us the armoury to choose when we contend daily with Satan on the battlefield.

✠

For further reflection:

> To celebrate thy praise, O King of Heaven,
> Let all our band harmonious unite,
> Our whole assembly singing hymns to thee
> On the renewal of high festival
> In Michael's honour, he whose ministry
> Gives lustre to the mighty universe.
>
> (from the Sarum Sequence)

Satan, the opponent and obstructer of all that is good, is given life in man's weaknesses.

'An angel stood near the altar of the Temple, having a golden censer in his hand: and there was given to him much incense, and the smoke of the perfumes ascended before God.'*

(from the Offertory of the Day)

In Festo D.N. Jesu Christi Regis
The Feast of the Kingship of Our Lord Jesus Christ

'Give to the King, O God, thy justice, and to the King's Son, thy judgement.'†

Proper of the Day: Introit: *Apocalypse 5:12; 1:6; Psalm 71:1*
                        Epistle: *Colossians 1:12–20*
                        Gradual: *Psalm 71:8, 11*
                        Alleluia: *Daniel 7:14*
                        Gospel: *John 18:33–37*
                        Offertory: *Psalm 2:8*
                        Communion: *Psalm 28:10, 11*

'Regnum meum non est de hoc mundo.'‡

In 1925, His Holiness Pope Pius XI drew attention to the waywardness of the world in turning away from God and his Christ in its obstinacy, in placing itself outside the realm of Christ, organizing its life as if God were not. He reflected that man's pride removed God from his consideration; man's self-satisfaction caused him to ignore his neighbour. In instituting this feast, Catholics of the world would be encouraged and, in

---

* Apocalypse 8:3, 4.
† Psalm 71:1.
‡ John 18:36: 'My Kingdom is not of this world.'

turn, could encourage others in the knowledge of the Universal Kingship of Christ.

Sadly, those reflections hold good today. We need look no further than the constitution of the European Union, which refuses to recognize the Deity. And it is not alone. Indeed, not only is God excluded but there is a seemingly inexorable movement to promote the most unhealthy, unchristian and anti-Catholic legislation. Signs, perhaps, of the disintegration of western civilization, for whence God is excluded, there Satan sets up his kingdom. These are the outward signs. Is all hope of the Kingdom gone?

This feast was itself a bold, emphatic pronouncement of the royal rights of Jesus as the Word Incarnate, of Jesus the Redeemer and the Royal Priest. How does Jesus royally claim his territory – with an army and on horseback, the traditional mount of kings? No, on a donkey, the foal of an ass, the kingly mount when on a mission of peace. Our duty, on behalf of our King, is to help communicate the joy of this feast to the world by encouraging the faithful, our fellows. Of course, there is higher authority than a European President, than any prime minister, than any sovereign – and the good ones faithfully acknowledge the fact – but, in any event, they have no need to fear for their positions, for Christ arrives on a donkey and not on a war-horse. Christ gains territory for his Kingdom in a rather different way. For the territory Christ longs for is the heart of man. It is there that Christ plants his Kingdom when invited to do so. We tread the heavenly path when we live our lives as though we were in Heaven, in accordance with heavenly virtues and values. That is the territory of the Kingdom where Christ yearns to reign. To offer this territory willingly to Christ and, further, to extend the territory in others by taking Christ to them, is the general vocation of all followers of Christ.

The Heavenly Father is so much more than the most perfect father we can imagine; so Christ the King than the most dutiful monarch – and we, in the United Kingdom, are most fortunate to know a monarch whose life is dedicated to her people, who possesses an unswerving sense of duty. But how do we ensure that we have a suitable place for Christ? The answer we find in the Beatitudes. The poor in spirit possess the Kingdom of Heaven. They live their lives in modesty; nothing is placed between them and God. Pride and self-esteem are not their idols. They win territory for the King, by opening their hearts to Christ. Satan can gain no foothold there and Christ is welcomed. If we strive to love God and our neighbour, we find it more difficult to place ourselves first, and we gain territory for Christ the King within ourselves and, by example, within others. To help us, we have the wonderful graces provided by the sacraments.

Now we see more clearly how the King comes to us. We see our King as the Monarch not of this world but of Heaven and those on earth striving to live by the heavenly virtues, often out of step with contemporary values and standards. The throne of Christ we see as the Cross upon which he hung in degradation. We kneel at its foot hardly daring to look up, but when we do so we see the benevolent and loving Universal King of inexpressible majesty. He is dressed in Eucharistic vestments to show us his royal priesthood and how he nourishes his Church and the least worthy of us; a crown of pure gold is upon his head; his arms outspread in a merciful embrace. This is not a King by force of arms but by supreme love, the love that is the very bond of the Three Persons of the Most Holy and Blessed Trinity.

✠

For further reflection:

Lord, when thou as King shalt come,
All the universe to claim,
Grant us, devotedly we pray,
Thy beatitude for aye,

In that land of saints, where we
May alleluias sing to thee.
                    (from the Sarum Sequence for Ascension Day)

Now we see how our King comes to us . . . his arms outspread
in a merciful embrace.

'The Lord shall sit as King for ever: the Lord shall bless his
*people in peace.'**
                    (from the Communion of the Day)

In Festo Omnium Sanctorum
The Feast of All Saints (1st November)

'Come to me all you that labour and are heavy laden, and I will
refresh you.'†

Proper of the Day: Introit: *Author unknown; Psalm 12:1*
                      Epistle: *Apocalypse 7:2–12*
                      Gradual: *Psalm 33:10, 11*
                      Alleluia: *Matthew 11:28*
                      Gospel: *Matthew 5:1–12*
                      Offertory: *Wisdom 3:1–3*
                      Communion: *Matthew 5:8–10*

☩

'Gaudete, et exultate quoniam merces vestra
copiosa est in caelis.'‡

Throughout the course of the liturgical year, we rejoice in the memory of the numerous saints whose feast days

---

  * Psalm 28:10, 11.

  † Matthew 11:28.

  ‡ Matthew 5:12: 'Be glad and rejoice, for your reward is very great in Heaven.'

pepper the Calendar: martyrs, confessors, doctors and virgins, all of whom give us a clear example of what it means to be a Catholic Christian. The lives of some are well known to us, while others are little more than names whose deeds and deaths are barely a memory in the Martyrology. Today, however, we do not celebrate any particular saint, but *all* the saints, especially those who are unknown and unsung heroes of the Faith. Like the Ascension and the Assumption, this feast day is one that helps us look Heavenward. It is a celebration of hope that the promises made to us by the Lord will be fulfilled, and a firm reminder that one day this feast day will be our own, provided that we persevere in our quest for holiness '*without which no one can see God*'.

There is an unfortunate tendency in us to envisage a huge gulf between us here and God's holy ones there. This is a mistake, because it makes us faint-hearted and liable to give up trying, saying something to this effect: '*It was all right for St So-and-so to say or do such-and-such a thing, but he or she was a saint and I am not.*' That may be so, but we ought to remember they were not born saints: they were mortal too, like us. And they were not saints because they were good, but because they loved God, and it was because they loved God that they became good.

Never think that the saints were without sin – only one can make that exalted claim and she is the one we call the *Refuge of Sinners*. No, saints were men and women like us, who recognized that they were sinners and did something about it. Is that not what we are striving for; to fulfil that command of Our Lord, '*Be perfect as your Heavenly Father is perfect*'? Such a demand sounds so utterly impossible to us, does it not – to become perfect like God? There is a translation that renders this verse rather freely as, '*Let your love have no limit as your Heavenly Father's love is without limit.*' Again, we might think such a goal unattainable; it does, nevertheless, point out to us a way in which we should try to fulfil this difficult command of Christ, which means nothing less than keeping the two great

Commandments on which hang all the Law and the Prophets. Love God and love your neighbour. It is their struggle to do this daily which makes the saints so helpful to us in ours. It is from the example of their Christian living, their faith, the way they faced problems and handled difficulties, that we can draw hope and inspiration, rather, perhaps, than from the miraculous elements of their life stories. This is not because we necessarily disbelieve the accounts of their miracles; in fact, such things are signs of their sanctity and of the Lord's approbation. Yet, miracles do not make the saint; it is the holiness of life that counts – the saint's love and virtue, the saint's response to the gift of grace. St Philip Neri used to say, *'Never say what great things the saints do, but what great things God does in the saints.'* He was, of course, quite right. It has been said that the occupation of the saint is to disclose God's presence in the world – and this is something we can all do. How do we? St Francis de Sales said, *'Where God's will is done, he is always present.'* Our business here is the same as that of every disciple of Christ – past, present and future – and that is to do the will of the Father, thus disclosing the presence of God to the world.

Let us think for a moment of those saints whom we most love and admire, and why that is the case. It may be that there are certain aspects of their lives and personalities which resonate with ours. For example, the mother of a difficult child might find strength in the example and prayers of St Monica, whose prayers and tears won the grace of conversion for her wayward son, Augustine. It is perhaps because they help us see and experience how God is present in our own situation and difficulties, that we love and admire our friends in heaven. We see in them what we are called to be, and are encouraged because they too experienced failure, trial and sin, yet by God's grace were strengthened to overcome the weakness of human nature.

Precisely because they struggle as we do, and are now in the presence of the One who loves to share his glory, they can be the truest, most sympathetic friends we have, as they intercede for us before the throne of the Most High. Like the figures in stained-glass windows in many of our churches – and there, most probably, the resemblance ends – saints are people through whom the light of Christ shines in the world; and we who are called to love God have been given the mandate by Our Lord, who is the light of the world, to be a light to others. *'So let your light so shine before men, that they may see your good works and glorify your Father who is in Heaven.'**

Let's not be afraid to seize the torch he offers. Let's carry it and pass it on. And, please God, the 1st November will indeed be our own feast day. Meanwhile, let us not forget that, *'He that shall persevere unto the end, he shall be saved.'†* And it is always easier to persevere if we are in the right company.

For further reflection:

To Christ, the glorious, let our white-robed bands
Sing hymns upon this holy festival,
Extolling all the company of saints.
Let them hold us in their ceaseless prayers,
And lead us to true joys in Heaven above;
Let the redeemed devoutly sing, Amen.
(from the Sarum Sequence)

Saints are people through whom the Light of Christ shines in the world.

'Rejoice in the Lord, ye just: praise becometh the upright.'‡
(from the Introit of the Day)

Missa Pro Defunctis
Requiem for Remembrance Sunday

'Eternal rest give unto them, O Lord, and let perpetual light shine upon them.'[*]

Proper of the Day: Introit: 4 Esdras 2:34, 35; Psalm 64:1, 2
                             Epistle: 2 Maccabees 12:43–46
                             Gradual: 4 Esdras 2:34, 35
                             Tract: Collect
                             Sequence: Dies irae
                             Gospel: John 6:37–40
                             Offertory: Collect
                             Communion: 4 Esdras 34, 35, etc.

✠

'ut omnis, qui videt Filium, et credit in eum, habeat vitam aeternam.'[†]

S uch words are of extraordinary comfort and power from today's Gospel. They are unequivocal: he who sees the Son and believes in him – that is, believes that Jesus is the Son of the God. What strength for the bereaved and for all who hear the words! But how do we show that we believe that Jesus *is* the Son of God? Indeed, how can we now see Jesus? We are not contemporaries of Christ's sojourn on earth, or are we? Well, he has declared that he is with us until the end of time. But how do we see him? When do we see him? We see him clearly in Scripture, and can see him in the priest at Mass, in others fulfilling their God-given vocations, in the poor and in the wretched, the hungry, the sick and the dying, when we minister to them. Others, likewise, will see him in us as we fulfil our vocations through life. Indeed, it is our general vocation to be 'other Christs' and to radiate his brightness and love in our

---

[*] 4 Esdras 2:34, 35.

[†] John 6:40: 'that everyone who seeth the Son, and believeth in him, may have life everlasting'.

very demeanour. (How we usually fall short of this!) But, in any event, is all this no more than a mere reflection of Christ, an imitation of his action? No, *'when did we see thee a stranger, and took thee in, or naked, and covered thee? Or when did we see thee sick or in prison, and came to thee? And the King answering shall say to them: Amen, I say to you, as long as you did it to one of these my least brethren, you did it to me.'** Jesus makes it clear in this passage that we most assuredly encounter him in these circumstances. And, of course, we encounter him in his most Blessed Sacrament: the gracious gift to adore and take into ourselves. Christ as truly in the form of bread as he walked in the flesh of humanity.

November, the month of the Holy Souls, gives us in addition to All Saints' and All Souls' a most sobering of days set aside for reflection – Remembrance Sunday, the second Sunday of November, the Sunday nearer Armistice Day. Remembrance Sunday was so designated after the Second World War in order to remember war dead of that conflict. It now embraces the memories associated with all battles and wars up to the present day. But for all who gather on these occasions – whether bereaved or not – there must be something more than mere remembrance and recollection. These things are useful in that they concentrate the mind and cause us to meditate upon the horrors of war, man's greed and evil, and man's heroism; and that meditation, in turn, prompts and guides our prayer. However, our prayer on this day is primarily prayer for the souls of those who have departed this life suddenly, without preparation, in the midst of war, and for those who have died after the agony of all-consuming injury sustained in battle. We offer Mass for these souls and we pray earnestly for them. This is the very least we can do, to intercede for those in their place of purification and refreshment. Some of the fallen have, of course, already achieved the Heavenly Realms. Most we do not know. Some, however, we do know – the saints and martyrs of the world wars and other battles and conflicts, are numerous

---

* Matthew 25:38–40.

and their stories often terrible, soldiers and civilians alike. We think of St Maximilian Kolbe, to name only one example, but there are many whose shining examples inspire and humble us. We can be sure of their prayers for us. As for those who wait, we pray that they will soon feel the loving embrace of Christ the loving King.

St John the Baptist bade his disciples to live their lives in the fear of God, making proper use of their talents and expertise; if a soldier, for example, a good soldier and all that that implies. It may be – whether soldier or not, during war or not – we are called to show a soldier's heroism in our own walks of life while fulfilling our own vocations. If so, then with God's grace we shall do so. But as we truly believe that God sent his Son, we strive to do what God asks of us and, inevitably, we shall see the Son and receive the gift of life eternal promised in today's Gospel.

✠

For further reflection:

> *Vouchsafe the prize*
> *Of sacred joy's perpetual mood,*
> *And service-seeking gratitude,*
> *And love to quell each strife or feud,*
> *If it arise.*
>
> (from Hominis superne Conditor – tr. JHN)

This is the least we can do, to intercede for those in their place of purification and refreshment.

'May light eternal shine upon them, O Lord, with thy Saints for evermore.'

(from the Communion of the Day)

In Anniversario Dedicatione Ecclesiae
For the Anniversary of the Dedication of a Church

'This ... is the house of God and the gate of Heaven.'*

Proper of the Day: Introit: *Genesis 28:17; Psalm 83:2, 3*
       Epistle: Apocalypse 21:2–5
       Gradual: from an unknown source
       Alleluia: Psalm 137:2
       Tract: Psalm 124:1, 2
       Gospel: Luke 19:1–10
       Offertory: 1 Paralipomenon 29:17, 18
       Communion: Matthew 21:13

✠

'Quia hodie in domo tua oportet me manere.'†

The choice of the Gospel for the Dedication of a Church – the account of Our Lord's encounter with Zaccheus – gives an immediate indication of the value and purpose of a church. A church is above all else a sacred building consecrated, dedicated, set apart for the worship of Almighty God. Jesus bids the chief publican, the man of small stature, *'festinans descende'*: *'Make haste, and come down: for this day I must abide in thy house.'* The truth is that Christ, who seeks us out before we ever think of searching for him, desires to pitch his tent, as it were, to make his dwelling with mankind.

His Church, that is his Mystical Body, present throughout the ages and in all places, gathers to offer the sacrifice of Calvary. And it is for the celebration of the Mass and the other sacraments that the physical building of a church – comprising the bricks, mortar and stone – is thus set apart and made holy. When a church is consecrated or solemnly dedicated, it is

---

* Genesis 28:17.
† Luke 19:5: 'For this day I must abide in thy house.'

Christ himself who says, as once he said to Zaccheus, '*I must abide in thy house.*'

When Zaccheus, overjoyed by the presence of Our Lord in his abode, promises to make right his misdoings and, what is more, act with great material generosity, Jesus replies by assuring him, '*This day is salvation come to this house; because he also is a son of Abraham.*' Abraham, our father in faith, was the one who first received the promise of salvation. Christ himself is the fulfilment of that promise, and now he bestows his mercy and redemption upon those who seek him and welcome him. And it is within the sanctuary of buildings dedicated to him that we can most fully begin to do so.

The act of consecration of a church, be it a mighty cathedral or a humble chapel, reveals and celebrates the presence of God in the midst of a wounded world. The building is made holy by the various acts of consecration, by the sacraments subsequently conferred therein, and by the constant recourse to its walls by the faithful. The building, once sanctified, is a visible sign and an anticipation of the hope of Heaven, of the Kingdom of God. It is a sign of the temple of living stones built up by God, those stones formed not from hard inanimate material but constituting the souls of the saints. Yes, in our consecrated buildings the new and Heavenly Jerusalem breaks forth. That is why our churches ought to be worthy, both within and outside, of their holy purpose, places where the presence of God is both evident and tangible.

The Communion Antiphon today declares: '*My house shall be called the house of prayer.*' It is to fulfil such a sacred, solemn and joyful duty that we gather in this church today.

✠

For further reflection:

To this temple, where we call thee,
Come, O Lord of hosts, today;

With thy wonted loving-kindness
Hear thy people as they pray;
And thy fullest benediction
Shed within its walls for ay.
                                    (from Angularis fundamentum – tr. JMN)

The building is a visible sign and an anticipation of the hope of Heaven, of the Kingdom of God.

'Grant that whosoever enters this temple to ask blessings of thee may joyfully obtain all his petitions.'
                                    (from the Collect of the Day)

Index of Scriptural References

Genesis

Hebrews

Isaiah

James

Jeremiah

Job

John